THE PAPER CHASE

HAL PORTER

The Paper Chase

UNIVERSITY OF QUEENSLAND PRESS

First published 1966

Reprinted, with corrections, by University of
Queensland Press, St Lucia, Queensland, 1980

Printed and bound by Silex Enterprise & Co.,
Hong Kong

Distributed in the United Kingdom, Europe, the
Middle East, Africa, and the Caribbean by
Prentice-Hall International, International Book
Distributors Ltd, 66 Wood Lane End, Hemel
Hempstead, Herts., England

Originally written with the assistance of the
Commonwealth Literary Fund

National Library of Australia
Cataloguing-in-Publication data

Porter, Hal, 1911-
    The paper chase.

    First published, Sydney: Angus & Robertson, 1966.

    ISBN 0 7022 1504 X

    1. Porter, Hal, 1911- — Biography. 2. Authors,
    Australian — Biography. I. Title.

A828'.3

FOR SUNDAY REED
who is younger than I'll ever be

WHEN Mother dies in late March 1929, I am newly eighteen. Although I have already blandly participated in, or artfully avoided participating in, enough impure enough or ludicrous enough experiences to be as case-hardened as a stripling can be, Mother's death and the unromantic form of it affront me deeply. No Lady of Shalott she. Writers with their aesthetic inventions about death and death-beds—*I am dying, Egypt, dying* and so on and so on—are, it is too clear to one wading heart-deep in fruitless tears, charlatans. This latest experience in which I resent participation is startling. The fairy-tale forests of childhood are behind. That blossom-hung and sun-striped era, at least and at last, is over for ever and ever.

It is not only startling, it is agonizing.

At least that's how, in March 1929, it appears. My knowledge of agony is, however, and to this very today, nearly forty years later, meagre—the dialect of grief is a hard one to learn. My death-side agony may not be authentic agony at all. Agony, grief, sorrow, whatever it is, may be something else yet to accomplish or never to accomplish. Does one—does a writer with his eyes in his heart, and his heart in his brain—ever really get to know? Perhaps, eighteen, and considering myself and the earth cruelly deprived, I am putting, as Westerners are inclined to do, an excessive, maybe an extreme, value on individual life.

As a quick lesson-learner I don't put it for long. By autumnal May the leaves of my sorrow are falling too. Dressed in black like an early Julien Green character I am walking, late at night (midnight?), along the Gellibrand Pier, Williamstown. There is a suitable fog, moveless and rich with chill, and the prehistoric baying of fog-horns. Now and then, far from the lamp before, a pier-lamp appears in its fog-bow. Now and then, below and regularly, the bay water slaps at the pier-piles like swags of cold

cold flesh. There is nothing to feel with the eyes but the discernible nothing. Into this salt-spiced lateness and desolation there comes a consoling and informative revelation (doubtless it is canny self-information to self-console) that eternity is what goes on behind one's back, that living is what goes on behind the backs of the dead. Cold fleshy water, blazing flesh, shrivelled flesh, passion and loss, crystals, rocks, barnacles and butterflies, laughter and screams and songs, footsteps on fog-damp pier-planks, all things go on and on and on no matter who—Mother or somebody's mother or Caligula, Mary Queen of Scots or drummer-boy at Waterloo—are filed away among the used-up. Oh yes, the used-up, the blue-pencilled, the dead dead. It is (the revelation continues), it is, however, impossible to kill the dead. Indeed, it is only the dead, salted down for ever, pickled in the vat of time, who illustrate how immortal mortals are, and how unavoidable is resurrection, how immediate and permanent, with no three days required, and no hope necessary—hope, the last and most terrible of all the evils let out of Pandora's box. No need at all for hope: although as dead as mutton, Mother has come upon the earth, a very Tmu from the Book of the Dead, and with her two feet has taken possession of it.

"Clean the *backs* of your shoes," she says. I obey—1917, 1923, 1935, yesterday, today, tomorrow, as long as there are shoes and shoe-polish and me.

"Lucifer, Star of the Morning, was a fallen angel," she says. "Grace Darling was a brave girl. Those stars—see, there, above the cherry-tree—are the Seven Sisters." He, Lucifer, is. She, Grace Darling, is. They, the Seven Sisters, are. Mother, therefore, also is because she has her resurrection in them and such unforgotten lessons or legends or lies. She lives in old words to old tunes I catch myself singing in new places and new years which hear thus the errors in word and tune she taught me. She lives in the woodbine and the picotees which have followed the family, sentimental cutting by cutting, from her country garden to this, that and the other garden. She has being in the chipped petals of a white china rose she loved, in an appalling supper-cloth she crocheted, in a Cacao Grootes tin still filled with her blouse-buttons—carved mother-of-pearl, jet, cat's-eye agate, in a silver teapot inherited from her inheriting, in blankets she bought as a young wife over half a century ago and which, threadbare, with faded stripes top and bottom, now lie folded beneath the mattresses of grandchildren she never knew.

Ah Mother, up to your tricks, vital, inexorcizable ghost! As all women are, you are born solitary. You must, as each woman does, mulct a man of his identity. You must, as a mother does, use the subtlest temptations to mulct a son of his identity. A writer son, a marked man, needs particularly to brush aside these temptations. He must round on himself, and bare his unlovable strengths to the bone with the insolence of one baring lovable weaknesses. He must say with finality, "Listen, you there, *woman* . . . Mother . . . it was a short and merciless happiness, given merely to be taken away. Gifts from Heaven are also gifts from Hell. Be comforted, Mother. Be comforted, immortal. Nature is, after all, not so much cruel as not kind. Now, *now*, I must try to avoid whatever repugnant Utopia you might have wished lovingly or with maternal zeal on your first-born, and defend my right to suffer or not to suffer. Let me find out for myself if I shall come to regret a desire not to live better and better but only to live more and more."

Goodbye, immortal.

Goodbye, Mother.

Eternity will go on behind your back.

Already, 1929, April, May, June, July, December, it goes on. Compulsory military training which began in the year you bore me is abolished in the year it should begin to affect me. The tumbrils of the Depression are now audible. Words you've never heard are beginning to be heard: cellophane, gaga, beau geste, babbittry, Grand Guignol, mentalism, scanties, superego, heebie-jeebies, proletarianization, sexy, tommy-gun, mike, and penicillin.

It is, then, 1929.

I return from my first devastating yet exhilarating foray with doom, with unaesthetic death; I walk out of the fairy-tale forest, Hamletishly "sable-garbed" and consciously "doleful of mien", to my job as a Junior Teacher at State School 1409, North Williamstown.

On a plane above the sorrow I seem to feel, I counterfeit, when I don't forget, an additional public sorrow. Now, all these years later, when my past is already decades longer than my future, it is amusing though discomforting to recall how impressive, then, my bad manners are. I take to smoking Sobranie cigarettes—black ones. I buy boxes of black-bordered, hand-made writing-paper at the final sale of Cole's Book Arcade. How worn the wooden floors of this place I loved as a child, how dim the aspiring columns of brass, how forlorn the iron-rimmed risers of the stairways and the echoing emptying galleries! It takes years to use up this mournful hoard: startled acquaintances of the nineteen-forties are the final victims of the bargain. It takes a far shorter period for me to put myself out of mourning, Sobranies and all, public and private. Off with the black! On with the motley!

I remain at State School 1409 until 1937 and, moreover, remain as a Junior Teacher. Without tiresome research it is not possible to state if this stationary decade, from 1927 to 1937, as a Junior Teacher, ten years deliberately on the lower rungs of a ladder easy to climb, is not some sort of grotesque record. It may well be, and almost certainly is. It does indicate my dearth of material ambition. At the end of ten years of energetic work I am earning about £2 a week. Do I care? No. Do I think of Rolls-Royces, castles in Spain, a harem of Clara Bows and Colleen Moores, a Tahiti of my own? No and no and no and no. This decade of apparent marking-time also indicates a lack of domestic ambition or, maybe, since fear and sex are so closely handcuffed together, it indicates fearlessness. Wife? Children? Backyard with lemon-tree, Congoleum square, Royal Doulton figurine, Genoa velvet three-piece suite, ice-chest, wirless set, electroplated rose bowl? The opportunity till death do us part to wound and re-wound, to be wounded and re-wounded by the weapons of devotion? Decidedly no. Why flee from freedom? Better to be imprisoned in freedom than to be free in jail. Wife, children, roof-over-heads, Iceland poppy plot, and pea soup on the gas-ring seem the threads that could enmesh Gulliver on Lilliput. Or, to be fair to all, a Lilliputian in Gulliver Land.

Anyway, with no one to egg me on, and lacking at least two

4

of the multiplicity of ambitions which could jolt me into starting from cover, I remain at State School 1409. I chaperon myself pretty competently most of the time, and keep myself alive and lively by a nickel-plated belief in myself. I am sustained also by my love for and fascination with the school and with Williamstown. The microscopic uselessness of everything I do in those years is no more than the microscopic uselessness of what everyone does.

In writing of Williamstown during the nineteen-thirties, and of the Depression, one requires of oneself no more than to commit an act of lucidity, and of lucidity that is limited by one's own nature, one's own shortsightedness, one's own conviction that, while a form of compassion is seemly, life is too short for the exercise of outright pity or unpruned tolerance. One must, as well, not philippize nor concoct emotions and "thoughts" that a dedicatedly omnivorous and intelligent but nevertheless ill-informed Jack-o'-Lantern of a brat cannot possibly have had. After all, in those years, there is never a toneless day, never a filleted evening, and my line is empty-headed gaiety, chatterbox shallowness with one eyebrow—the left, of course—raised like Lew Cody's. This is the exhibition part. Alone, I am without a thought. This makes for happiness. About the evaluation of happiness I feel more competent and confident than about an assessment of agony. Happiness has been practised for years. As a writer it occurs to me, right here and now in the country kitchen where this is being written, the wood-stove vibrating with heat, two cats folded into identical designs of peace on the hearth-rug, that nothing can be more tragic than the life of a man who has condemned himself to the solitary confinement of happiness, contentedness.

It is from this cell that I look out on the Depression. As though through a pane dazzlingly lit, and on which my own all-too-important reflection fuses with the images beyond, I see some of the effects, some few only, of poverty on the minute section of time and space confronting me. Poverty, however relative, is, I see, a brake. It slows movement. It deadens and mutes. Trios of ascetic-looking louts too languid to spit loll at street corners. Women shoppers trudge by. The Williamstown beach, bigger than that at Juan-les-Pins, is strewn like

Juan-les-Pins, on Depression summer weekdays, with the expensive-looking, sun-ripened bodies of sussoes—young Adonises on unemployment relief. Prone and moveless, they have laid themselves out like pumas or corpses across the castor-sugar sand, by the lisping silky sea. Impossible for me, the poor employed scurrying in shabby clothes towards work in sun-less rooms, to read their rich unemployed minds. What goes on behind their blissfully closed eyelids and calm Hindu-brown foreheads and sun-bleached forelocks? Has the sun, day after day, dried up the fluid of emotion? Are their minds breathing or holding breath? They themselves breathe, no more than that. For the rest they do not agitate one single artist's-model muscle. Other sussoes, who have worn mud and lice and terror for God, King and Country, for England, Home and Beauty, do move. They trail the streets with blighted suitcases, and plead with bright desperation and grinning fatigue at the sub-urb's front doors, offering for sale strange tin-openers and apple-corers, strange insurance policies, strange hair-crimping devices, home-made toffees, gaudy soaps reeking of jasmine, ylang-ylang and otto of roses, paintings of camels sneering on dunes, toys of Cro-Magnon crudity soldered from kerosene-tins and jam-tins, or carpentered from the wood of packing-cases. Un-fishermen lean, attempting to fish, against the bollards of piers and wharves. All women of all ages wear cheap berets. Men begin to take shamelessly to hatlessness. Notices, discreet as pain but adamant, and childishly lettered on boot-box lids or the backs of writing-pads, appear between the lace curtains and the front window panes—BOARD & LODGING; SINGLE ROOM to LET; ACCOMMODATION for RESPECTABLE LADY (Protestant); DRESSMAKING; KNITTING for INFANTS; LAUNDRY TAKEN IN (Dress Shirts). *Do any-thing*, say the advertisements in the newspapers: *Do anything; go anywhere*. The pawnshop windows become more and more crammed with gravy boats, tan riding-boots, silver-topped walking-sticks, goblets made of carved emu eggs set in German silver, tureens filled with fish knives and Apostle spoons, amber necklaces, Nellie Stewart bangles, wedding-rings and MOTHER brooches, and banjo-mandolins that surely, at Jazz Age beach parties sizzling with mosquitoes and ill-lit by moon-

6

light, must have been strummed to the semi-tipsy caterwauling of "Barney Google", "Betty Co-Ed", "Bye Bye Blackbird", "All Alone", and "Me and My Shadow".

Me and my shadow—what unfitting and diaphanous shadows the writers of the nineteen-twenties and early nineteen-thirties cast. At least, what non-human shadows of authors fall from the shadowy books I am able to find in the Williamstown Mechanics' Institute Library where the Reading Room is peopled by out-of-work men wearing fissured patent-leather dancing pumps, puce Oxford bags on their last legs, out-at-elbow navy-blue twill coats, and knitted white silk scarves with fringes from which some of the teeth are missing. They sit there vacant and dazed before the tender young fire in the art noveau fireplace, reading of dukes in *The Tatler* or of West End plays in the *Illustrated London News* while their solitude grows more and more obese, and the lean wind from the sea roams outside in the world of the wind, and the diaphanous and curious shadows float from the books on the shelves—ubiquitous Pan, Pan and satyrs and nymphs and sly, sidelong, lustless lust; pierrots and harlequins and columbines tripping under honey-coloured moons; Blind Raftery; Douglas Fairbanks pirates; silver shoon; perukes and pomades; elegant highwaymen with Valenciennes ruffles (*Stap me!* and *La, sir!*); slender gipsyish women with long green eyes, arched insteps, husky voices, and secret slanting smiles. There seems a whiff of inferior incense or scented snuff in the middle air between the chestnut-glossy linoleum and the untouchable upper shelves of calf-bound Dickens, Scott, Thackeray, Mark Twain, Ouida, uncountable biographies of David Livingstone, and books on South Sea Island cannibals written by portly Anglican bishops with eyes like onyx whose frontispiece, steel-engraved portraits are veiled in tissue-paper.

Meantime, as I seek among the cheaply scented and shadowy —James Branch Cabell, Donn Byrne, Jeffery Farnol, Rafael Sabatini, Georgette Heyer, Marjorie Bowen, Eleanor Mercein —for a Henry James or a Vicente Blasco Ibañez I haven't read (I am getting too old for Guy de Maupassant and Constance Garnett's Chekhov), outside, in the indigo twilight smelling of October lilacs, or the uneasy night alive with running elm-

7

leaves yellow as bile, or the night packed to its eaves with the snoring and odour of a sea impassioned by late summer, the street-corner violinist is to be heard execrably sawing out, as though on the tendons of his own begging throat and the strings of hunger, "Roses of Picardy", "After the Dawn", "Little Grey Home in the West", and "Till the Sands of the Desert Grow Cold".

I remember, really, little unpleasant about the Depression in Williamstown, although more than a quarter of its population is out of work, because I am not punished enough by it to remember: its cat-o'-nine-tails leaves no mark on my thirty-bob-to-two-quid-a-week shoulders. I have no wife playing landlady to a mysterious stranger in the spare room of her belly. I have no brood of children clamouring like billeted troops for fish and chips, vanilla ice cream and kola tonic. I keep no mistress, greyhound, saxophone or motor-bike. It does become necessary to learn to clean and press my own trousers, and to try to remember to walk on the grass plots, which do not seem to be called nature strips then, in attempts to save shoe leather. Beyond that—almost nothing. I am, however, persistently half-aware, even in the most blinding midsummer high noon, of a touch of twilight—somewhere—someone else's twilight—somewhere; and, even at moments of absolute cessation, at dawn, say, with dew-soaked suburban tulips still dead-asleep on their feet, I feel there is a bleakish wind blowing—but not for me—somewhere high up, high above a weakened and narrow-gutted world, a streaming, ever-blowing, unheard gale that tears to tatters the unseen banners of someone's life, of many lives, and showers down no fiery petals, no bluebird's feather, no warm tears.

During the day, at school, it is impossible not to know that many of my pupils live on the bread-line, it is impossible not to observe the home-cobbled shoes, the darned elbows of boys' jumpers—heather-mixture jumpers just too tight and short of sleeve, the don't-be-ashamed-of-a-patch trousers and turned shirt collars, the chapped patent-leather belts and scrubbing-board-dimmed colours of girls' dresses, their skirts home-made from some obviously adult material. No one is, however, not neat; there are speckless fingernails and polished shoes; no one

gets emaciated; all are ebullient and happy-go-lucky, or unde-
tectedly pretend to be so. There may have been hand-outs of
milk at school—I have no recollection of them. There are free
exercise books, donated by Williamstown tradesmen, the *Sun
News-Pictorial*, the Wool Board, and a biscuit manufacturer
. . . *Ben the Baker offers a Malvern Star Bicycle*—The Bike that
'Oppy Rides—*as prize for the best essay on Brockhoff's Malt
Biscuits*. Printed on and within the covers of the exercise books
are the supplications of the tradesmen: a chemist, a builder,
wood and coke merchants, a ham and beef seller (delicatessens
are ham and beef shops or smallgoods shops in the nineteen-
thirties), a hardware merchant, and a maker of liquorice cigarettes. *Parents!* says a discreetly conspicuous notice, *support the
advertisers who have made this distribution possible.*

During the early years of my prolonged Junior Teacher
career I am still well within earshot of my own boyhood, and
therefore learn from the children I teach nothing that cannot
be disdained as very old hat, and scarcely any more about
children than that as a mob—and any mob is a mechanism, a
juggernaut capable of bulldozing itself down—they contain a
quality of danger and a fuel of frenzy. The many teachers I
work side by side with during my ten years at this state school
are, most of them, adequately equipped to smother the danger
and transform the frenzy. The equipment is the diamond-cut-
diamond one of intimating a more dangerous danger and a more
skilled frenzy. In this, each teacher to his own technique: steel-
lined sweetness, bullocky shoutings, fishwife screechings,
Shakespearian denunciations, but mainly the iron control in the
velvet manner, the suggestion that just beneath the patient mask
of the Archangel Gabriel are the lineaments and fangs of Attila
the Hun.

Since the nineteen-thirties the abandonment by those in
authority of this Attila quality is something that seems to one
of my generation and training not only an irresponsible giving-
away of the tribal rights of adulthood and the powers due to
experience but a gesture of great impropriety and greater
danger. Children, being born lawless, cannot make themselves
law-abiding. In London, in 1965, I see with distaste and contempt something of what happens when archangelic tolerance

gets out of hand. In these days of England's decadence, when sections of London are also out of hand, there infests Trafalgar Square, side by side with the tourists and pigeons, a horde of barefooted minors, male and female, in a sexless uniform of duffel coat and skin-tight trousers. They infest also the railed-in concrete island surrounding the Eros statue in Piccadilly Circus. The males wear ear-rings; their clotted hair hangs to their shoulders; the backs of their hands are tattooed; each finger, and sometimes each thumb, has its Woolworth ring. In London one becomes used to such people as the Duke of Wellington's ex-son-in-law earbashing one in an upper-crust accent about what he obviously feels is the Australian perversion of cleanliness, one becomes used to the unwashed Englishman, to the smell of feet and armpits and rancid hair-oil in the Underground, and learns to accept physical scruffiness as being as English as eccentrics, tepid beer, spring greens, bad manners, hard water, over-long twilights, vapid beef, public love-making in Hyde Park, and a general cynicism of almost Gallic size. The Eros Islanders, however, the London young in their elderless tribes, out-English the dirty English, and are—surely, if one omits the Parisian *clochard* and the Eskimo?—the world's filthiest and smelliest bipeds. I watch from Swan and Edgar's corner, with the sense of watching a nightmare, a pack of them, a wolfish twenty or more, Medusa-haired, slouch away from the meanly dribbling Eros fountain into the dinner-and-theatre traffic of the Circus and, with the sinister self-possession of cranks no one will upbraid, caper primitively as Zulus among the taxi-cabs, buses and motor-cars. No one does upbraid. The drivers, their faces set at an imitation of forbearance, devote themselves to the difficult job of not running down this next generation, to the process of being blackmailed by youth. The policemen look down their noses. The passers-by pass by with eyes deliberately looking at nothing. Meantime, for twenty minutes, for half-an-hour, while the neons perform and reperform their miracles of ugliness and vulgarity overhead and all around, the untouchables, uttering animal sounds, padding on nigger-black feet, jerking tattooed hands about, continue their hideous and undecodable defiance. Why are they not called to heel? Who is to call them to heel? The cynical and bewildered adults trotting cinema-wards up from the bowels of the earth into Shaftesbury Avenue? The Queen? The Archbishop of Canterbury? The Coldstream Guards? A posse of warders from Holloway Prison? The two neat London bobbies posed a yard away from me and the plate-glass of Swan and Edgar's? Standing there, I think—and it breaks the nightmare—of how this lawlessness might have aroused to disciplinary action people not thought of for years: Mr Goulding of Grade Eight, State School 1409, Miss Graham of Grade Six, Miss Glew of Grade Five, Miss Benson of Grade Four, and Madam, the Headmistress of the Infant School.

The Headmistress is Miss Margaret Lindsay, but Junior Teachers, bleeding from the knout of her tongue with its barbs of chaste logic, call her Madam—such is the grandeur of her style they cannot call her anything less. She is a tartar: were she ever to say, "A little bird told me!" one would know the bird a vulture. Madam wears most often a patently expensive tailor-made costume of barathea-like cloth on the left lapel of which hangs a cloisonné watch, gunmetal-grey silk stockings on her ageing elegant legs, kid shoes embellished with oval buckles of cut steel, and a sapphire and diamond dress ring of almost Rajput gorgeousness. Her pompadour, long before the era of lacquer, sustains itself in steep mathematically disposed ridges, and is apparently an arrangement of platinum and pewter no tomahawk can dent, and no exercise in violence disturb a hair of. An indubitable lady with a voice like a cutlass, Madam has no gentilities, and is incapable of embarrassing herself. I see her, once, under the sweetness-and-light gaze of the Merrie England inhabitants of Margaret Tarrant pictures, pursue an eight-year-old vandal and rebel around the Kindergarten's assembly hall, and catch him by the upright Bechstein as an old vixen catches a gosling, as fate and the law must catch the sinful and stupid. This pursuit and capture is a nice illustration of the proper use of fate and the law, of the old, the trained, the inexorable, the unruffled, the speedy. In less symbolic a manner this spinster of over fifty whose jabots, although of chiffon or *crêpe de Chine*, seem carved from whiteness itself, pursues her staff of younger spinsters until their imperfections become exhausted and their blackboards perfect—meticulously arranged multiplication tables, copperplate sentences in coloured chalk . . . *The cat sat on the mat. A fish is on a dish* . . . and polychromatic friezes of illustrations to nursery rhymes and fairy stories. Madam, and each of us lesser teachers, believe that children can be taught to control themselves and material. None of us believes, in those days, before Jewish-Mittel-European and "progressive" American notions of child education hit Australia, that education is fun-fun-fun and sugar-and-spice, or that a splodge of poster paint on a piece of butcher's paper is anything more than a splodge. ("And what is that, dear? An elephant? An umbrella? Little Miss Muffet? Oh, it's your Uncle Albie drinking a glass of tomato juice. Very good, dear.") Even though some of the less courageous teachers pretend to rave about Van Gogh's "Sunflowers" there is still enough courage remaining for them to mock the suggestion that an aimless swirl made by childish fingers dripping with coloured goo is Art, or training for anything except swiping soiled fingers across clean surfaces.

From Madam and the older teachers worked with during my suburban state school decade, I learn many tricks of the trade. I also learn much from them as human beings, reluctantly absorbing medicinal lessons in kindliness, honesty, courage, forbearance, and humility. Piecemeal, I acquire a little of the much I lack. I pick the pockets of those who have hard-earned a handful of wisdom or a shillings-worth of nobility. On the other hand I steer clear in myself of weaknesses, coarsenesses and gaucheries observed in others.

The Headmaster, Percival J. Green, despite the fact that he is, as I am, a Gippslander, is a man I nearly respect yet do not wholly admire. I am offhandedly fond of him as one is of a big cuddly toy. This is largely, perhaps, because he seems to have taken a shine to me, the least tractable and most wilful member of the staff. It is impossible to know why he has this affection. Indeed, it is always impossible for me to see why any other human being likes me—this is written without any humility whatever. It is far easier to understand someone's dislike—this is written without any pride. I know enough about me neither to like nor dislike me.

12

I suspect P.J.G. always of acting the Headmaster as well as being the Headmaster. He has a wide, apple-cheeked, yeoman-farmer face with peasant-shrewd blue eyes, and a brow which mounts roundly into a thinning undergrowth of baby's-hair bull's-wool. A middle-aged, bulky man, he indeed resembles a well-disposed bull. His wife and his two grown-up daughters are, on the other hand, waxen, chiselled of profile, and elegantly got up. One feels that, transformed into creatures of the Reign of Terror, the three females would disdainfully descend from the dung-carts of Paris, and disdainfully mount the steps to the guillotine while a tricolour-sporting P.J.G. roars from the gutter, "*A bas les aristos!*"

He has had some sort of partial stroke and, always on the go, limps and stumps up and down the long, wide corridor between the class-rooms, booming like a bittern, and duelling at space with one of those point-to-point-meeting sticks. State School 1409 is, all in all, a noisy monkey-house of a school, but it is with the noise of work, the noise of a factory, the din of dedication.

Every Friday, mid-morning, as apart as Napoleon, in the centre of the playground, he sits tripodically on the opened-out stick-handle. Meantime, class after class, all following the school brass band playing "Colonel Bogey", the school marches round and round and round, over the cindery ground, past the peppercorn trees, past the boys' lavatory, past the shelter sheds and the drinking-taps, round and round again and again until with an imperial gesture P.J.G. waves an enormous handkerchief. The band expires. The school halts. In the silence he announces with the voice of God's own major-domo the name of the most soldierly class.

P.J.G. chews peanuts constantly. Since he sprays as he bawls Othello-like into the mouthpiece of the office telephone it is ringed with peanut specks. He bawls with such outsize vehemence that "Why bother to use the bloody phone?" say the more twitchy members of the staff, the ones who were gassed at Passchendaele or still contain grits of Gallipoli shrapnel. By Friday afternoon, after five days of bawling and roaring and stumping about, P.J.G. slumps. So, in a sense, does the school which now occupies itself with manual matters—sloyd, chip-carving, basket-making, knitting, needlework, and plasticine-modelling. P.J.G. appears at the window in the door of my class-room, his expression both wistful and despotic, and beckons with a stubby finger. When I open the door he whispers, in a manner adroitly pitched between plea and command, "Come and talk to me, Laddie." I put the class on their honour to behave well. This means, God help you Young Turks if I hear you. Skilled in the diplomacy of behaving honourably, they misbehave with the stealth of dingoes. Meantime I undergo a weekly experience which is perpetually interesting, partly because P.J.G. means "Come and listen to me, Laddie. I'm tired and alone," partly because he calls me—on Friday afternoons only, and a sheer accident—by my childhood pet name, partly because I sit, a decorous stooge with permission to smoke, on an arse-mortifying Public Works Department chair while he lies on the floor beneath a Public Works Department table, his head on a cretonne-encased cushion of superior grubbiness which rests on a cartridge box, eating peanuts, and talking. What these years of monologues are about is largely beyond recall, though it is recallable that the monologues are not always fresh, that any one Friday's soliloquy can be any other Friday's *réchauffé*. There are certainly long analyses of his two favourite books, *Origin of Species* and *The Martyrdom of Man*, and affectionate reminiscences of his favourite schoolmaster, Spielvogel. He presents me also, from under the office table, as from under a nabob's palanquin, with his own schoolmasterly trinkets of wisdom. Of these I retain but few:

Never keep in one girl only after school.

If a message is to be run send one boy only because one boy is one boy, two boys are half a boy, three boys are no boy at all.

A teacher has to repeat and repeat and repeat until repetition becomes an absurdity—and then repeat again.

A man who stands on his dignity is standing on a balloon.

Not once does he offer a peanut. The large brown-paper bag of them near his hand on the abraded turkey-red mat continually rustles, the shells continually splinter, and the litter on the solid upcurve of his clerical-grey waistcoat and on the floor continually increases and spreads, and so offends my strong streak of Teutonic neatness that it is difficult to keep from using the feather duster hanging on a hook at the side of the glass-fronted cedar bookcase. All the time, behind the rustling and the splintering and P.J.G.'s sonorous and over-modulated voice, one is aware of the turbine of the school week running peacefully down. There is briskly mournful singing from class-rooms nearer or farther away from the office . . . "The Ash Grove", "Strawberry Fair", "Molly Malone", "John Peel", "White sands and grey sands", and "London's burning". Farthest away, thread-thin as the choiring of infant angels on settees of cumuli, the Kindergarten children can be heard. One knows that their soiled little hands are pressed together prayer-wise, and their lustrous eyes closed, as they sing:

Now the day is over,
Night is drawing nigh,
Shadows of the evening
Steal across the sky.

Any minute, the bell will tinnily ring, and all hell will be let loose. The mob will flee towards Saturday and games. Already, in the nineteen-thirties, many of the games of my childhood have become as unfashionable as jazz garters, meerschaums, sun-bonnets, ludo, and trilbies. The Depression children of seaside and dockland Williamstown no longer totter on stilts, or play tip-cat or spin tops or bowl hoops. The streets are no more to be picked over for gilt-and-vermilion cigar-bands; cigarettes are not accompanied by silk-covered cigarette cards; Tobler chocolates at a penny a slab have disappeared, and with them the enchanting picture cards—*Petit Poucet, Contes de Fées,* Robinson Crusoe, Cascades, *Perroquets, Metropoles Comiques, Chiens de Chasse, Navires de Guerre,* and the series of the three children in sailor costume who, attended by a night-gowned female (an angel? a fairy?) with the wings of an inferior moth, and holding a camera, are pictured globe-trotting at such places as St Petersburg, Amsterdam, the North Pole, and the Jung-frau. Skipping is still mildly modish, and jacks are still dyed with Condy's Crystals, but marbles are no longer the gem-like

15

spheres of my time, and the game is less elaborate, less fervent, an agate-less and colourless match fought out with the grey-green glass stoppers of lemonade bottles.

P.J.G. with his peanuts and point-to-point stick and his maxims (Good, better, best; never let it rest, until your good is better, and your better best) is a shrewder and much more powerful headmaster than his fatherly exposure of himself as an eccentric windbag suggests. Even now I don't care to turn any of his maxims on its back. State School 1409 runs like a souped-up Daimler, and the showiest of the staff "personalities", even Madam who transmogrifies herself into a gracious and charming Grande Dame in his presence, are well under his blunt thumb.

For some of the older men on the staff, returned men from the Great War—one is actually a steak-faced, pot-bellied colonel with hands like Mona Lisa—I insist on myself having just sufficient respect as a form of gratitude for not having to goose-step, eat frankfurters boiled in pilsener, or salute the German flag. I do not, perversely, let this unfair minimum of respect show even a whisker nor do I reveal that my deepest feeling about them is one of masculine timidity. They are the veterans of the tribe, the old-stagers and warriors, scarred not only by actual woundings of lung and limb but also by experiences I have not had and cannot imagine. A number of the elements of their maleness have been, at Ypres or Cairo or Villers-Bretonneux, welded into a design that must differ from the unwelded elements of maleness in my nature. They and the dead who steamed away in puttees and dashing khaki hats to the tune of "Goodbye, Melbourne Town" make the fence behind which I and my generation put down roots in bloodless soil, and put out young leaves in an air free of mustard gas and dum-dum bullets and foreign notions. They could justifiably be sickened by the knowledge that a flibbertigibbet whippersnapper too wily to display respect or timidity is one of the creatures they ate skilly for, killed other men for, and laid themselves open to the inconveniences of trench feet, shell-shock, limblessness, Egyptian or French gonorrhoea, and the risk of unbelievable death. They disquiet me because I am jealous of their knowledge, because there is perceivable in the depths of

16

their eyes—which can see children playing with yo-yos, and men of my age playing miniature golf, puffing at gold-tipped cigarettes, and wearing silk socks—the damped-down lights of appalling yesterdays in shattered landscapes drenched by cloud-bursts of metal and flame. Until I understand more, I am apprehensive of them because they mock what seems to me their own courage by monosyllables of obliquity, by changing the subject, by outright silence. They may drink their tea like horses, hold knives and forks like fountain pens, and belch as publicly as babies, but in the matter of war, their manners are flawless, their reticence masterly. Because I'm a blabber-mouth at this stage, reticence disturbs me. This is my first inkling of what is now a conviction nothing can shake; in situations involving the sensibilities and sensitivities of others, Australian men are the best-mannered men in the world: oaves maybe, gentlemen indubitably.

If I fortify and amuse myself in the presence of these more seasoned males by impersonating a dissolute and flashy young bohemian this is not so with the older women teachers to whom the impersonation is that of a giddy spark who is really a very nice boy. Politeness—the opposite of love!—is all. I am almost orientally polite, pushing chairs under female bottoms, leaping at door handles, carrying feminine parcels even if they be wrapped in pink tissue paper, walking on the gutter side of the footpath. For some of the older women I sustain varying degrees of affection, but platonic, purely. Having been rather baldly and incompetently seduced at the age of seventeen by a temporary teacher with the morals of Catherine the Great, who plucked me as it were *en passant*, I am momentarily somewhat at a loss about women, and certainly very cagey of women over forty. Fastidiousness? A Greta Garbo standard? Immaturity? Selfishness? Conceit? I am at the level-crossing stage of *Stop, Look, Listen*—'tis safer so.

With Miss Glew who is older than I but is certainly nowhere near forty there flourishes a kind of cultural relationship. Pastels have come into vogue as a medium in the school art lessons; she and I are rather dabs at executing with these gritty crayons very glossy Jonathan apples, bunches of Lady Finger and Black Hambro grapes, copper kettles, and artistically run-

17

down windmills with scarecrow sails. Armada galleons on James Elroy Flecker seas, and Viking ships with dinosaur prows and billowing striped sails also excite our attention. One Saturday afternoon we brazenly sketch the bluestone backside of a church in a lane off Little Collins Street; sometimes we go to the middle-brow theatre together—Margaret Rawlings in *The Barretts of Wimpole Street* at the Athenaeum Theatre sums it up. Miss Glew is friendly with some of the famous and quarter-famous of the day, and is accepted as the school authority on art. This fazes me not a tittle and, once, I now recall with some astonishment, while eating mushrooms on toast at the Cavalier Restaurant I passionately uphold to her Frank Brangwyn as a more overwhelming painter than Rembrandt. It is not until the Headmaster's plum-duff Friday voice from the nest of peanut-shells under the office table informs me that Miss Glew has called me a promising young man that her support of Rembrandt seems less the act of a deluded woman. "Promising!" roars the Headmaster Falstaffianly. "Promising, eh! You'd promise anything, Laddie, anything!" He is so amused with himself he nearly has a second stroke. I sit mum and bleak with a smile as small as a mouse's.

The nearest I get to love of a woman a few years older than myself is with Miss Graham whose Christian name of Amy is so not-her, for she is forthright and downright and a brilliant teacher, that we call her Tommo which is equally not-her. She is just old enough to be young enough for me, at one period, to meet her at a level of almost compulsive puppy-love. On my side only, this is. Just outside my range of vision which scarcely extends an arm's length beyond my own wonderful, subtle, perceptive, multi-gifted, et cetera, et cetera, et cetera self, she is tracking square with Mr Roberts, a small, handsome, pipestem-chewing teacher whom—to my absolute amazement —she ultimately marries. Mr Roberts lives in a suburb on the other side of Melbourne, a long way in those carless days. The Headmaster is the only one of the staff of State School 1409 who owns a motor-car, a sort of beige hearse with buttoned-on isinglass side curtains. Mr Roberts being thus far removed— and maybe he is a non-dancer—I apparently serve as a fill-in cavalier for Williamstown dances and balls. Regard me, there-

18

fore, albeit cagey and as naïvely hard-bitten as a shop-soiled romantic can be, in the florist's buying a spray of non-U pink carnations for Tommo with whom I am nearly as besotted as with foxtrots, the Blues, circular waltzes, one-steps, and such revived Edwardian dances as the Gipsy Tap and the Oxford Waltz. Politely or bravely Tommo attaches the carnations to the shoulder-strap of her evening dress of apricot taffeta. The front of the dress is just below her knees, the back descends in ruffles to touch the beeswax polished hardwood floor of the Williamstown Town Hall or of the something-or-other Tennis Club Hall while the saxophone yearns out the melodies of the day: "If You Knew Susie", "Walking My Baby Back Home", "In the Valley of the Moon", and "I'm Alone Because I Love You". Despite my poverty I have had a dinner suit made, at what stern denial of belly or necessity I cannot now imagine or remember. In wing collar and porcelain-fronted shirt, a clove carnation or a cornflower in my lapel (a touch picked up from gossip about the Prince of Wales or Noël Coward), suffering divine sartorial discomfort, and hung with the ritual scarf of knitted white silk, I hasten through the effervescing night to the lights and the balloons, and the scented and painted women in golden or silver shoes, and the hours of dancing until "Good-night, Ladies" is played, and "God Save the King". Now and then during these evenings, and to my dismay, for Tommo and I seem to me to be the Ginger Rogers and Fred Astaire of the suburb, there is a Canadian Barn Dance. If I do not get, in the changeover of partners, a tight-lipped undertaker's daughter in acid-green who dances like a penguin, there enfolds me a matronly bolster in the royal-blue satin councillors' wives are prone to wear on which is pinned a spray of the same muni-cipal-pink carnations, stems in silver paper, I have bought for Miss Amy Graham, the basketball-playing and Galsworthy-reading teacher of Grade Six who gives me *Zadig* for my twenty-first birthday.

With the other Junior Teachers, the young men and women nearest me in age, my relations are unelaborate and, in retro-spect, strangely pure, curiously devoid of friction, keep-off-the-grass friendships.

During the ten years in which I calmly acquire the notoriety

19

of being—surely—the oldest Junior Teacher in the Victorian Education Department if not the most elderly one south of the Tropic of Capricorn, I inevitably encounter several waves of Junior Teachers fresh from country or suburban high schools, their youthful pimples and ideals still showing. Most of them, being the children of lower-middle-class or upper-working-class parents born in the nineteenth century, have absorbed with a mother's milk and had beaten into them by a father's razor-strop a clean-cut acceptance of the decencies fashionable to those classes in late-Victorian and Edwardian times. Even if born, as most of these young people have been, to be no more than minor characters, they are minor characters of the astute and solid salt-of-the-earth kind who are to become other versions of Madam and P.J.G. Looking back with tenderness and affection on them it is astonishing but warming to recall the placidity, offhandedness and frivolity of the relationship which is, at one and the same time, articulate to a degree and absolutely inarticulate. After school we talk and laugh together for hours. What we talk about and laugh at is lost for ever. It is only possible to recall, and vividly, what we do not talk about. Politics and religion are taboo, so is sex. The young men do not even swap dirty yarns. The Depression—which reaches rock bottom in Victoria in November 1931 with 26·8 per cent of the population on the Unemployment Relief Fund —is never spoken of. What then, apart from ourselves and our restricted doings, are we endlessly articulate about? Maybe we touch on Amy Johnson and *Jason's Quest*, and the appearance of the first neon signs on the Regent and Plaza picture theatres and the *Argus* building, and the disappearance of Bert Hinkler into a grave in Florence, Kingsford Smith into the mystery of Burma, and King Edward the Eighth into a blinding and shameful sunset. The scandalous newspaper, nasty-green *Beckett's Budget*, also disappears, so do white celluloid eye-shades lined with green, and hair-ribbons, and—except on film stars like Ann Harding—long hair. The first air-mail and the first chilled beef from Australia reach England. Couéism goes out of fashion. An odd Irishman, Francis Edward de Groot, whom I meet nearly thirty years later in Dublin where he runs an antique shop, makes himself conspicuous by slashing the

20

ribbon at the opening of the Sydney Harbour Bridge. Oxford Groupers come into being, and such expressions as go-slow, motivate, pylon, what's yours?, donor, says you, whodunit, Nazism, nitwit, loopy, and advert.

These newly minted words especially fascinate me as words have especially fascinated me from boyhood. In 1934 I learn to use wizard, pickled, and pansy in place of gorgeous, molo, and queen. Ascorbic arrives, and more uncomfortable words like Pakistan and Brownshirt. In the same year the Shrine of Remembrance is dedicated by the Duke of Gloucester, and Egon Kisch, a Communist being deported from Australia, jumps from the ship, and breaks his leg on the wharf. Neither of these events much stirs me . . . it has just become nearly clear to me that Communism and the Soviet Union are something to do with Bolshevism and Russia, and that Russia is no longer the Russia I know from books and films—Turgenev and Chekhov, Stephen Leacock, Emil Jannings in *The Patriot*, William Boyd in *The Volga Boatman*—any more than it is the country of Rasputin, kulaks, St Petersburg, gaudy garlic-headed churches, Don Cossacks, and wolves chasing sledges through a landscape of Christmas trees and snow. In 1934 too I first meet one of the people of my generation who is later to become famous. He comes to teach at State School 1409, and it is instantly obvious that he possesses qualities lacking in the other young teachers. His surname is Dargie. Although he has two Christian names and is only twenty-two, the staff, young and older, call him Dargie to his face, and discuss him behind his back as Dargie rather in the manner of one saying Gains-borough or Grock. Whether this is something that he, confident of his future, compels us to do, either by direct or tangential means, or whether this is mass-prognostication and pre-recognition of his future, eludes me, quite. He is decidedly, we see, someone to prognosticate about. Miss Glew and I, hitherto the Pastel Queen and Pastel King of S.S. 1409, hastily descend from our thrones: Dargie is crowned the sole monarch. He can really draw.

Dargie is, in 1934, my 1934 idea of handsome, and has a proud, neat countenance informed by intelligence, and adorned by a shapely beard of a deep colour hard to put a name to, some virile tint between cedar and ox-blood, a composed negligence of ripples at the heart of which live two sensitive red lips. For some reason now too remote for capture he seems to resemble Dante Gabriel Rossetti, or some romantic bravo composed—half-words, half-paint—by Rossetti. He is going through a period of wearing nut-brown tweeds, a period I have momentarily put by for a farcical get-up of plus-fours, brogues enlivened by straps and buckles, and lumber-jackets with leather buttons. He and I, both eschewing the bestial gods of luck, and set, almost from the threshold of the womb, on being members of success, are each too occupied by our own developing natures to require to be deep and interdependent friends, but we are, because our witch-doctor natures compel us towards steeper paths than those to be trodden by the other young teachers, close acquaintances and—in the mode of the era—garrulous about much, secretive about much. We sense that it is action, not knowledge, which transforms the world, but support knowledge. This is, ultimately, to make us into older men who are coolies to more information about hell than those in hell.

He has his kingly beard, I my pallid imperial and Ronald Colman moustache. My fingernails are affectedly long, his are trimmed straight at each side and across the top in the shape of a demi-hexagon. Our literary tastes are as different as our finger-ends. He is a devotee of Ezra Pound, Auden, Spender, and T. S. Eliot, none of whom, as poets, enthral me in the nineteen-thirties. I prefer Swinburne, Herrick, *haiku*, Edith Sitwell, Gerard Manley Hopkins, and the more woe-struck of Masefield's poems. About painting and drawing I have not the information to hold opinions worth a cracker—Tissot excites me more than Turner, Delacroix more than Dégas, Vermeer more than Van Gogh, Guardi more than Gauguin, and my rabble of favourites includes Edmund Dulac, Böcklin, Ida Rentoul Outhwaite, Hieronymus Bosch, Gustave Doré, Albrecht Dürer, John Austin, Arthur Rackham, and Elioth Gruner—eclectic to vanishing point. Dargie, on the other hand, is infinitely knowledgeable, and has the firmest convictions which are all the firmer because he is absorbing technique along with the results of technique.

He has what he calls a studio in one of the disintegrating mansions of a bygone sea captain or wealthy ship's chandler along The Strand, a double-cube 1850 drawing-room. This has a chimney-piece of carved white marble from Belgium, and a deep bay-window through the hand-made glass panes of which the silt jetties at the mouth of the Yarra River are to be seen, and dredges and buoys and pilot-ships, and P. and O. liners, and yachts from the Royal Yacht Club, and seagulls and cormorants, the wastes of Fisherman's Bend shimmering with noon-flowers in summer, and a Port Melbourne Whistlerishly etherealized by distance. At night the twinkling fires of a raffish encampment can be seen inland from Fisherman's Bend —Dudley Flats, a squalid Alsatia of shelters made from packing-cases, fish-crates, oil-drums and corrugated iron in which the more gipsified and degenerate victims of the Depression and their own weaknesses re-enact Gin Lane, swigging methylated spirits from triangular bottles, gnawing Cornish pasties and shark-and-chips, and consummating goatish amours in nests of newspapers and sugar-bags. I often see these fuming stars of fires as I lope along the sea-cold Strand to sit for Dargie, sometimes lugging a kitbag of Mallee roots stolen from the school woodshed to feed his fire in its arched frame of marble. The ex-drawing-room is, however, too vast to be much de-refrigerated by these pilferings: Dargie's breath, as he paints, is sometimes visible mist; now and then he must unhook his thumb from the palette, and beat his freckled hands together.

In 1965 I sit again for Dargie the O.B.E.-holder in his Famous Painter's studio cosy as mink, furnished with a full-size reproduction of his portrait of Queen Elizabeth II, and the treasures he has picked up during his many circlings of the world. Now that we are older we no longer need beard or imperial, those disguises—oh-so-carefully nurtured, oh-so-carefully pruned in narcissistic looking-glasses—behind which young men try to conceal their doubts or encourage their delusions about themselves. Our fingernails are conventionally filed. Our habiliments are expensive and seemly. We talk of our younger selves with mocking affection as of sons we ruefully indulge but would not like to be. Young men are bores, we decide, however charming, and crass amateurs. Indeed, one is

23

never fully professional until one has accomplished all, until one is dead and, for the first time, properly visible. Dargie digs up one of the Williamstown portraits. It makes my nerves run cold to look into my own very clear, very steady, tell-nothing eyes which have, a mere half-hour before, watched the Depression fires blinking on Dudley Flats, the fires of other people's gehenna. It is chastening to confront the unwrinkled face, seemingly ascetic, incorruptible, and private, and amusing to observe that I am wearing a pale trench coat with preposterously wide lapels, a garment the young men of my day are much given to, and which it is necessary because fashionable to wear grimy.

Later in 1965 Dargie is in London again, this time painting the Queen on a horse which poses separately from Her Majesty, and indolent with drugs. I am also in this haunted city of grimy stone and grimy history to sit through with fascinated astonishment, and what once would have been—in the days when it was breathtaking to own a fountain pen—disbelief, the rehearsals at the Royal Court Theatre of a play of mine being directed in the neurotic West End manner by a young man needing to be as heavily bearded as Rasputin. He directs on literal tiptoe, seeking, and thinking to find, subtleties not there, bulldozing subtleties already there, and having the time of his life. I am staying at one of the numberless South Kensington middle-class terrace mansions which have been converted into hotels. This hotel sticks to the pattern of all the many hotels within lasso distance of the Victoria and Albert Museum. Minute Bar. Minute and spastic lift. Chintz lounge with stopped-short grandfather clock; painting of windjammer buckjumping on bottle-green and yeasty billows; Chinese vase, *circa* 1908, tall as a four-year-old girl, and holding an insufficiency of plastic delphiniums. Pebble-eyed manageress with pseudo-Knightsbridge accent veneered over Cheshire. Irish porters, waitresses, and chambermaids all being very top-o'-the-mornin'-to-you-sir, and all smelling of un-recent sweat. Library for Use of Resident Guests—Sheila Kaye-Smith, James Agate, E. Phillips Oppenheim, H. V. Morton, Edgar Jepson, Denis Mackail. Silent permanent guests—elderly and English. Talkative transient guests—Germans, Turks, Scots, Dutch, French.

My room, a double-cube first floor front with french windows opening on to a long, narrow, wrought-iron-bounded balcony, is indubitably the ex-drawing-room. Its chimney-piece, of white marble from Belgium, is of precisely the same design as that in Dargie's Williamstown studio—this, at least, stirs me.

Dargie, who is temporarily using a Buckingham Palace drawing-room as studio, fittingly has more distinguished accommodation than I—a mews flat hung with paintings of the Heidelberg School family, and within a few blocks of the ormolu and Canalettos of the Wallace Collection, Madame Tussaud's, his favourite Greek restaurant, Queen Mary's Garden, and *le cinéma bleu*. At 9 Wimpole Mews it is only a few rubbish-tins and butcher-blue doors away from 17 Wimpole Mews where Mr Profumo visited Miss Christine Keeler; in the next street, at 50 Wimpole Street, Mr Robert Browning visited Miss Elizabeth Barrett whose ringlets flopped on her jaws in the same way as her spaniel Flash's ears flopped on his. While Dargie and I sit drinking retsina at 9 Wimpole Mews, I raving about Malmaison, he about Princess Marina, it dawns on me that I still, after thirty-odd years of it, affect the kind of garment he once painted me in. Lying on a chair is the trench-coat I have arrived wearing, a pale trench-coat with preposterously wide lapels. It is, however, spotless.

As one who is concerned with the truth rather than the facts I find both trench-coat and chimney-piece apposite elements in the Williamstown-London-Dargie-me relationship. Their accidental duplication—another trench-coat, another chimney-piece—does not, of course, affect the relationship but does intensify my conception of the relationship. No matter how invisibly fine is the thread strung from, say, coat A to coat B, it is a straight, a dead-straight, thread passing through thousands of miles and thousands of hours, and connects the centre of my consciousness directly to yet another dimension of the world I am composed of. The quality of one's connection with people through their relation with things, tunes, scents, sounds, and so on is a subject of great allure, its existence a great blessing. Being thus connected, thus braided into a web composed of sumless such unseen and unbreakable threads, it is not possible ever to be lonely. Moreover, reined in and informed by these threads, one is more aware of one's destiny, and cannot suddenly and brutally collide with it.

The decade spent at State School 1409, a longer period by years than I ever spend in one job or at any one place in the world, provides so many connecting threads that one is constantly being put in immediate touch with what time cannot alter, and which nothing can annihilate until one's consciousness is itself annihilated. Walking, for example, a quarter of a century after I cease being a Junior Teacher, through The Meadows in Edinburgh I come on a cartridge box lying near the whalebone arch over the path to the University. Instantly, there is the feather duster hanging on the cedar bookcase. The pewter inkwell and the rectangular bottle of red ink are there on the Public Works Department table. The brown-paper bag rustles. P.J.G., years ago dead and silent and skeletonized, crushes another peanut in his fingers, and intones plummily from beneath the table, "*Vestigia nulla retrorsum*, Laddie. Remember that always: *vestigia nulla retrorsum*." He turns his jowled chawbacon face towards me, and his sharp blue peasant eyes. There, in a Williamstown no one else sees, there, in The Meadows sodden and green with Scotch autumn, I see face and eyes and cretonne cushion and cartridge box—GRAND PRIX SPORTING CARTRIDGES, SCHULTZ, and NOT LIABLE TO EXPLODE IN BULK. I hear, for the threads can be fittingly subtle, Miss Greta Benson's Grade Four singing "Over the Sea to Skye".

Williamstown in the nineteen-thirties is, however, not entirely a matter of singing children, Madam, Dargie, P.J.G., pastel lessons, the modelling of relief maps in papier mâché, and a nine-to-four existence within the walls of State School 1409. I spend a mere thirty hours a week there, learning much never to be forgotten. I learn also things long ago forgotten—something called the Seven Herbartian Steps, for instance, and how to use a tuning-fork, and a curious sort of singing called Tonic Sol-fa to which is allied an even more curious sort during which one makes finger signs while chanting in monotone expressions such as ta-ah-tay-tafatete. I pass examinations in this. What it is for is now arcane.

All in all, my adventures within the walls are mild.

Outside—ah!

Outside, the adventures have that smell of fantasy which I now know is the smell of daily reality, the smell of life. Outside, I am playing one of the many parts I find myself, at the drop of the coin, playing in those days, this time as a Simple Simon to that eternal Greek chorus of women tricked out as landladies.

Until Mother dies I live in the art nouveau comfort of 60 Victoria Street, W.16, with Aunt Rosa Bona, Mother's sister, who is married to Uncle Martini-Henry, Father's brother. Mother's disappearance is the disappearance also of any obligation to comfort her by remaining under the eye of her sister and Father's brother. Aunt Bona and Uncle Tini have known me for ever. They have dandled me in their courting days when I am plump and portable in a bonnet threaded with blue ribbon, a smocked gown twice as long as I am, mittens and bootees threaded with blue ribbon, and a padded bib of Swiss lawn embroidered with forget-me-nots. At the age of four, in a sailor suit adorned with anchor-embossed brass buttons, I am at their wedding and, intending both kindness and neatness, throw confetti not on their new clothes but into a golden-privet hedge near a lich-gate. When I come down from the country to be a Junior Teacher they take me in, feed me well, and do not once question my comings and goings. I love them both but, Mother dead, I drop them without a twinge.

I order the first taxi-cab I ever order and, feeling extremely polished, very man-of-the-world, set out on what is to be a longer paper chase than I could have foreseen. I set out to live with strangers. I have, since that day in 1929, spent most of my life living with strangers in the houses and hotels and boarding-houses and flats and ship's cabins of strangers. Right from the jump I receive many shocks, and many kinds of shocks. The first kind is with domestic practices never before encountered.

Since Mother and Aunt were both brought up in the same house in the same country town, and picked up their house-keeping habits from Grandmother Ruff, I can perceive no great difference between Aunt's and Mother's way of doing things. Aunt Rosa Bona uses the same recipes as Mother does for Christmas Pudding, Jubilee Pudding, Tomato Sauce, Banburies,

Melon and Pineapple Jam, Fruit Salad, and everything else. Her millet broom wears a stocking top, a species of stays, just as Mother's does. Aunt also tests Genoa Cake or Madeira Cake with a broom-straw, and goes through the rituals of bed-making, sheet-stretching, brass-doorstep-polishing, hearthrug-beating, and clothes-boiling in the same manner and at the same sacred times as Mother. She buys things long familiar to me—Bon Ami, Champion's Malt Vinegar, Red Feather Cheese, cracknels, rump steak, sirloins, Schweppes' Lime Juice in conical bottles, Monkey Brand Soap, Wright's Coal Tar Soap, Zam-buk, Rose's Marmalade, Uncle Toby's Oats and Kruse's Fluid Magnesia. Although quasi-aware that there are other sorts of soap, lime juice, and vinegar, I've scarcely encountered them. That period is over. In strangers' houses the other sorts are to be encountered, along with foods and housekeeping customs which often rattle or repulse me, while at the same time displaying to me that what and how people eat in the privacy of their own boxes, and how they behave within those boxes, are the sharpest pointers to what they are.

Transfixed at State School 1409, I inhabit Williamstown for ten years. During eight of these I am far from being transfixed in one house, one bedroom, one bed. I seem to spend a dispro-portionate amount of time in a mustard-yellow taxi-cab. It is raining. I hear the sea thrashing about, and do not at all feel suave and a man-of-the-world jammed in among my belongings which have been temporarily thrust into inherited, run-down portmanteaux or zinc-lined tea-crates bearing such statements as TJARENNANG, PRODUCE OF JAVA, TARRA 14, NETTO 82, BRUTO 96. With the bronze statuette of the Goddess of Mercy Grand-father Porter gave me, a pewter hotwater jug, a Lionel Lind-say woodcut of toucans, half-a-dozen wine glasses from Webb's, a secondhand Daimler-black Remington typewriter almost as cumbersome as a linotype machine, and always a lap-ful of books I cannot squeeze in—Daisy Miller, The Great Gatsby, S.S. San Pedro, The Story of an African Farm, Madame Bovary, Roget's Thesaurus, The Ugly Duchess—I am fleeing, raddled of cheek and ice-eyed with rage, after a volcanic showdown with the latest landlady.

What am I always fleeing from?

In the physical sense I am fleeing, largely, from the very people I have stepped outside the family circle and class deliberately to attempt living with; essentially I am fleeing from standards of existence which throw me. Most of all I am fleeing from what interferes with my placidity, and kindles emotions I prefer leaving dead wood. It is not that there is any fragment of desire at all to re-enter the briarless glades and moss-cushioned dells of boyhood; to hell with racing backwards. "Onward!" is the unuttered cry, "Press on!" and "Ex-cel-si-or-r-r-r!" Oh yes, I am in dead earnest about toting the banner with the strange device, but lugging a picnic basket of familiar victuals in the other hand. It is, nearly always, the subject of food that leads to quarrels and, next step, the taxi-cab. I cannot and—more definitely—will not compel myself to pretend relish for, or even grin-and-bear-it satisfaction in, the dishes put before me. Many of the dishes are new to me. None have I had to face up to before. Were I the subject of charity, or the traveller hounded by night and storm, the situation would be fair enough. I am, however, paying more than half of my small wages for what has been advertised as comfortable bed and excellent board. Excellent board, I discover, generally means black puddings, mutton birds, stuffed ox-heart, flap, Digestive Meal cooked in water, grey potato soup, bread pudding, fish and chips, tinned jam, sometimes a few square inches of a wizened and fibrous steak called Equal-to-Rump, and sometimes veal which, as most people from the country do, I regard with some repugnance.

Within a week after leaving Aunt Rosa Bona's table it is obvious that, unless the right landlady is discovered, I am to perish of an irritation not hitherto experienced, or of slow starvation. I am always putting down spoon or fork, and excusing myself from any more than the trial taste of one (one!) under-sized egg with a yolk of musty primrose, or a reeking slab of braised liver, or the curried gobbets of unidentifiable parts of an unidentifiable creature to which my mind inclines to put a name such as goanna, Labrador, tomcat or auk. Within a fort-night I am wedged again in a taxi-cab nursing the books I cannot pack—*Crome Yellow*, *The Garden Party*, *Pears Cyclopaedia*, *Sussex Gorse*, Perrault's *Fairy Tales* illustrated by Harry

Clarke, and a bundle of copies of *Le Sourire* containing the sort of advertisement that catches my impure attention:

J. homme 26 a. journaliste étranger, robuste, des. conn. dame. JOE au *Sourire*.

MADAME curieuse et moderne, si possible disting. êtes-vous lasse du banal et souhaitez-vous du nouveau? NIX c/o Iris, 22, rue Saint-Augustin.

L'INDEPENDANTE et originale CAPRICE aime trop le renouveau. On peut la conquérir une fois mais jamais plus. Ecr. CAPRICE, c/o Iris, 22, r. Saint-Augustin.

DEUX dames broient du blanc et ont les idées noires. Elles dés. conn. deux gentl. NIRA au *Sourire*.

Thus laden, I have begun, in earnest now, a vagrant's life, a paper chase existence.

In the next two years I move nine times, in and out of back-street maisonettes furnished with bitter lies and bitterer truths, and flock-filled sateen eiderdowns, and firescreens of stamped brass whereon, in low relief, a Teniers scene of guzzling and gorging mocks me as I wait for the dinner of three wafers of Strasbourg sausage, five sopping brussels sprouts, a wedge of ironbark pumpkin, a "sweet" of junket and prunes, a cup of cheapest Ceylon tea.

I find out that, behind the starched curtains and the half-drawn blinds and clipped prisms of privet and brasso-ed door-bell, lies a slum world run largely by Methodist widows, English, unintelligent, shrewd as pickpockets, a world where milk is poured into cups before tea is, where electric-light bulbs are thirty-watt, bananas black, apples shrivelled and flecked with acrid beauty spots, lavatory-paper a scandal sheet, and table napkins never used. Fortnightly a pretence of changing bed-linen is made, and one fresh sheet, and one fresh pillow-case appear. The fresh sheet is the new upper one, the used upper one becomes the lower. Pillow-cases are similarly meanly trans-planted.

Those of the landladies who are not widows, own husbands. Of four enchained males whose roofs and discomforts I briefly share, all are smallish, all are teetotallers, one only of them smokes. The smoker is a tally-clerk; the others are a clicker, an upholsterer, and a railway porter. We talk sleet or humidity, we talk about cricket or football scores; we tell each other that a storm has washed away some of the Williamstown Baths, and that the condition of the footpaths in Hanna Street or Stevedore Street is disgraceful; in short, we tell nothing, and talk about nothing. Why, anyway, should they talk through the bars to free and foolish puppies? They are concealed within themselves and, almost certainly, from themselves.

This is frustrating to me as a young man because, not only am I tracking spoor as a writer, I am after information that will stop me from becoming the sort of man each of them seems to be. Point the way you walked, and I'll walk elsewhere. I inwardly wince and inwardly flush with anger when the landladies—in front of the eighteen-year-old or nineteen-year-old stranger—order their husbands about, rebuke them as though they were bad children, and denigrate them to their faces. Politely, I show none of the anger or embarrassment felt when the little, middle-aged men also show neither embarrassment nor anger in situations where I would have my rapier out. Seeking answers both as writer and enquiring primitive I retreat to posing questions to which, then as much as now, I am uncertain of the answers. Are these men, viciously emasculated before my very eyes, also being polite? Or, having been cut at so often, do they no longer feel pain? Do they ever think murder, or flight? Is it that, having sold themselves, they have bought only what they have the price for? Certainly there can be no answers from them to questions one asks only of oneself. The single conclusion I arrive at is a dreary one and lopsided— the conclusion of a young man flummoxed by but interested in the antics of an Adam and an Eve of a certain kind—that rats know the way of rats, that all putrid flesh has the same taste, that all fifth-rate people live in the same way, exercising their talent for meanness, nagging, petulance, self-pity, evasion, and —oh, all the fifth-rate practices. Admittedly, I dine out on skilfully over-tinted accounts of Life as a Paying Guest, as eater of the uneatable, and can be—must be, I now suppose—very amusing about what is not really anywhere near amusing. In fact, since I prefer to believe that it is Man who is ultimately

the great poet—not Shakespeare, not Milton, not Homer—the
unending exhibition of domestic pettinesses is sad and sicken-
ing. Each taxi-cab seems to take me merely deeper into the
weed-sown wastes of this cheese-paring underland, but each
taxi-cab takes a more knowledgeable me.

By the time I am ready to leave the ninth landlady and her
charred rissoles and tin bath and sallow rubber-plant and a husband henpecked until there is nothing left of him but monosyllables, I have acquired a little finesse in paving the way for
and making a cool departure. Towards this end I have re-
invigorated and burnished a lapsed ability for lies. This means
no more than that instead of leaving the house in a willy-willy
of accusations like splintered glass I leave it in such a lucid
blaze of white, grey, and jet-black lies that the truth is as visible as if it had been shrieked out in words of acid and verdi-
gris.

My tenth landlady, Mrs Bachaus, is a lucky find but her
cottage is not in one of the back-streets I set out so enthusiastically, two years before, to make the experiment of living in.
Mrs Bachaus's street is lined with old elms, and smells of baked
seaweed and evaporated waves and the resin of pine trees for
it is only a block away from the beach and the Public Gardens.
On hot days the asphalt footpath outside her picket gate melts
soft, the cicadas burr on and on and endlessly on in the elms,
the pigeons in the Norfolk Island pines of the Gardens endlessly
and contentedly repeat the one clause they know to the sea
captains and pilots and military officers who largely inhabit the
street, living in slate-roofed bluestone houses with look-out
towers up the sides of which Virginia Creeper or green-and-
white ivy swarms. From within these houses there stride
shingled middle-class daughters, Younger Set daughters, Swimming Club daughters, Red Cross and Victoria League daughters, in white fuji silk dresses, and swinging Slazenger tennis
racquets thumb-screwed into weighty wooden presses.

In this street, twenty or less houses away from Mrs Bachaus's,
is the hearty *ménage* of Father's half-sister, Aunt Gwendoline,
and her military husband, with whom live Aunt Nell, Father's
spinster sister, and Father's stepmother who, being of an indefinable relation to me, I call Aunt Kate. The sideboards are

32

loaded with brass vases made from shell-cases, and filled with statice.

From time to time, during my two years' wanderings in the off-colour wasteland of Board-and-Lodging-with-Refined-Private-Family, I have, when hungry, broken my vow of being absolutely independent of the family, and have appeared at Aunt Gwen's early enough not to appear to be hanging around, as I am, for the solid dinner served in a room with burgundy wallpaper, the almost Edwardianly solid dinner—oyster soup, grilled garfish, lamb and green peas, gooseberry tart and cream, Gorgonzola and Limburger cheese and Thin Captain biscuits. Should I, after a dinner of this sort, still feel that a cracked vow might as well be used to the full, it is only necessary to suffer several hours of playing the not-quaite-naice games—Five Hundred, Solo, Pontoon, or Show Poker—Aunt Kate is addicted to and, when the decks of cards are stacked away at eleven o'clock in the box covered with porcupine quills, to hoe into the large bed-time supper she is also addicted to: welsh rabbit and steins of cocoa, or crayfish and brown-bread-and-butter and Foster's Lager. I rarely use my cracked vow thus because card-playing, any sort of gambling, any sort of superstitious call on the guild of gods bores me. Anyway, it is only when the solace of old-fashioned food seems necessary that Aunt Gwen's ringing post-mortems are bearable, or Aunt Kate's hawklike pouncings and tart pronouncements on a wrongly played Knave of Diamonds.

Mrs Bachaus's meals, those of an Australian country woman brought up on Mrs Beeton, make vow-breaking and Pontoon-playing unnecessary. This new landlady is a tall, lumbering widow of about seventy with huge bones from which the flesh sags earthwards as though under a particular attention from the force of gravity. The sparse, creamy floss of her hair is Eton-cropped; her luminous eyes are deeply set and far apart; eye-brows and eyelashes are invisible. The effect which, in 1931 with "Little White Lies" and "Love Letters in the Sand" being whistled along the bare-deck streets of night by unemployed lovers, could be macabre is not so. Mrs Bachaus merely seems to have an afterglow of grace as of someone freshly scrubbed which, in fact, she almost always is as those who have a passion for gardening almost always are. I remember her most as wearing a kind of shift or jibbah, a vast cotton dress, waistless, with short sleeves. It has been so often and so vigorously boiled, and so savaged on the glass corrugations of the scrubbing-board, that the original pink and white stripes have almost vanished in a soothing anonymity.

My attraction to her is immediate and instinctive. Her unusual appearance does not impose itself between me and her core, that core of a human creature instantly clear to those who do not let considerations of a worldly sort fog the vision. To this day I have utter trust in these instinctive assessments, and should regard myself lost to living should instinct be injured by anything, logic and common sense included. On the few occasions in life when I have turned a deaf ear to instinct, and listened to the animal in the loins or to a lesson of tolerance taught by fools, or to pinpricking reason, the aftermath has been disastrous and life-wasting.

I like Mrs Bachaus. I like her cottage which has its name *Shalom* in blistered gold-leaf on the fanlight of the front door. I like its contents which include china dogs, Mary Gregories, an eight-day clock, a cane-seated Vienna rocker, photographs of Mrs Bachaus resembling a Scandinavian princess with a waist like a whippet's, a marble-topped rosewood chiffonier, and a late-Victorian doll's house as overfurnished in exquisite detail as any in the Bethnal Green Museum where—ah, those threads resistant to space and time!—she returns to life after years in the grave, and longer years hung up in the warehouse of my mind. I like my bedroom with jasmine and honeysuckle unbelievably and Wordsworthianly dangling from the window-shade, with its Persian bed and feather mattress and honeycomb quilt, a rattan chaise-lounge, a cedar chest-of-drawers, and two kangaroo-skin mats which skid on the Shinoleum-dangerous lino patterned with bouquets of roses and fern the outline of hairy crabs. After two years of meagre buffalo grass lawns, primulas in lozenge-shaped beds, soapwort, and Exhibition Border, her garden enchants me, partly because it is, at its peak, the romantic Anne Hathaway's Cottage garden of the grocers' calendars but also because it waxes and wanes with the seasons, and has its after-life in ginger jars of home-made potpourri. Lining the brick path to the lavatory there are green-painted kerosene tins cunningly cut into curled strips at the top, and containing molly-coddled geraniums. The lavatory, white-washed within, and bridally hung with snail-flower creeper and mandevillea, contains a shelf of lavatory rolls: Mrs Bachaus is convinced that the antimony of newspaper print is piles-encouraging. Unlike the five mean widows and four mean wives who preceded her in the role of landlady she has other seemly convictions. There is the country one that it is a female sin not to feed young men as lavishly as *foie gras* geese. There is the one which leads her to say, "The Lord God gave us on'y one set a peepers, and don't expect us t' be silly enough t' ruin 'em with piddling little no-watt bulbs," and to light the house brightly. She has never heard, she says, after I have revealed some of the habits of the nine, of women who don't change all the bed-linen each week, never ever heard of it. "But w'at can you expect from the dirty pommies," she says, "w'en they feed you all that offal they fed ya. There should be an inspector."

It is from this direct and simple woman I first hear the word pommy. It is, she tells me, a term of pre-Great-War birth derived from immigrant—immigrant, pomegranate, pommy. Mrs Bachaus, enclosed in sombre marocain, lisle stockings, nurse's shoes, gloves, and a dark straw hat enlivened by a clinking bunch of black-red cherries, rolls off to the Church of England every Sunday morning with the gait of a master mariner, yet, despite her clear sincerity as a church-going Christian, she has the Australian farm-woman's lurid tongue, and none of the sour gentilities of my former landladies. From her, not only do I hear unbuttoned expressions heard since the days when I toddled, but ones brand-new to me.

As a boy I lacked the invaluable social refinement of being able to swear with aplomb, and when I first meet Mrs Bachaus am still going through the inelegancies of a mealy-mouthed phase which requires that one convince oneself that any sort of vocal bawdiness sets up a reaction of distaste. This is utter affectation. Heady language has surrounded me always: my parents, my rustic uncles and aunts and cousins, my schoolboy friends, all swore like troopers. It is signal of my admiration and affection for Mrs Bachaus that there is no reaction of distaste when she is lavishly cursing the Jerusalem artichokes or vilifying snails and that, moreover, very soon, inspired by her finish, I am myself able to swear with ease. Perhaps because her three middle-aged sons were killed, childless, in the Great War it pleases her to take on the part of that old domestic monument, a free-tongued and heart-of-gold grandmother, for the young motherless boarder. At night, wearing steel-rimmed spectacles with enormous circular lenses that make her look like Red Riding Hood's grandmother, she sits reading *The Old Curiosity Shop* or Helen Mather's *Comin' Through the Rye*, and knitting me a crimson cable-stitch sweater with the newly modish crew neck which I am to wear flamboyantly with the very long points of the collar of a white shirt showing over the neck rim in the collegiate-collegiate-yes-we-are-collegiate manner of talking-picture heroes like Johnny Mack Brown. Meantime, on the upright Schiedmeyer so old that the ivory of the keys is buff-colour and, in the central octaves, worn down to the wood, Stella, also wearing steel-rimmed spectacles, violently beats out Moody and Sankey hymns or, in less uplifted a state, "Mélodie d'Amour" and "The Last Rose of Summer".

Stella, in front of whom Mrs Bachaus never uses a coarseness, or a profanity bluer than "Sugar!", is her niece, and also boards at *Shalom*. Stella owns a packing-case-sized Fancy Goods shop in Douglas Parade, North Williamstown, to and from which she pedals with angular ferocity on a bicycle with a carbide lamp, and a frame of saxe-blue lacquer on which are flowery designs like those on early Singer sewing-machines. The seat wears a crocheted and padded cosy of ginger wool. The wheels are partially screened in a kind of sunburst of string. A black tape somehow attached to Stella's waist, and slanting down between her busy bony knees to the front of the machine, keeps her skirts in order. Stella is not Church of England, but is demoniacally active in, I think, the Baptist Church. As tall as Mrs Bachaus, she is about forty, gawky, intense, noisy, a mistress of platitude, and has anguished and beautiful and sensual eyes set beneath thick eyebrows in a skull-like face. Apart from her eyes, which are desperately female and years younger than the rest, she is the most unfeminine woman I have, in the nineteen-thirties, yet run across, and almost the

36

archetype of dottily religious old maids. In an age of berets and felt cloches she wears navy-blue straw hats with brims which are hat-pinned to her black-and-white-striped hair. This hair is strained back from her soap-and-water forehead and face, and screwed into a bun scarcely as big as a doughnut. From this missionary-lady coiffure she sometimes picks a black hairpin to scoop wax out of the recesses of her large, lobeless ears. This she does publicly, in front of me or anyone. She has a just perceptible moustache. Once, on a steamy Saturday afternoon when she is helping Mrs Bachaus in the garden, I see, protruding from the split at the armhole of her working-dress, a pointed tongue, a Vandyke beard of black hair. It matches, in an animal way, her eyes, her yelping voice.

From Stella's bedroom, which is across the front passage from mine, there is nightly heard a monotonous mumbling. I presume she is not talking to herself but to God. It could even be that she is discussing me with Him because, having often enough returned to *Shalom* and dinner from drinking beer in the Bristol Hotel, I am obviously, though far from drunk, more high-flown and flushed than usual. About this Stella looks tracts, and says nothing, but I do find, always a day after my three or four sixpenny pots of draught beer with the ex-A.I.F. teachers who are interested in making their sort of man of me, that there is a force interested in making another sort. Anti-drinking pamphlets are on my pillow, or little cards on which, inside a border of ill-printed forget-me-nots, is the information WINE IS A MOCKER. It seems too that Stella, for it is doubtless she, has prayed by the bed of the tosspot. In the honeycomb quilt are two depressions: with her knobby knees on the kangaroo-skin mat, and her elbows on the quilt, she has fervently done what she must, and left her sad odour of spinster sweat. As she has said nothing, so I say nothing either by word, eye, or attitude. I am getting older. I have turned twenty-one. Let her pray. Let me drink. Let her hot-headedly pray. Let me cold-bloodedly drink.

I have been drinking since the age of seventeen. More precisely, since the age of seventeen I have, now and then, drunk a little wine, a little beer, and experienced the lifting of a veil or two from the senses. The wine is drunk at Camillo Triaca's

Latin Café in Exhibition Street, Melbourne, or on Saturday visits to a sow-fat, vivacious, French-speaking Madame Jorgensen, born in Vraa, Jutland, a Conrad character who runs a wine depôt on the Williamstown waterfront. At Madame's, with a sang-froid and fearlessness which, considering my youth and appearance (sometimes garbed in plus-fours, or a squire-of-the-village suit of sorrel-coloured Harris tweed), still amaze me, I brazenly mingle with, and openly hang on the words of, and unflinchingly stare at the brawls between Jack London seamen from every sixteenth of the globe: Creoles from Mauritius, Scotsmen in navy-blue Sunday-go-meeting suits, Scandinavians in cumbersome, high-necked sweaters, Japanese with teeth edged by what appears to be aluminium, all sorts of teak-textured but curiously innocent men tattooed with anchors, thistles, windjammers, roses, and S-curled scrolls bearing the word Mother. While I eke out two or three or, at devilish most, four port wines or clarets—Madame keeping a sly slit of maternal eye on me—the seamen drink deep, offering me hair-on-the-chest potions Madame will not let me accept. It is handy to have her refuse for me, it saves the embarrassment of cissily refusing myself. At six o'clock Madame's jelly of a face switches off its professional animation and charm, and sets like cement into a Hindenburg mask, and the symposium is over. Some of the men from the sea swagger zigzag across the plantain-ruptured asphalt to the railway station and the train that will take them and their bottles of muscadine to Melbourne, where are the brothels of Little Lonsdale Street, or the sly-grog-and-prostitute joints of Carlton. Others reel away, they and their reeling sunset shadows, through the fennel, along the old groaning wharves to orgies of dark singing and spiceless brawls in their own fo'c'sles.

In 1931, aged twenty, I begin to drink as it were more formally, more conventionally, at the Bristol Hotel, a block away from school, with the older men on the staff, with the Anzacs. It is usually a pay-day stint, every second Friday. The other Junior Teachers are far too morally cautious, financially prudent, parent-controlled or wowserishly inclined, to take this risky step. They cannot guess how dull and ritualistic it all is, and with what faultless regularity nothing happens except

38

shop-talking. It is not, of course, of *course*, revealed to them that, in putting my foot on the brass rail beside the feet of these older men, these practised boozers, I am far less interested in gulping draught beer than in seeing what goes on inside the Bristol and, more to the point, what goes on inside my beer-companions. This ignorance of my reasons, and of the gentlemanly rules of the bar which are more stringent than the gothic rules of teetotalism, allows me to assume for the other Junior Teachers the air of a hard-drinking, flashy worldling. It actually pleases me that they have the feeling that a headlong descent on the road to ruin has begun, that just around the next bank of primroses is the downhill run to a Night Refuge and the bread-and-margarine ministrations of the Salvation Army. The truth is far otherwise. However factitiously big-man my bar performance is, however embroidered with blokely details of tapping ash from cigarettes, and flicking matches—zing!—into the bull's-eye of a spittoon, and balancing florins on edge upon the bar-counter, and not revealing that the fourth pot of beer has had the effect of anaesthetizing my upper lip, no one at the Bristol is fooled, not the returned soldiers, not Peter the Roman Catholic barman with the countenance of a world-weary circus clown, and certainly not me. They and I know I am acting—and learning. It is nevertheless necessary for the two-legged, outrageously healthy, almost-extrovert who loves solitude to explore the Bristol and anywhere. Why? Embedded deadly deep in that visible creature, two-legged, ten-fingered, slant-eared, beak-nosed, is the writer, the mechanism whose spring needs no re-winding and will not run down, and for whom the external animal must move on to whatever next-scene-please the mechanism directs him to; the Bristol saloon bar, Madame's Wine Depôt, the Latin Café, boarding-houses in back-streets, other people's bear-pits and man-traps and velvet-hung cellars of dreams, trite and secret gardens where lust can be vile and private, the air terminals and clip-joints and outrageous cathedrals and bombed-out cities and blood-irrigated fields of the terrible and glamorous world, the lane beyond the lane beyond the lane beyond the crippled tree, the lane that leads to nowhere but the tombstones twinkling like bitter salt at its end.

39

In 1932, because my parents mated twenty-one years and nine months earlier, I am compelled to vote, be responsible for my debts, and am—legally—a man: I need no one's permission to marry. There I am, then, happy as a silk-worm in a cocoon at *Shalom*, happy as a ring-master at S.S. 1409, altogether as happy as a fool. It does not make me unhappy to know that I am undeniably an Australian philistine, a born reactionary, and already possessed of the useless information that opera, ballet, Apollinaire's 1917 surrealism, Picasso, and Bach mean less to me than irises, a blossoming almond tree, Alice Faye, or a flotilla of mulberry-coloured clouds anchored in the golden harbour of a sunset sky. It does not make me unhappy to know that, about this imperfection of taste, I can do En-Oh-Tee-Aitch-Eye-En-Gee. I have reached the milestone XXI without playing two-up, losing a tooth, breaking a limb, burgling a house, being an agnostic, having a headache or an illegitimate child. I have never seen a horse race, a musical comedy, a vaudeville show, a dirty postcard, a motor-car accident, a marathon foxtrot competition or a pole-sitting contest. Nor, on the other hand, have I read Tolstoy, Dostoevski, Marx, Ethel M. Dell, Steele Rudd, or *Gentlemen Prefer Blondes*. The back-rooms of my being are, in short, lined with empty shelves, and pigeonholes nothing will ever be put in.

There are shelves I do try to fill. Towards this end I beach-comb at the edge of the sparkling and sub-bitter shallows of what, then, appears to the magnifying eye of ignorance to be Sophistication. In this quest I am accompanied by some fresh Williamstown friends of about my own age, all of them equally exhilarated by a brief venturing away from firmer ground— Terry, a newly arrived Junior Teacher whose real name is Isobel, and who has bobbed yellow hair, green eyes, a querulous American mother, and a prickly sailor father; Barclay, an ironic intellectual who is studying Japanese with Professor Inagaki at the Melbourne University; and Nora, Barclay's sister, who is secretary to the Williamstown High School headmaster, W. M. Woodfull, the Test-cricketer. Nora and Barclay, orphaned young, live with a battle-axe of an over-religious aunt. The four of us seem to the four of us to be pretty smooth, deliciously witty, and well-informed tourists in the

40

country mapped by Evelyn Waugh, Frederick Lonsdale, Michael Arlen, Aldous Huxley, and Noël Coward. "Some Day I'll Find You" from *Private Lives* is a near-enough theme song. Norma Shearer and Robert Montgomery are the demi-goddess and demi-god of this demi-fairyland. In retrospect, it is interesting that the ears of four young people, all intelligent and gay, are so exactly tuned in to the more acid and edged sounds ricocheting from the surface of the shallows, and that we can catch every intonation of these clever-clever echoes from a society divided from us by several classes, the Equator, and our minimum of discreet colonial-suburban experience. The effect of Messrs Waugh, Coward, Lonsdale, Arlen, Huxley, and of *Punch*, and the tunes of Cole Porter does not last long. For a while we become an aloof quartet, mocking and superior, imitation sophisticates, at Junior Teacher dances in The Palms which is a sort of larger Afternoon Tea Kiosk with ballroom attached, in the Alexandra Gardens on the bank of the Yarra River in Melbourne. We are equally aloof, more from youthful self-consciousness than from superiority, at Naval Dances in the Williamstown Drill Hall because, we know, we are surrounded by time-kippered commodores blasé enough to carry silver-plated hip-flasks of pink gin, whisky, or brandy.

Each of us has had some unsatisfactory and minute experience of alcohol, largely beer, a beverage we regard, in our Huxley-Coward-*et al* period, as plebeian. My Latin Café and Wine Depôt ventures I have, at this stage of the relationship with Terry, Nora, and Barclay, kept quiet about, because wine is, in Australia of the nineteen-thirties, generally considered to be only one cut above methylated spirits. Plonk, steam, bombo, Red Ned, or Red Nell are among the derogatory names for wine. It is not that there are not many superb Australian wines being properly drunk. It is that there are many crude ones, saccharine and fortified, which provide the nearly cheapest form of intoxication, and which are the tipple of no-hopers, blackfellows, poverty-stricken alcoholics, and swagmen.

Enfevered as we are by notions of "sophistication", neither forgotten-man plonk nor plebby beer nor, indeed, drinking as such, interests us at all, but we are intensely interested in getting rid of one of the devils of ignorance that possess us. We are determined to get drunk, privately, and on—what else, what possibly else?—cocktails. Where? We boggle. We bide our time, certain that something will turn up. While biding, Terry and I take to collecting cocktail recipes from sources now unimaginable to me: Martini, Manhattan, Bronx, Chevy Chase, Virgin's Kiss, Coral, à la Ritz are recallable, as well as Enrico Caruso's favourite of one-third sherry, one-third sweet vermouth, and one-third gin. I forget Sinclair Lewis's favourite, but it is on the list.

Suddenly, beautifully conveniently, during the September holidays of 1932, something turns up. We sadly abandon the idea of cocktails à la Gertrude Lawrence as beyond us. We decide that whisky-soda for the males, gin-and-lime for Terry and Nora, are drinks that qualify for the experiment.

Mrs Bachaus, in deciding to make a week's country visit during the school holidays, provides the opportunity, the setting, the as-it-were laboratory. During her absence Stella is to do what essential landlady chores she can; for the rest I am to fend for myself. Mrs Bachaus is to leave on Friday, the late shopping night when Stella does not scorch back from her fancy-goods shop until after ten o'clock. We four conspirators, come Friday, will have our looked-for gift of time and a private place.

Mrs Bachaus, in a nimbus of eau-de-Cologne, topped by the Sunday hat and its clinking cherries, carrying a millstone fruit-cake in a string bag, a disproportionately small suitcase for one so large, and a sheaf of her own daffodils, lumbers off.

"Now, you be a good boy, young fellow-m'-lad," she says, and I am never to hear her speak again.

She walks away under the aged elms pretending youth with their tissue-paper flowers; she and her tall old body and eau-de-Cologne and daffodils turn the corner, and I never see her again. I am to see Stella once again.

Mrs Bachaus gone, I hurry to meet Barclay at the grocer's where we are to buy, with the air of having often bought thus, what we think is enough to make four people drunk: two bottles of whisky, two bottles of gin, two siphons of soda water, and a bottle of lime juice. It seems hardly enough. We therefore choose, from the ceiling-high shelves behind the long cedar counter rimmed with brass, a bottle each of Tokay, Frontignac Sauternes, and Shiraz. The celebrated names blind us, perhaps, to the fact that we are buying plonk, the tipple of the seedier working class.

The shop is a nineteenth-century one at the sea end of Ferguson Street, and has a sawdusted pine floor, biscuit tins with glass windows, brass scales flanked by graduated brass weights of which the larger have handles, and bins of flour, sugar, pearl barley, cream of tartar, Lima beans, and split peas. From the ceiling depend bunches of scrubbing-brushes, hearth-brushes, stove-brushes, dust-pans, cobweb-brooms, and turkey-feather-dusters. Outside the entrance stand hessian sacks of potatoes, swedes, bran, pollard, and wheat. On the pavement, at the bases of the sacks, are whitewashed thick semi-circles to disencourage peeing dogs.

Across the street from the grocer's is a two-storeyed house, balconied and bay-windowed conventionally enough but also lit by windows of less ordinary shape—ogival, hexagonal, port-hole.

As we are passing the house, still in have-we-bought-enough? state, I notice, pinned to the dramatic cretonne curtains (black with life-size foxgloves soaring and flaunting) of a ground-floor window, a notice: FLAT TO LET. The notice is trimmed to the outline of a scallop shell; the lettering is Lombardic.

By three o'clock, shut away from the sunny spring day, and the sussoes dreaming or not dreaming on the sand, and the falling elm flowers, and the sensible world busy at buying and selling and corrupting and muck-raking, we are ready to drink.

We are in the room where Mrs Bachaus knits and reads, and Stella flails at the Schiedmeyer like a lustful animal, a room scented with potpourri, Shinoleum, and the diminishing last of the departed landlady's eau-de-Cologne.

Talking of our experiment, thirty-odd years later, when Nora is a mother and a headmaster's wife, Barclay a father and a member of the Australian Embassy in Tokyo, and I childless and still footloose, it is seen that each of us, on that Friday in spring, crosses the frontier between sobriety and drunkenness at a different place, and that the untrodden shire into whose

43

unreliable landscape we hurl ourselves for the first time, wears a different climate for each of us. For me, then as now, too many drinks affect most—whatever and however else they affect—my sense of time. Sober, I am sharply aware that each second is a thrilling addition to my past, an equally thrilling subtraction from my future and, above all, a second that brings me nearer, in a manner literally breath-taking, to the excitement of death. Drunk, this awareness of the reward awaiting me disappears. Reality is, on these occasions, unavoidably all around one, but is bestowed on situations one's real self is apart from. One spins, exhilarated, in a whirlpool of others' experiences. This exhilaration cancels out one's own exhilaration in the consciousness of advancing towards the glorious and tantalizing secret.

I forget, therefore, alas, my own feelings about being drunk for the first time. It is impossible to forget the happenings. They are preposterous, trivially preposterous. Revelations? Intimations of immortality? The miraculous acquisition of sophistication and wit? *In vino veritas?* Far from it. Wine is a mocker? Perhaps, perhaps.

We open bottles. We pour. In our ignorance we pour portions fit for the heroes of Valhalla. We lift our tumblers. On the edge of the abyss, we look at each other with nude eyes and unwritten-on faces, and clink the tumblers together. We drink. The taste dismays us but, having committed ourselves as guinea pigs to our own curiosity, we continue to drink.

Time, for me, loses its juices, dries out like pemmican.

In what seems no more than half an hour, the magic lantern slide of afternoon has been replaced by those of late afternoon, early twilight, late twilight, electric light. Nora and Terry, having early tossed aside their shoes, are prancing on the colonial sofa as proudly as mad-women. A broken Chinese vase, red and gold, lies on the floor. Barclay says, now and then, dreamily, "*Mono no aware wo shiru*—that's Japanese for 'the Ah-ness of things.'"

Oh we agree, we others shrieking with the unstitched laughter of children, we agree. Someone, or each of us, uses the dirtiest of all dirty words.

44

We drink on. It is, thinking back, amazing that none of us is sick, for we violate every section of the drinker's creed. The clock strikes eight.

Stella!

Two hours away, Stella!

We yell with reasonless laughter, but accept the clock's warning to leave. *Shalom.* I stumble to the wash-house for a gallon jar into which we pour, willy-nilly, what remains— gin, whisky, lime juice, Frontignac, Shiraz, everything. With the glittering-eyed wiliness of maniacs we put empty bottles in my bedroom, and lock its door. We leave the key in the door, the shards of vase on the floor, the light on in the desecrated room where once upon a time Red Riding Hood's grandmother knitted, and Stella on homely Wednesdays played "Mélodie d'Amour." Arm-in-arm we roister down the street to the beach, past the shuttered weatherboard shops which will open in summer to sell ice creams, liquorice straps, water wings, hot water, corned-beef sandwiches, tin buckets decorated with Felix the Cat or the Three Bears, wooden spades, tubes of Lanoline, ginger nuts, saffron-yellow slabs of factory cake, tins of cigarettes, and peppermint walking-sticks. The moon sits on a platter of cloud above the silent Ozone Picture Palace—a tonight's Williamstown moon the ancients did not see, but the moon that nevertheless shone on the ancients.

In the house we have become childishly, honestly, earnestly drunk in a non sequitur fashion. In the street, linked together, staggering under the moon and the Esplanade tamarisks, we are not merely drunk, we also are acting the part of drunkards, moving-picture drunkards, postcard drunkards, and we yowl together the orthodox songs: "Sweet Adeline", "Misery Farm", "Show Me the Way to Go Home", and "I Belong to Glasgow". We lack little but the crayfish on the ribbon.

The beach attained, that soft floor, our mood alters, our swagger loses tone. We recline on the cool sand rather in the style of Romans at a feast, the gallon jar of Walpurgisnacht brew centrally disposed. Languor possesses us. No more helpless and near-hysterical laughter. No more hot-time-in-the-old-town-tonight baying of drunk's songs. We attempt, as we had promised ourselves *Before*, to analyse what we feel. We become loudly earnest, but *After* is against us. Our minds flicker, wane, vaporize. Our sentences have broken tails.

One cannot therefore, now, remember what, at the scene of the crime, the feelings were. Nor, now, can one estimate if the experiment had any more value than providing the means to murmur nonchalantly, "Oh, but I've *been* drunk!"

Lolling stupefied in the moonlight, the film of water at the mill-pond sea's rim rustling seductively as taffeta, we reach a smudged conclusion that in gaining something we have lost something, but we cannot decide what the something lost or gained is. Our questions hit the mind as weakly as winter-bound blowflies hit a window-pane. I recall one only clear-cut conclusion—our experiment, regarded as a possible form of playtime, smacks, we think, of the immediate pleasures of the poor and the unintelligent and, maybe, the depraved.

No sooner have we cast this shadow across the tangled currents of debate than, across our sprawled bodies, falls an actual shadow, and a cruelly clear voice says, "Depraved is *right*! You are dis*gusting*, *all* of you!"

It is the voice of Terry's seventeen-year-old sister Lalla, who is fond of consciously solitary walks (brogues with flapping fringed tongues, tweed skirt, Pringle jumper) before going to bed with Rupert Brooke's poems and a mug of Ovaltine. Plastered against the sky, she harangues us with intensity, skill, and pleasure. As she walked, she heard *common* people, larrikins, street-corner *louts* and *their tarts*, in the midst of a *drunken* beach orgy. About to double back so as not to become involved with the re*volt*ing creatures, she *thought* she recognized voices she knew. She paused. She listened. She came nearer. Disbelief! Belief! Realization! Horror! Dis*gust*!

Prone on the mattress of sand, we hear and watch with a polite and languid stupidity, as though Lalla is a talkie projected on the sky. She is competent in invective for one so young, and her vocabulary is interesting. We say nothing and do nothing until, at the apex of a sparkling sentence about immorality, she swoops out of the screen on which she has reared like a voluble two-dimensional deity, and plucks the gallon bottle from our midst with three-dimensional talons, and strides to the water's edge, and hurls it horizon-wards. As she

46

strides, we scramble on our knees a little way after her, crying out, "No, Lall! No, Lall! Bring it back!"

These cries for something we no longer want bring us to.

If this be drunkenness, this exposure of ourselves on our knees calling out, like Colombo beggars, and for something we have already had too much of, it is time to retrace our steps to the other side of the frontier. We get to our feet. We brush sand from ourselves. We become charming about goodnight, about tomorrow, about time and place. Lalla and Terry depart to not face parents. Nora and Barclay depart to not face an aunt. I? A chill enters me, the chill of guilt—the first I recall experiencing. I cannot not face. The drink is drunk. The vase is smashed. I walk and walk and walk, but the chill remains in my being, all that remains is the chill.

One cannot walk for ever on the cold crack in the jigsaw. One must step over it, and onwards. I return to *Shalom*.

It is dark within. It is silent within. Outside, the scent of Mrs Bachaus's violets is a different scent, just as the dark and silence within are a different dark and a different silence, a false dark chafing to be freed, a false silence. As I open the back door, the dark and the silence are broken. The light flashes on like lightning.

There stands Stella.

Her hand is on the switch—how long has it been there? Over her winceyette nightgown she wears a gabardine overcoat which she holds closed at the neck. Her hair is plaited into a meagre, pathetic pigtail. Her great eyes, without spectacles, are terribly uncovered, fermenting, the eyes of a feverish seraph. Since it is after midnight, these eyes, as mine must also do, contain still the stale lights of an unextinguished yesterday.

She is to speak, and I set calm in preparation for a shower of Hosea-inspired rebuke. I am out-calmed.

"You have abused Mrs Bachaus's hospitality," she says in a horizontal, dusty voice so unlike her usual yawping and gobbling that it seems dubbed in. "You have abused it while she's away. That's despicable. She trusts you. You've been a traitor. And you've had a cocktail party."

Could I toss off a flake of laughter—I can't—this would be the moment to. Cocktail party! Traitor's cocktail party!

47

"The neighbours told me. Mrs Kellow nearly went for the police. She was terrified. People pounding on the piano. Drunken women screaming with laughter. Foul language. I just couldn't believe her. I said, 'Mr Porter is a respectable young man, and very well thought of. I just don't believe it, Mrs Kellow!' She said she saw you and another young man, and two drunken women, come out of the house staggering and shouting. She was very upset, and insisted on coming in with me, just in case."

I find myself listening to the slow, soothing account in the same interested way as, slack on the sand, we listened to Lalla's more theatrical oration. An itch to ask questions has to remain unrelieved—just in case what? what was Mrs Kellow wearing? where was she when she saw us leaving *Shalom*? which expressions of dismay did you use when you saw the broken vase?

"I took the liberty of looking into your bedroom. You know what I saw. Murder will out, Mr Porter. And another thing: you, or one of your evil acquaintances, broke Mrs Bachaus's vase, the one she bought at the bazaar."

She pauses. Somehow and inexplicably, I find myself mollified by a lonely and full-blown beauty in *evil acquaintances*; my mind licks at it; and the delicious and repulsive thought of raping Stella arises like a vapour, and instantly disappears. She is speaking again. Only her lips move. She does not, has not.

"Mrs Bachaus was very fond of that vase."

I know this is a lie. I have heard, and Stella has too, Mrs Bachaus saying to it, "Ugly thing you are. Don't know w'y I bought ya. See if I care if ya fall over and break yaself, you and ya squinny-eyed dragons!"

I don't bring this up, but I do say, crackling out a lie for a lie in a voice that is mine and not mine, the voice of some insolent demon imitating me without a considered permission, "The cat!"

"There is," says Stella, unruffled, still as an image, her voice remaining down and dusty, "no cat. You don't mean that. You don't know what you're saying. You are still intoxicated."

I am. I say no more. "The cat!" are the last words Stella ever hears me say. What else to say? Anyway, it is preferable to stare at and listen to the unexpected. If there has been anything

48

to expect from Stella on behalf of the ravished *Shalom* it is not this subdued and mature-sounding voice, these limpid eyes out of their aquariums of glass, this sculptured stillness from a woman never seen before, this column of forgiving blood.

"I can see," she says, her voice loitering more and more, "that you are exhausted and bewildered. It's well after one o'clock. Go to bed. I've tidied your room, and put the bottles in the rubbish-tin. Go to bed. And try to pray for guidance. I'll pray for you too. I'll call you when I'm leaving for work tomorrow morning. I've bought some nice spring lamb chops for your breakfast. Don't forget to put out the light. Good morning." To remember that night is morning!

She goes.

She is gone.

The frame of the doorway contains no talking statue holding gabardine lapels closed over sapless, uncaressed, unsuckled breasts. Although I live in Williamstown for another six years, I never see Stella again.

As one sleepwalking I go to the bathroom. The toothpaste is already squeezed on to the brush when I notice that the soap-dish of the bathroom washstand is shaped like a scallop shell. A page turns over in my mind. There, with a whole old house and a partial new-world behind it, is the cardboard trimmed in the shape of a scallop shell—FLAT TO LET. When a decision has to be made, a painter cut, I do not shilly-shally. I go to my bedroom, noiselessly as a hollow man, carrying my packed sponge-bag. Beyond the closed door, which I shall never open again, across the corridor, beyond her closed door, Stella prays, grumbling like a kelpie. I hear her while I pack. I hear the prayer sink, and her with it. When I sense that she is, beyond all doubt, asleep, foundered, fathoms under, her eyes shuttered by their purple lids, I put suitcases and portmanteaux out of the window and, in slippered feet, carry them to the beach still dented by our drunken soles and bodies. Since tea-crates are out of question, four trips are necessary—I carry on my back, bowed over like a peasant fleeing an army, a number of ridiculous and useless possessions I regard as essential and useful bundled up in my rug. I leave two majolica Toby Jugs

49

bought in a secondhand shop on my—on *the* chest-of-drawers, and a note: *These are to replace the vase. I'm sorry.*

Am I sorry?

My belongings stacked about me, I lie on the beach, refugee-swaddled in the rug and, as open-eyed and sober as a snake, for the first time in my life do not immediately sleep. Do fish sleep? Where do the seagulls sleep? The water of the sea begins to talk of a million years ago, to talk and shrug its shoulders.

The moon sets.

One by one the hours set.

Am I sorry?

The east bleaches and curdles, and the horizon reappears, preoccupied with its own agelessness. Now, too late, I sleep. I am awakened, too soon, by racehorses bathing in a foam of gilt and sunrise, posturing like a quadriga. I drink much water at the bluestone drinking-fountain set in a coprosma hedge glittering all along the Esplanade. At six-thirty I walk to the telephone kiosk near the ramp leading to the Baths. In twenty minutes the taxi-cab arrives. An hour later I am fast asleep at 2 Ferguson Street, North Williamstown, not only in the first flat I have ever rented, but also—as far as I know—fast asleep *upstairs* for the first time in my life. Upstairs, at last. Ah well, it's time enough—I am twenty-one years and six months old.

Am I sorry?

In the final count, and at the harshly styptic core of my nature, under the coating of detached frivolity, I am not at all sorry.

It would be false to pretend that the simple comforts of *Shalom*, and the grandmotherly cosseting of Mrs Bachaus, and the entertaining antics of Stella, are not far outweighed by the stimulation of moving on or, rather, of creating the illusion that one has moved on, that one is advancing of one's own free will on fate, instead of waiting on one's backside in the wing chair by the never-failing fire, with ears half-cocked for the sound at the closed door, the discreet tap, or the musket-butts, or the scratch of an evil oriental fingernail, waiting for the poisoned goblet of milk on the papier mâché tray, the voices shouting, "We have come to get you," or the stinging kiss from unknown lips.

If I am a little sorry, it is as all men must be a little sorry when they wittingly lay aside for the final time something still capable of use that has nevertheless outlived its usefulness. I am also a little sorry, perhaps, that Nora broke Mrs Bachaus's vase —this is no more than an atavistic leaning towards animism. Ultimately, tenderness and whim aside, I consider that it is a wise man who feels no pity for what or whom dies, what or whom lives, unless—yes, unless he pities only those who love him. Oh, those fools in peril, those reckless eyes and hearts! One must, on the other hand, judge severely those one loves.

In abruptly and for all time dropping *Shalom* and Mrs Bachaus and Stella to take on the upstairs front flat at 2 Ferguson Street, and Landlady Eleven, Mrs McArdle, I am, in a way, giving that particular part of my masculine nature which has an inborn yen for no-strings-and-no-connections full rein. The inconveniences are minor. I do have to learn, at the age of twenty-one, to make a bed, and how to do some cooking for myself. It is scarcely difficult—during two decades of existence in women's houses I have, without ever performing them, unconsciously noticed many of the tricks of the game females have to play as servants to males. A bachelor with no one to impress except me, I take no time to strip these housewifely tricks of the hanky-panky and superstitions women decorate them with.

If I cannot be bothered getting myself a meal, it is easy enough to sing for one's supper. Bachelors do not mind encouraging women to believe in their woman-made fiction that men do not know how to look after themselves. In those days I am sure that although women may dress largely for women, they cook largely to cajole or stupefy men. In singing for suppers, I grade my songs with care—an unstinted repertoire to those who cook for the belly, an equivocal tune to those who cook for the heart. Knowing that the heart is the source of the greatest disasters, I keep mine, during most of the nineteen-thirties, as firmly under control as I can. Although it strains often at the leash, I have no intention of letting it impulsively drag its keeper into any more than a touch-of-sleeves-in-passing relationship with—who knows?—a Medea, a Cleopatra, Madame Bovary, Ethel le Neve, Delilah, or a Clytemnestra. There is record enough of the various sorts of discomfort they brought to Jason, Mark Antony, Doctor Bovary, Crippen, Samson, and Agamemnon to warn one to read again the sign: BEWARE. WOMEN AT WORK.

I pay ten shillings a week for the flat. It has a living-room thirty feet long by fifteen wide which contains such out-of-date refinements as a marble fender, a marble chimney-piece topped by a gilt-framed looking-glass, a sideboard with blue-velvet-lined drawers, and a leather ottoman that sighs when I sit on it. Adjoining this room, beyond a curtained archway, is the bed-room out of which, by a glass door in the side of the bay-window, one walks on to a balcony-veranda fenced by cast-iron filigree. Off the stair-landing outside the living-room door are, east, the kitchen and, west, the bathroom with its lead floor, claw-footed porcelain bath, corrugated-iron shower-screen, and a copper gas-heater that has dripped from its beak an ex-quisite green stain on the porcelain. The lavatory is far away and communal, downstairs, off the back of the house to which it is connected by an elongated conservatory, a glassed-in pas-sageway lined by racks of pot-plants, and floored with en-caustic tiles, blue and white, bearing fleuron-like designs. The lavatory bowl, Doulton, has its white overrun with particularly involved acanthus leaves. The horse-collar seat and the lid have been enamelled white, and decorated by replicas of the tortuous acanthus. This, like the scallop shell advertisement, is the work of Mrs McArdle who pussyfoots about, marionette-frail, pink-and-white-faced, fiftyish, in a well-ironed artist's smock of the same black-and-foxglove cretonne that curtains the windows of the ground-floor front flat where lives a lecherous and up-all-night-eyed reporter whose grey flannel trousers are urine-stained at the fly to the same colour as his nicotine-tinged fing-ers. Mrs McArdle abhors him, and he her.

What currents have swept Mrs McArdle and her white eye-lids and bony ankles and flawless accent—the purest and least affected I think ever to hear—into landladyship of a near-folly built by a retired Captain Pearson in the eighteen-seventies I do not find out, although aching to. I do find out that the name Margaret Elphingstone-Fyffe on the paintings hung on each wall of the up-a-step, turn-a-corner, down-a-step corridors is her maiden name. Her paintings have a childlike, William-Blake-cum-Douanier-Rousseau air. Lily-stalk seraphim with long, crinkled margarine-coloured hair, and dressed in robes like Botticellian tea-gowns, are in every painting, as are robust under-angels with Judas-coloured page-boy bobs, and bare male arms in which too many muscles, anatomically misplaced, are punctiliously painted. From the outskirts of a jungle of striped, spiked, fringed, serrated, and criss-crossing foliage these beings, all with alertly sad aniseed-ball eyes, stare towards a well-lit glade. Here, on the daisy-dotted turf, a pinafored girl and a Norfolk-suited boy play stiffly with toys already, even in 1932, out of fashion—wooden horses, Noah's Ark giraffes and dromedaries, parti-coloured balls, china dolls, and pogo-sticks.

I should like to think, but refuse to let myself be convinced, that seraphim and under-angels stand in for Mr and Mrs Mc-Ardle, and the children for the children she tells me they have not had. Curiosity nudges me to ask, but I've not the crude cheekiness needed. Nor can I ask if Miss Margaret Elphing-stone-Fyffe married beneath her. Mr McArdle, whose stage-Scots, Glasgow accent can be heard in the wings, but whose face I never see, is a big parcel of a man. I catch back glimpses of him. He has a duchess's hump under his cardigan, and a cannonball head of which an ebbing tide of grey-and-ginger hair reveals the pink skull, and he moves with an orang-outang gait as towards some task of heavy work. I should like to ask as well if, besides dealing with my rubbish-tin, which Mrs Mc-Ardle tells me he does, it is he who also polishes my kitchen floor and brass taps, and wipes the china finger-plates and door-handles decorated with moss roses, and black-leads the Mappin grate, and unnecessarily raddles the slate hearthstone. Someone does this every Tuesday, and it is difficult to imagine that it is Mrs McArdle, with uncrumpled smock and the cleanest of fingers, like a consumptive child's, whom I never catch at any task more sordid than watering, from a Wedgwood teapot, the pot-plants in the conservatory passage. These plants all have the sort of foliage she paints, the sort women often prefer, and pander to: striped, dotted, blotched, lacy—queer foliage and perverted colours.

I stay at 2 Ferguson Street for four of the six more years I

53

am to remain in Williamstown, and leave only after the Mc-
Ardles sell the place to another man-and-wife. This pair I take
an immediate dislike to: instinct tells me that they and I belong
to different tribes. It is true. Within their first week they reveal
themselves as members of one of the tribes for whom I have a
disdain so engraved that the most searching surgery could do
nothing to reduce it. These bright-eyed Goths ask me to their
flat for what they call a cosy snack—bloater paste on fingers
of toast, curried egg yolk perched on little dry biscuits, and
tea in thick red cups with solid triangular handles. Drinking
tea, one drinks the hosts as well. They say this gathering is "to
get to know the tenants". They spend two hours letting me
know them, and they let me know with confidence, pride, and
a zest that makes my mind weary, and wipes my face blank.
Weary because there is nothing my mind can offer theirs: it is
pointless preaching to the unconverted; blank because the house
is theirs, and a penurious tenant possesses no right to display
distress on its behalf. To me they are foreigners, and out-of-
gear ones. Modernization is their enthusiasm. They use the
word often, little knowing that each time they press the button
marked *modernization* it rings *vandalization* to me. Bubbling
over in anticipation of their crime, they tell me, one by one, the
things that are to go. All in all, they are pleasant, happy people
and, although loathing their clever stupidity, I can almost admire them for the perfection of their clean-sweep, scorched-
earth plan. The eyes of the house-killing tribe they belong to,
trained in heaven knows what hygienic annex of hell, miss nothing that appeals to the eyes of the tribe on the other side of the
ravine which separates one taste from another. Their list of
what they call, their voices pulsating with a sincere dislike,
horrors-that-must-*definitely*-go is, item by item, the same as the
list of things I find particularly enchanting—the conservatory
alley with its panes of hand-made glass in cathedral-window
colours: ruby, castor-oil-bottle blue, emerald, olive-oil yellow;
the cast-iron balcony and the french window leading on to it;
the marble chimney-piece and fender; the non-rectangular windows covered by transparencies of medieval Germanic jousts
alive with Dürer knights and Holbein-sturdy margravines; the
curtained archway to my bedroom; the tiled front veranda and

54

its wrought-iron supports; and the sixty-year-old elm standing before the house. Unentitled to comment on what they excitedly tell me they will be starting to do tomorrow, I say nothing —they are years older than I, the house and the elm are theirs. Shall I tell them, while they are in an ecstasy of self-praise because they have so quickly tracked down all the faults of the house, that tomorrow I shall be elsewhere? Why waste words? I put down the coarse, modern, red cup. I go out of the panelled door they are going to cover with three-ply. I run upstairs, deadpan and in a hurry, and telephone friends to bring suitcases, and help me pack, so that I can be elsewhere before what I like to remember has been wrecked into what would make me not like to remember. All this is, however, in 1936.

Meantime, from 1932 to 1936, I am able to go on enjoying 2 Ferguson Street. It stands high on the inventory of other people's houses I have enjoyed living in. The affection I have for it is not only because I spent untrammelled years under the lichened slates of its ridged and valleyed roof, but because of a preference for older nests. Since it is inexplicable to me, I cannot explain this straightout preference for the time-worn over the brand-new, for patina above rawness and, therefore, cannot and do not defend it, any more than I can defend a vigorous affection for the milieu of many of my temporary nests.

Take, for example, Room Seven in the Pensione Bucintoro, Venice, a room to which, however one's feeling for Venice itself waxes and wanes with the seasons, it is impossible to resist returning every now and then. Room Seven is directly over the tiny church of San Biaggio: the room's red-tiled floor is the church's ceiling; the bathroom with its enamelled *bidet*, and continental shower like a telephone-receiver, is plumb above the comic-opera altar. While one is looking out of the window, straight ahead, over the humped stone bridges of six canals, to distant Saint Theodore sitting bleached on his bleached crocodile high above the Piazzetta, one can sniff the incense winding muskily out through the open church door beneath one's nose, and has only to look down to see Venetian crones in black bebobbled shawls shuffling in to pray—for what?—before San Biaggio's starry pyramid of candles and plastic roses. How can one, except to oneself, defend an affection for a boarding-house so absurdly situated? There are middle-aged Swiss women drinking hock, and vivaciously gabbling in their *chuchichästli* accents, under the curtailed Muranese chandelier in the stiff little terrazzo-floored parlour; there are French sailors sitting outside the front door, with their legs apart like tongs, at the circular tables furnished with triangular Martini ashtrays and shaded by Martini beach umbrellas; a hundred yards away Greek and Spanish liners catnap at the wharves, two hundred yards off is the Arsenale, five the Doge's Palace, six the Piazza San Marco, and the ugly ghost of Wagner in silk underwear drinking at Florian's.

Take, now, the Manx Hotel, San Francisco, set in the centre of fake-Edwardian or fake-Gay-Nineties rosy-gloomy piano bars, shoeshine arcades, cable-tram-shaped flower-kiosks, taco and enchilada counters, and deep narrow shops where one buys pepper-mills, butter-pats, bullfight posters, blinies, *Lady Chatterley's Lover* and photographs of nude men, gramophone records of the cries of masochists being whipped, figures of life-sized borzois, ecclesiastical fabrics, crab sandwiches, white china Kwannons, Filipino straw hats, Mexican jumping beans, and tin models of the cable trams which clang past the entrance to the Manx at twelve miles an hour, up Nob Hill, by-passing Chinatown, to the crest from which, seemingly more wildly though at the same pace, they descend to the pigeon-and-tourist-populated waterfront. Here is Alcatraz offshore and, on the wharves between the parked fishing-boats, here are the Sicilian fish grottoes, the Walk-away Shrimp-cocktail stalls, the waxworks, the sukiyaki joints, and the shops selling salt-water taffy, baby turtles, Coney Island Chowder, and atrocities ingeniously contrived of shells—poodles on their hind legs, herons, galleons, albatrosses, tortoises, trinket-boxes, and niches for plaster figurines of the Virgin Mary. Who contrives, and who buys, are those one never sees.

It strikes me, right now, that the off-the-cuff choice of the Bucintoro and the Manx—merely to point up the fact that the writer segment of my nature, the itchy-footed, wind-blown and hungry-eyed part, seems to need to find its fodder in places as chock-a-block with objects and human beings as a Brueghel painting—also illustrates something I've not noticed before.

56

Although I have—a robot on the mission of the writer—gone far, and perhaps too often too far, down morally dirty and dangerous alleys of life, and have broken strange meat with strange animals, and made unmentionable covenants, I have, it now seems, always denied the writer at least one thing. I will not, even on his most tempting or be-a-man-my-son kinds of errand, move for long far away from the sea. Hinterlands and their edgelessness confine me, and blunt my joy. Once again, I cannot attempt to explain why, nor why I must, for utter contentment, be able to sense the sea's nearness or, at very least, the nearness of a large river or lake.

Perhaps this quirk explains more my serenity at 2 Ferguson Street, that old nest in a Brueghel-lively tree with the brine-saturated winds of the sea always twiddling its branches. The flat is one house and one road's width away from the Ferguson Street Pier. This road, curving along parallel to the sea-rim, is lined, on the land, by the stationary buildings of the steadfast land, and on the sea by the restless buildings of the wayward sea. These are to be seen from the end of the elm-shaded balcony—white liners sliding as on well-oiled castors towards Port Melbourne, tugs, fishing-boats, tramp steamers, freighters, monkey-boats, and lighters. When the elm-leaves go yellow, and go, it is then possible again to see the grocer's opposite and, on the corner next to it, the lofty weatherboard pawnbroker's with its crow-stepped false front and arched shop-windows behind the soiled glass of which, among the more domestic and suburban pledges of jardinières, shaving-mugs, fusee cases and horn-handled carving-sets, are arranged nail-studded seamen's chests, barquentines in bottles, Fijian cannibal forks, Samoan necklaces, scrimshawed whale's-teeth, and nautilus shells. It is here I buy for a shilling a Portman decanter covered, as is everything in the shop, by a gauze of mouse-coloured dust, and, for half-a-crown, a set of ebony and ivory chessmen. I go through a born-but-to-die period of chess enthusiasm with unusual rapidity, playing sometimes with a highly intelligent schoolboy called Edward Livingstone Jones who invariably beats me, and sometimes with Lesley Thompson, the ex-Olympic diver who is, for a while, a Junior Teacher at S.S. 1409, and who also invariably beats me. With her, as with

Terry and Nora and the schoolboy and his grown-up sisters and such Junior Teachers and other young friends as are addicted to the then fashionable Saturday and Sunday exercise of hiking, I walk miles. How we young ones walk—and talk! What we talk about—all gone. God knows what the thousands of words, the passionate interruptions, the trumpetings of laughter, the exaggerations and confidences and confessions and lies are about or for—but all gone, blown out of the thistle-down air, blown out of the closets of memory, all gone. And all gone the houseless paddocks on the plains between Williamstown and Altona where we wade for miles through the metal-blue sea-holly, and the horehound and charlock, and the scented and tasselled grasses, while skylarks sing among the curls of cloud, and cuckoos in the boxthorn clumps, and we contentedly wail the overseas, sweet and melancholy songs we enjoy even though we are Australian, unsweet and light-hearted—"Twentieth Century Blues", "Gloomy Sunday", "Smoke Gets in Your Eyes", "Black Moonlight", and "Remember My Forgotten Man". We wail too the songs we hear on the wireless from a young singer—a young *crooner* called Bing Crosby whom we like better than Rudy Vallee, but whom the generation before ours, signing itself *Disgusted* in letters-to-the-editor columns, unmercifully cries down.

On some Saturday or Sunday mornings, when in a less gregarious frame of mind, in a the-world-is-too-much-with-us mood, I trail to the waterfront, the boat-building yards, the docks, the wharves, and piers with their barnacle-and-mussel-stockinged legs, and their rows of bollards wearing iron bands tight around their foreheads. Wheat grows peakily in the cracks of the wharf planking. Sparrows peck among the horse-manure, and flirt about. Seagulls sail and skim between the red funnels and black masts, now and then uttering cries of a disinterested defiance. All else is drugged by the smell of oil, wheat, blistered tar, and the sea deep-breathing sensually under the wharf—rich, black-green water in which whitebait flicker like particles of thought. Farther out, rarely and slowly, a wave-top flashes its jewellery, flutters a vague and farewell hand. To the thin, human squeak of the mooring-hawsers on the bollards, and the insect whistling of the tin rat-guards on the hawsers, outdoor sleep edges nearer, Saturday noon or Sunday noon—one must push siesta and solitude ruthlessly aside, and move, and go to find out what lies on the other bank, who is to be the next creature to say "Hello!", what make-up two o'clock will wear, and an answer to "Little man, what now?"

An answer one has. One contains it. It is in a million bits which have only to be put together. For many, who sagely and safely take an easy way out, the answer is Life, and Life, they say, is merely living, merely filling in time until. The answer I contain, yet cannot put together, is—I think, then—not the gather-ye-rosebuds, filling-in-until one at all. Life for me in the nineteen-thirties is not merely living of this sort, although it does appear to be no more than a filling-in of time. There are other things to do besides teaching children, those brief and impermanent animals, other things besides dancing and drinking, walking and talking, fondling parts of bodies, kissing mouths, sleeping in beds owned by others, watching the sea or swimming in it, becoming devoted to inanimate objects, singing silly songs, and smiling smiles at silly and lovely people. One cannot be forever and only trimming one's moustache and buckling on one's trousers for one sort of living, and trimming one's moustache and dropping one's strides for another sort.

This is man-shaped man stuff, a leaf-shaped leaf simplification.

I am young enough and—therefore—fool enough not to want to be no more than a leaf-shaped leaf among sumless leaf-shaped leaves on the leaf-weighted branch of my generation, any more than I want to be a firefly trying to hide in a blaze of moonlight.

I remember, with some amazement at my younger self, that, as the years of the nineteen-thirties flutter frivolously and oh-so-quickly off, I encourage the highfalutin notion that it would be more soul-satisfying to be a crystal, whatever the danger of being broken, than to be a safe brick in a wall of bricks. Being a crystal means to me—then—being able to be seen through, and being able to see through myself to some means of arranging the million bits of the answer into One Answer. Should this One Answer, rather than turning out to be Life, be something more classy such as, say, the Art of Life, then there is certainly a great deal more to do than merely filling in time, hiding in the moonlight, making green no greener by a contribution of nothing but green. This Art of Life, as half-conceived by my skippy-boy younger self, seems, if memory is not dropping stitches, to be the art of making use not only of one's Adamic self but of everything, no matter how relative everything is to everything else—poverty, ugliness, falsity, cruelty, and so on, as well as beauty, benevolence, purity, and so on.

I would not, even to save the world, care to be that young man again—as tiresome, or more tiresome, than most young men.

I do pull my forelock to him, just once, and unsmilingly, for recognizing that, by choosing to stay stubbornly for a decade in one small, decaying, seaside-and-port suburb, he is choosing to live cheek-by-jowl with most of the people who have ever lived—give or take a little—in any place, in any time, since people began drawing together in flocks for the betterment of their own needs to sin and sacrifice and create and control and glorify. They are all there, closely scattered over Williamstown's meagre acres—saints in wheelchairs; murderers who have never murdered; passionate young friends rehearsing for misery and loneliness; future beauty queens and spivs and lady mayoresses and small-time tycoons in perambulators; prostitutes and nuns and Boy Scout leaders on tricycles; lechers and embezzlers and Average Men—*ni ange, ni bête*—disguised as children playing French cricket with a piece of paling and a sodden tennis ball outside the Stag's Head Hotel; warriors and sluts and prophets and knights' ladies running to catch the clerks-and-typists' eight-thirty-two.

At night, late, alone, when lust has had its fill, or the visitor who talked too long about Thomas Wolfe has gone down the stairs into the starlight, or the late-night walk in the sea-lacerating gale is over, when filling-in-time is over, I write about these people. They glow in my mind with such an intensity that it seems the simplest of labours to get them down clearly, in glowing sentences, and as though I do really see them clearly, and glowing. It is, alas, a more brutal and ego-tripping labour than it seems when leaning on the gale, or abstractedly making love, or not listening to the garrulous visitor. I am not the panted-after crystal able to be seen through by myself, but a grime-clouded pane of glass—the pawnshop window!—on which my own reflection intrudes, with the grime, to defile the glowing images, and make them secondhand. Secondhand objects may be valuable, secondhand people are valueless. How many botched stories are written and destroyed no one, not even I, know. Of the many written about Williamstown four only remain—"Waterfront" about Madame and her Wine Depôt; "Miss Brockel" about an odd old woman who lives in a blue shop of which the door is always locked; "Gone Away" about a pixillated middle-class young woman who, for a while, is in love with the idea of being in love with me, but is not in love, my hands and mouth soon prove, with even the idea of me; and "Miss Rodda" about a music teacher with whom I spend some months finding out that a musical sense is yet another of the senses I lack.

In callously lighting fires with sumless short stories, poems, and—fortunately, my God!—vignettes, I am early trying for a balance-restoring attitude to writing. Having already seen, by the time I am twenty-five, too many writers defrocked by the public after a period of adoration, too many gods of the academics torn from their plinths, I learn to doubt both public and academic judgment. By doubting one arrives at a truth: doubt first and most one's judgment of one's own work, strip vanity to the buff, destroy oneself before others destroy one, regard the kink for writing as a form of leprosy, ring the little bell, cry "Unclean!", and walk straight through the marketplace.

No one can outcry, "Unclean!"

If I cut myself down to size by accepting my own decision that a fever to write is less a God-bestowed gift than an inconvenient ailment, and if I doctor the ailment by panglessly putting a match to years of observation and hours of writing, it is because of a young man's desire to find out what remains of self-confidence after self-surgery.

I do not stop there. In those years-off, yesterday-seeming, oh-to-be-a-crystal days I am all too aware that, although one cannot become perfect even in a hundred years, one can be corrupted in an hour.

I remember—with raised eyebrows—deciding to avoid many of the vaunted pleasures which, for reasons too esoteric to stick in the mind, I then regard as somehow corrupting, and certainly as bamboozling, (and therefore, crystal-clouding!) to me. I try, earnestly and suspiciously, as one trying hashish for the first time, two musical comedies, *Bitter Sweet*, and *New Moon*. They so discompose me that I've never tried another. It is impossible to defend this sort of amputation. It is impossible to defend a profound disinterest in this sort of entertainment, or an indifference to comic opera, the grandest of grand opera, or the sleaziest operetta. The art-form—*Turandot* or *Tea for Two*, Mozart or Gershwin—is one in which the enlargements, distortions, and out-of-this-world conventions conceal perhaps a truth from one as blind as I, but reveal a number of magnified falsities I am not quite blind enough to miss.

What does scandalize me, now, is not that I can lightly scrap the vanity-massaging notion of being gifted, and much more lightly deny myself operas, greyhound racing, musical comedies, symphony concerts, cricket matches, circuses, and such entertainments because they bore me and clutter up a clear vista, but that I can wear a self-bestowed see-what-a-good-boy-am-I halo while double-facedly involving myself in goings-on quite as trumpery as the ones given up so easily, quite as trumpery, quite as boring, not so easy to give up.

I partner doctors' and bank managers' nearly nubile daughters in débutante sets, performing before illiterate suburban mayors tricky gavottes I've no memory of rehearsing, whirling about with females now nameless and faceless who wear white camellias and long white kid gloves, and whose never-again part in a ritual so fleeting moves almost to tears the half of me that does not mock. I must have liked or loved these nameless ones—otherwise why spend so long tying the black butterfly bow? why shave so closely? why whirl at all with an armful of tulle and camellias and mummy's borrowed scent? Or is it the whirling I love, and my own Al Jolson gloves, my own white camellia?

I go to Artist's Balls, drunken and circumspectly abandoned occasions from which, reeking like an abo plonk-merchant, red-eyed, trembling with post-gaiety fatigue, and still dressed as

Harlequin or a melodrama villain or an over-tattered pirate, I return from Melbourne in the paper-train, the charwomen and newspaper-boys and street-cleaners and milkmen and early workers on their way to unguessable jobs not noticing me with such delicacy that I feel more invisible than unoriginal fancy dress, which cancels out one's own nature, has already made me feel.

The last time I experience this feeling of invisibility is the last time I go to an Artist's Ball, and leave Melbourne at two o'clock in the morning to walk the eight miles to Williams-town. I am depersonalized in a borrowed Mephistopheles get-up, vermilion cloak and tights, and a thickly sequined vermilion doublet but look less like a visitor from the bottomless pit than the Demon King from the stage trapdoor of a Christmas panto-mime. After leaving the outskirts of the city I see no one, not any human being, in the whole distance which—once one is through the stinking, houseless, treeless area of fellmongeries and putrid marsh between South Kensington and Footscray—is lined, mile after mile, with jam-packed houses, unlit, blinds drawn, sealed up, battened down behind their picket fences and pittosporum hedges. I wonder, passing house after house, all those blind witnesses, in my fiery cloak, with my torso of flame, if anyone hears my footsteps, the soles of a fake Satan too poor to afford a taxi-cab sharply rapping on the asphalt, or if no one, not anyone, no one at all of all the hundreds in their front-room beds an arm's length away hears anything of the passing. It is the first time I am deeply conscious of existing only to my own senses, of having the exhilaration of being the one alone in the whole world who knows of me during those hours and miles filled with the morse of my heels on the narrow footpaths, and nothing more except, once, the dry sound of a sheet of newspaper dancing and gyrating by itself in a twist of dustbin-tainted air. I whirl and caper for a moment, dawn-struck, with this solitary other living thing, and then stride on, unobserved, unheard, invisible even to myself, in the absurd and glorious garments.

If I am not able yet to give up dancing as I give up watching ballet and three-act sparkling comedies with Aldwych-baronial or french-windows-on-to-the-terrace settings, I am able, at least, to make the excuse of being active, of personally participating in a folly instead of doing no more than gawk at the activity of others.

I cannot excuse myself for the two-faced behaviour of being a movie fan and, as well, a fan—with an inclination to translate *fan* into *connoisseur*—of movie houses themselves.

Melbourne, then, has ten theatres, and fourteen picture theatres, eight of the picture theatres being in Bourke Street. I know the picture theatres well, and love them all, from the flea-pits to the ones in which the feast of Belshazzar could have been fittingly empalaced. The flea-pit sorts have bosomy nymphs, and bare-bottomed *amoretti* with wings like pullets', reclining above the proscenia to the right and left of a central jumble of lyres, corrugated ribbons, clarinets, mandolins, and pipes of Pan. The seats are wooden, or cast-iron and leatherette; the floors wooden or oil-cloth-covered; the spearmint-chewing cashier who tears off tickets from a carrot-coloured roll of them has spit-curls, and eyebrows plucked almost to a line of single hairs; the men's urinal exhales the smell of ammonia and Phenyle to intertwine with the smell of threepenny pies being eaten by out-of-work men who sit through the continuous sessions, out of the rain, out of the revealing sunlight, out of the mismanaged world. If they lack the ninepence to escape into flea-pits such as the Melba, the Britannia, the Star, and the Empire, they read the finger-grimed pages of *The Psychology of Abnormal Sex* in the Public Library, or outstare chunks of pretty quartz in the museum, or the busts of ugly men on the marble stair-landings of the art gallery.

Other picture theatres, of the Belshazzar's Feast sort—the Regent, the State, the Capitol, the Plaza, and Hoyt's de Luxe (where the commissionaire, hoarsely and non-stop, brays himself into fame and the Australian vernacular as The Man Outside Hoyt's)—are, at the height of the Depression, at the height of their magnificence. Commissionaires as braided, frogged, epauletted, and many-buttoned as Czarist generals strut in the sky-high foyers hung with larger-than-life photographs of movie stars; ushers in Ruritanian monkey-jackets and pill-box hats, and usherettes with superb legs abound; the stairways are marble, the carpets deep and gorgeous; on every hand there are

64

intimations of Versailles: walls of looking-glass, oil paintings enclosed in gilt, murals crowded with good-looking nobilities being level-browed and calm in Arcadia, fountains attended by bronze nudes, ormolu console tables sustaining urns of real flowers, brocaded settees and divans and love-seats, chandeliers, lavatories vast and scented, and sand-filled marble cauldrons from which, when the audience has gone, a favoured susso, shabby but cleanly, is permitted to pick the more-lavish-than-usual cigarette butts.

The films are supported by stage shows for which an orchestra rises from the underworld beneath the pit, or a Wurlitzer organ and the unceasing hands and feet of the organist ascend on a seeming cylinder of saccharine melody. Next, a series of extravagant curtains—velvet, then silk, then irisated gauze—slither apart on the adagio dancers, or the mouth-organist imitating Larry Adler, or the woman in a turquoise evening-dress who will invariably trill "Beyond the Blue Horizon", or the tenor in tails who will sing Richard Tauber numbers including—invariably—"Girls Were Made to Love and Kiss", or the dinner-suited male quartet intent on singing "The Riff Song". Taken, like a poor fish, by a morsel, I sit limply in this false and stupefying element, desensitized by the two-bob's-worth of public luxury and the incandescently lit movie stars I then think I have a tenderness for: Garbo, Ouspenskaya, Constance Bennett, Ruth Chatterton, Conrad Veidt, Polly Moran, Carole Lombard, Alison Skipworth, Robert Montgomery, and Claude Rains. The orchestra plays "God Save the King". The incandescence of the monsters made of light burns down, burns out. Their voices wind back into the containers. They withdraw from me, I from them. Or, since I do, in a sense, remain fixed and unmoving within myself, one endless chain bears them away and away behind me, while another bears towards me other idols, other transparent shadows, other places, other pointless pleasures, other everything.

Away and away too go yo-yos, miniature golf, club sandwiches, tea rooms, tortoise-shell-backed brushes, Eton crops, milk-billies, Edward the Eighth, vases of Iceland poppies and gum tips, stencilled suède table-runners, slave bracelets, xylonite, kewpies, Mary Webb, lumber-jackets, and 1935, 1936.

Towards me, whizzing bullet-like, come more and more new words: bazooka, quickie, and scram; swing, rhumba, and boogie-woogie; G-man, Führer, perspex, bomb-load, Bren gun, and appeasement.

In 1936, a quarter of a century old, with a rag-picker's swag of information I did not have ten years before, I leave the flat at 2 Ferguson Street and the copy of Böcklin's *Island of the Dead* I have painted on the bedroom wall so that it can be seen last at night, and first in the morning, and move to the Gem Pier Café, three blocks away, where I have a balcony directly overlooking the sea, and a large bedroom on the wall of which I paint a copy of Böcklin's *Island of the Dead* to be seen first in the morning before I look at the frilled grooves of the sea, and last thing at night before I see nothing or the paperweight landscapes of the dreamer through which one ranges, bound by none of the rules of nature, able to swim in the air, able to look on colours beyond the spectrum.

The Gem Pier Café is an easy-going home-away-from-home which does most of its business with the weekend yachtsmen from the Royal Yacht Club across the road, and with the less rakish of the seamen who, scrubbed as bright as orphans on an outing, wearing silk shirts from Singapore or Yokohama, lay-preacher suits, and gleaming, round-toed black shoes, bypass Madame's Wine Depôt for a staid ale or two at the Steam-packet or Custom House Hotel, and the soups, steaks, meat pies, and crayfish salads prepared by the landlady. After the meal, it is usual for those of the yachtsmen or seamen who have nothing wilder teed-up, who are not prowling for flesh, and who are acceptable to the landlady, to spend the rest of the evening in the small sitting-room behind the café, a room jammed with ragged-arsed and out-at-elbow armchairs, and a desquamating wireless-set on top of which sits a chipped plaster Bozo, and ashtrays made by denting the bottom of a red Craven A or white Ardath cigarette-tin under the point of a chair-leg. I observe that entrée to this snuggery, this it's-just-an-old-shanty, is bestowed only on amusing, not-*too*-tipsy bhoys, and nice boys. Nice means sensitive, shaven-and-shorn, and somewhat sentimental; boys or bhoys means men no older than thirty-two or so. One common factor is a love of the bluer

66

torch songs with a wry dying fall which are so numerous in the thirties—"With My Eyes Wide Open I'm Dreaming", "Melancholy Baby", "When the Rest of the Crowd Goes Home", "We Just Couldn't Say Goodbye", and, topping all, the eye-glazing number with its dramatic recitative, "Blue Bird of Happiness".

My twelfth and final Williamstown landlady is a buck-toothed, hard-working and charming woman who once a week transforms herself from a flushed, hessian-aproned cook with hair like the Witch of Endor into a stately dame in brown lace, bronze shoes, silk gloves, and fox furs with sharp snouts, mean glass eyes, and swinging brushes. Thus dressed, her hair mathematically crimped under a lacy hat, powdered, lipsticked, heliotrope-scented, she goes off, her 1908 shape inclined in an almost Grecian bend, to a race-course where she will back horses indicated to her by all sorts of omens found on the ouija-board of the kitchen.

Her husband, a gentle, grubby man too dark to shave only every second day, which he does, has limpid Rudolph Valentino eyes and a portcullis of china-white false teeth. When younger he must have been a lady-killer; older, his sensuality siphoned off, he ineffectually runs the fruiterer-and-confectioner part of the Gem Pier Café. The café-and-shop, built of two-foot blocks of bluestone in Williamstown's boom era, is so large that his small stock of cheap fruit and children's sweets looks smaller. This playing-shop is given an air of authenticity by the display cases, enormous ones, backed by looking-glass, and filled by dummy slabs of chocolate—Old Gold, Dolly Varden, Beau Brummel, Violet Crumble, Nut-Milk, empty toffee tins, empty chocolate boxes decorated with pictures of Persian kittens in sewing-baskets, dew-speckled crimson roses, village blacksmiths shoeing percherons, the Castle of Chillon, Gainsborough's "Blue Boy", and Lake Como villa-scapes spiked with cypresses. These are all arranged against elaborate backgrounds of crêpe paper, curls of gold foil, and cut-out placards.

The landlady's eighteen-year-old daughter, a head-tosser with a jammy accent and Marlene Dietrich legs, who has inherited her mother's buck-teeth, is the waitress, one with the put-upon air of a princess in bondage. Regular customers are used to her; the rare waterfront-slumming strangers who buy a meal cannot but be curious about the heavily made-up young woman who glides towards them like a mannequin, and coldly takes their orders for steak-and-kidney pudding, because she is dressed in the slinky black-*crêpe-de-Chine*-and-pearls manner of the manageress of a Collins Street boutique which is what she would like to be. She has ideas beyond the café and, although she has a proper enough affection for her parents, feels them a cut below her. This social discontent she seldom tries on her mother, who is too forthright and masculine-feminine to have any attitude but "If you think you're too high-and-mighty for us, your highness, you know what you can do. But before you take off in your Bentley, Miss, you get out there and wipe down those tables." On the other hand she gives her father Larry Dooley. His feminine-masculine nature, emotional and aimless, is unable to defend itself against attacks of a subtler sort than those I have already seen landladies use against their husbands. This young woman, with more oblique and more original hornet-stings, outdoes them; she is an adept at the death-of-a-hundred-cuts technique. I am not one iota less shocked than by the former landladies, but have learned the extra dodge of concealing shock not only from others but also from myself.

Those who spend idle hours in the cave-like half-gloom of the sitting-room, which borrows its ration of light, day or night, from the café-shop through an arch hung with a bead-curtain, accept her off-on, on-off moods—charm, petulance, disdain, cuteness, soulfulness, warm niceness, cold rudeness—with patience, a polite, resigned patience concealing the thought that a public spanking could improve her hopscotch manners and diminish her relish for embarrassment-making dramatization. Except on one occasion I sidestep any criss-cross with her that could involve me in her adolescent shadow-play.

Once, however, there I am, villain to her heroine. I can't recall how or why, but memory tells me to blame the weather.

It is the time of evening when the constrictions and down-bearing weight of a moody and muggy day are being broken up into hysterical greys scribbled across by signatures of lightning. She and I stand by the bead-curtain which the reflected lightnings turn to electric-blue rain. She has stung.

I am horrified to find myself flicking her, lightly but with the darkest of intentions, across the cheek with the back of my fingers.

I am more horrified when, in the magnesium-flare next flash, she narrows her eyes, and hisses something, like Anna May Wong playing a Somerset Maugham East-of-Suez character, and then, accompanied by a really splendid sample of thunder, begins fluently to elocute, "You filthy beast! You yellow cur! Father! Father! This *gentle*man has struck me! I've been assaulted!"

Although he is sitting well within earshot, in his favourite sea-grass chair at the foot of the stairs, the father does not come. After I have apologized, and attempted to soothe, I go towards the stairs. There he sits, another Somerset Maugham character, fanning his greasy face with a rat-gnawed palm-leaf fan. As I put my hand on the newel, he looks at me from *behind* the surface of his slippery wine-brown eyes, and winks one of them.

My mind is still somewhat shaken from its orbit, but I record that I feel more masculine than I should, and that the Ku Klux Klan feeling of maleness is something men can arouse in men by the mere flicker of an eyelid, a feeling no woman could arouse with her body or her loyalty, her guile or her scorn.

So, recording and learning, I advance on the day of departure, having piecemeal discerned that an addition of years, information and experiences, while making me older, more informed and experienced, certainly does not make me wiser. Suddenly, in July 1937, it seems to me that, after ten years of peering and partaking, all that needs to be known about Williamstown is known, stored away, and that the time has arrived for the storehouse packed hugger-mugger to the rafters to be tidied up. I must leave Williamstown so that this tidying up can be done without the danger of my being tempted into acquiring more Williamstown bric-à-brac.

I shall tidy the decade into a novel.

Without taking a breath, I resign from the Education Department.

Immediately the letter is written—*I have the honour to be, sir, your obedient servant*—Williamstown becomes no more than the subject of a novel, a little suburban ghost-city made of words, and peopled by ghosts made of words. Looking back, I see these ghosts as largely gentle ones, lovable, self-minified, vague ones with their imperfections as restricted as their perfections, their quarrels and ecstasies muted because of the neighbours, their sins small, daily, run-of-the-mill, and their greater vices and sharper honesties blurred. The sun of their solar system is a sun of fog. Self-respect seals their lips so that they dare not speak even against themselves. Who, therefore, will speak against them?

My letter of resignation written, I am immediately no longer Junior Teacher 26,727 of North Williamstown State School 1409.

What am I?

First of all, I am a twenty-six-year-old male who, between the extremes of being a restless picker-up and a ruthless pruner, has acquired a number of habits and convictions nothing will alter. These particular habits and convictions, chosen after much exploration of other varieties, now serve the purpose of bringing me to heel when different habits and newly fashionable convictions present themselves along with the unnecessary opportunity to spend myself in further time-and-spirit-wasting explorations. Old gods exact fewer dues than new ones. I am wary of being broadminded because those who profess broadmindedness are, it seems, professing it on behalf of their own appetites. I prefer to keep my inborn sense of sin unsmothered, and to be narrow-minded about forgiving myself when I do sin. Self-forgiving is unforgivable.

What else am I?

Out of work. Homeless. Practically penniless and, as it were, large with child, gravid with the novel which is to have twenty-four chapters, each covering an hour in a one day's red-hot wedge sliced from the lives of a number of characters based on Williamstown people. Each character is to be dealt with in a signature-tune style which is to involve me in imitations of James Joyce, Conrad, Henry James, Thomas Mann, Kipling, Evelyn Waugh, Mary Webb, Proust, and others I forget. The result is, of course, to be the Great Australian Novel. In short, I have shamelessly—but not for long—lost my head. I do not lose it long enough to find myself doing a Thomas Chatterton in an attic. Where, then, am I to take my Wright's Coal Tar Soap and Euthymol Toothpaste, and hang up my sponge-bag, while the months of labour drag on? How shall I buy more soap and toothpaste?

Cheap rooms in the city are, in those days, easy to come by. Within the inner city there are still nineteenth-century cottages, terraces of attics, old warehouses, ex-shops, haylofts, and delicensed pubs, all to be rented. Most of the cottages in Little Lonsdale Street are taken over by harlots. The buildings at the eastern end of Bourke Street house innumerable fishy one-room enterprises—passport photographers, spiritualists, doll-doctors, employment agencies, fortune-tellers, herbalists, theosophists, tattooists, and the ravaged and crazy-eyed teachers of elocution, tap-dancing, Pelmanism, zither-playing, Writing for Profit, conjuring tricks, and artificial-flower making. The attics and back rooms of Little Collins Street, Collins Street, and western Bourke Street are rented by young artists of every sort who use the places as studios, love-nests, pieds-à-terre away from mum and dad, or merely as settings for booze-ups. My need is for something less Bohemian and ratbag. I certainly have no desire to live in a place whose kitchen-sink discomfort is aggravated by a décor of Picasso prints, pseudo-Benda masks, Spanish oil bottles, lacquered seltzogenes, and the booty of Treasure Hunts: *No Parking* signs, newsagents' hoardings, railway station fire-buckets, and *Keep off the Grass* notices.

I inherit, from a Communist schoolteacher friend called Ann of whose Communism I am not yet aware, a third-floor back room at 28 Collins Street. From the window of what must have been a parlour-maid's hutch in the eighteen-eighties I can see over the high brick wall of the backyard of the Melbourne Club wherein plane-trees, denied municipal surgery, grow like superior weeds, and are as tall as London's oldest plane-trees in Berkeley Square. The rent, fifteen shillings weekly, includes the use of a communal kitchen I never use, a bathroom bigger than my cell, with water so boiling that steam jerks out when the tap is first turned on, and room service. Every morning at

71

eight a breakfast tray is brought in by a woman of about forty called May, who has the build of a ruckman but is dressed like the French maid of a bedroom farce—black dress, tiny frilled white apron, tinier frilled cap. She is always borrowing cigarettes, which she does not repay as cigarettes. Instead, several mornings a week, she brings in a peanut-butter tumbler of port wine with the tea and toast and marmalade, shouting, "That'll put back the roses. Get it into you. That'll warm the cockles. That'll put lead in your pencil." At first I regard this gesture as a preamble to seduction, and imagine her magnificent eyes, darkly embedded in a crumpled rubber face, to be glimmering with depravity, until it dawns on me that the port wine is partly a pleasure in maternally sharing her own favourite drink with which she is always semi-woozy, partly repayment for the cigarettes.

The owner of 28 Collins Street, Miss Beveridge, is almost the same height, shape and weight as May—four-square, high-bosomed, undumbfoundable, with legs like jeroboams—and is as near to being a Grand Duchess as a lodging-house martinet can be. Her fingers are kept as apart as frogs' fingers by thick rings, two or three to a finger, and no finger free—diamonds, diamonds, and diamonds. She wears beige jersey, her silk stockings dull side out, and crocodile-skin shoes. Her creamy dome of hair, steeply terraced, is ideal for the display of coronets or aigrettes, and would not have been amiss in the basket at the base of Sansom's guillotine.

Although there must be a dozen or more others in the house I get to know two only of them. It shocks me, now, to remember that I know them by surnames—they are women—and that their food is, then, their most alluring quality.

Schultzie is a doll-pretty young woman from a farm in one of South Australia's German communities, with a prettiness that will later, I know, be much amplified—double chins, dimpled arms, buttocks quivering like blancmange. She has a piping, little-girl voice in which she sings "Moonlight and Shadows", and must be the only other person at twenty-eight who does not own the Penguin copy of *A Farewell to Arms*. Every so often she gets a hamper of farm food which she plays Lady Bountiful with. I recall roast pigeons, roast fowl, pickled walnuts, ham loaves, biscuits bristling with almonds, and dark fruit-cakes.

The other food-woman lives in the ground-floor front. Her door, always ajar when I come in late at night, opens off the entrance hall which is crimson-carpeted, mahogany-panelled, and smells of burnt toast.

"That you, Porter?" she calls as from the depths of a mine.

Her room fumes as though on the point of combustion because of the Turkish cigarettes she endlessly smokes, and glows like a furnace because of the red shades on her lamps, and is as hot as one because of the never-turned-off radiator and the constantly simmering coffee percolator, a device of glass resembling something from the laboratory of a science-fiction mad professor.

This woman, whose name is Abramson, and who huddles like a gipsy queen in the boiler-room fug, is a Jewess and a journalist, and is voluble in a jaded and overcultivated accent. I nearly see, then, and think I fully see now that she is one of the kind, too common, too self-pitying, which makes a pet of loneliness. Abramson drops lead-heavy hints of bygone tragedy and former Viennese grandeur, but I never lead her on to lift the dumbells and perform. There is enough to do in dissecting the subtleties and complexities of Australians, at one and the same time the world's most brutal sophisticates and fearless innocents.

The anguishes of the Old World are too rusted and creaking, in 1937, for an ear turned nativistically elsewhere. The anguishes of Jews, in 1937, are too obvious and showy and repetitive for me—I have already gone through the Bible twice. However, I act listening to Abramson's Weltschmerz incantations, keeping my eyes intelligently wide open, and directing at her the frank gaze that only the unfrank non-listener can convincingly direct. Meantime, with delicately managed gluttony, I eat, for she presses on me the exotic foodstuffs, of which she has a large supply all bought at Franz the Grocer's at the Eastern Market—rollmops, anchovies, caviare, salami, olives, rye bread, and the oozier cheeses. Irish stew would be preferable. A wallet of air and a tight belt drive me, however, to caviare, and Abramson's own blend of coffee from Quist's, and her own blend of enthusiasms which, in retrospect, seem

73

somewhat *Esquire*. Belly may be grateful for her hospitality (given on her own lonely-selfish behalf? given in pity, on my behalf? I'll never know); heart may be a little restless that something within her tosses in hungry agony: ear grows fatigued in paying for belly which does not have to listen to her on Nazis, pogroms, Dos Passos, Dreiser, Sinclair Lewis, Upton Sinclair, and Steinbeck, just as it does not have to listen to her vilifying Franco.

How do I pay for the right to live in a building that contains May to make my bed, and wash my socks and underpants, Schultzie and Abramson to provide money-saving snacks, and Miss Beveridge to be such an impressive all-seeing eye-of-God that, even when she is out or fast asleep, I never invite to my room anyone she would not approve of—how do I pay for all this?

I work, part-time and no more than is needed to keep my mouth just above water, for a firm called Arcadia Display Specialistes. The job, for which I have no really specialized training, is nevertheless a soda, and is engineered for me by my first grown-up male friend. His name is Leon Hogan. He is thirty-five, Roman Catholic, married, and Head Artist for Arcadia Display Specialistes. The he's-me-cobber bond between us is a new adult experience for me, and nothing has prepared me for its special quality. Boyhood friendships give no clues. These dexterously manipulated relationships between egos in unbreakable glass are no more than engagements of convenience tricked out in Tom Sawyer trappings. Later male friendships, easy-going and stimulating but without great depth —P.J.G., Dargie, Barclay, other teachers, art students I work and play with at the National Gallery School, saloon-bar companions—have all illustrated the shades of herd feeling between men. None of them has drawn me into the experience of being affected by or having an effect on another man. I suppose, too, that my younger eyes are not cleared enough of my own self-sufficient image, not humanified enough to see through to a mate. Moreover, in the early days of the friendship with Leon Hogan, it is not clear to me that the give-and-take directness and the sardonic you're-a-bloody-nice-bastard-of-a-friend intimacy are peculiar to Australian men. Years of observation,

74

later on, of the behaviour of non-Australian men unmistakeably reveals that their recipe for masculinity and friendship differs from the Australian one. Whose is right or better or truer or more honest I cannot know and, since I regard an open mind on subjective teasers as little more than a playground for the winds of other people's other opinions, close my mind, and do not want to know.

I can only praise Australian Mateship in reverse by recording that I have found men of other national groups lacking in what seems an important grace, a depth, an openness of mind and heart and hand. Their social masculinity is minus a fibre of sensitivity, a fibre of strength, a fibre of humour, a fibre of self-knowledge, a fibre of self-mockery and is, in short, much less trustworthy and vital. That the missing fibres have been replaced by strands of a *kitsch* and slippery polish is natural enough from the inhabitants of *kitsch* and slippery civilizations.

In 1937, then, my mate Leon Hogan gets me a part-time job as a cross between dogsbody and jack-of-all-trades at Arcadia Displaye Specialistes.

I have to walk nearly two miles from 28 Collins Street to the little factory. It is in a part of North Melbourne where streets are outnumbered by bluestone-cobbled lanes, more than usually underprivileged-looking lanes through which tomcats with tattered ears, and faces like Mr Hyde's, s-l-i-n-k rather than settling down to lick their steenkirks among the camp-pie tins and dogs' turds.

The Arcadia products, which are bought by suburban emporiums and edge-of-the-city corner shops and country town general stores anxious to get rid of their cedar shop-fittings, are of elementary and depressing design: plywood counters and display cases with one corner rounded, display boards with one corner rounded, nickel-plated *art moderne* display stands. These, though each looks the same as the other, are forever being emotionally designed by the Head Designer. He is the only one, just as Leon Hogan, Head Artist, is the only artist. The designer is called Rexie to his pendulous off-white face, and Rosie behind his undulant back. He has melon buttocks, one or other of which now and then winces through his chalk-stripe trousers as he stands in front of his patch of

75

looking-glass combing his hair into a Cornish-pasty arrangement: up from each side with a ruffle riding the centre. He wears thick-lensed spectacles, so that his eyes seem set in aspic. Rexie's cubicle (THE STUDIO, states his door) is as neat as a surgery but has enlivening touches such as a telephone he has enamelled mauve, a Lalique platter heaped with lacquered gourds, and a Beardsleyish black-and-white of a young man with amaranthine tresses, but otherwise as nude as a marrow. This nymph-man is on tiptoe.

As offsider to Leon my chores are various. I finically dash in the *minor* stars above his Three Wise Men—I'm not up to dashing them in dashingly; daub large white freckles on three-ply reindeer; spray stencilled curves parallel to the rounded edges of things; cut silk-screen lettering; paint cut-outs of Father Christmas, Mickey Mouse, Minnie Mouse, Peter Rabbit, portly chefs with Gallic waxed moustaches *circa* 1913, and, once, two hundred cardboard butterflies the size of pterodactyls.

There are also the more public chores. Doing them I often find myself knotted, before an undesired audience of quizzical street-strollers and troll-like errand boys, in shame-making conflict with inanimate objects suddenly gifted with a perverse liveliness, a maniac agility. There I am, for example, at eleven in the morning, sock-footed, confined behind the plate-glass of the South Australian Tourist Bureau shop-window, sweating like a stoker as I play ju-jitsu with an entanglement of many-elbowed real branches covered in tissue-paper blossom, two arc-lights, an apparent league of flex, a glass-eyed cutie of a dummy in pink organdie, and a placard—it has one rounded corner—defiled by such words as *picturesque, panorama, blossom-time, sun-dappled,* and *memorable experience.*

I quarrel in Henry Buck's shop-window with gesticulating and foot-stamping window-dressers who want to dispose Leon's painted backgrounds (lean, bronzed, white-moustached *Esquire* men in hound's-tooth sports coats toying with what one supposes are highballs) in an order he adamantly will not allow.

I teeter, dry-mouthed from vertigo, at the pinnacle of ladders while tacking Arcadia festoons of crêpe-paper wistaria to the

Babylonian pillars of Myer's Emporium, ringed about, far below on the plain, by shoppers stilled in a trance of delicious terror that I might dive down like Icarus.

In the back regions of Arcadia Displaye Specialistes are three or four men who noisily construct the rounded-corner furnishings, the silhouettes of chefs that are to stand outside the three-course-meals-for-tenpence restaurants, the kidney-shaped notice boards, and so on. They work under perpetual electric light, and are jockey-sized, quick-tempered, weasel-quick makings-smokers with witty, dirty, whiplash tongues. They have mutton and chow-chow pickle sandwiches for lunch, and Tamil-brown cups of tea almost mucilaginous with sugar. They can spit as brilliantly as llamas and, though it cannot be so, all seem to be called Arthur.

Since, for me, my job does not seem a real one—and, relatively, scarcely is—the factory does not have the air of a serious undertaking, more that of the occupational therapy quarters in an unorthodox guest house. Above the whining of the Arthurs's machines and the constant ring-ring ring-ring of the telephone rises the fracas of the squalls of temperament which, usually triggered off by Rexie, everyone enormously enjoys. In this coop of emotion and industry smelling of glue, shellac, sawdust, shavings, paint, and the hot metal of machines, my status is too low, my jobs too easy and soothing, and my nature too equable and what-the-hell for me to want to let off steam as the others do.

Leon rarely has noisy public blow-outs. His displays of temperament are private and subdued, and I learn, soon, that they are not caused by a tricky job or a botched painting but by emotions which have mounted in the pressure tube of self-control to the point of overflow. At such times, no matter the hour, no matter the task I have in hand, he comes to me, charged with melancholy, his green pork-pie hat on the tilt, his smile too devised, his voice too neutral, and says, "Wash your hands. Comb your hair. Let's get out of this dump."

Out means the New Treasury Hotel in Spring Street with the convict's fountain opposite and the temple-grave façades of the Treasury and Parliament House and, within, the 1860 bars with their wooden benches, sand-blasted glass doors, copper foot-rails, pictures of nineteenth-century racehorses, of Queen Alexandra and King Edward the Seventh, and of the Peter Dawson Whisky dogs dressed in fedoras, spats, watch-chained waistcoats and astrakhan-collared coats who are tippling, and playing poker for sovereigns at a baize-covered table. Sometimes, and it all depends on the pitch of Leon's distress, out means the Baltic Club, and cheap wine among chess-players, or the Greek Club, and ouzo among penny-gamblers playing colchina, agonaea, or pinochle.

It is in male settings such as these that I start to cotton on to the difference between the relationship with Leon, and the relationships with earlier men-friends, and begin learning properly at last, the syntax of the language of men. This is a study one cannot complete alone; it needs a countersignature.

I am never able to explain to myself, let alone anyone else, why one sample of a human being as something to look at is more satisfying than another. I cannot, either, find that there is a visual common factor in the many human beings who have delighted me. Hogan is no Adonis but his appearance pleases me: I know no more. I know, however, why my relationship with him differs from earlier relationships. The difference is, essentially, between what is told and what is not told. Earlier friends have colluded in agreeable games of social ping-pong, in the exchange of confidences so juiceless they can be painted up as large as Robur Tea advertisements for the mob to see, in the mutual exposure of only the skittish and you're-a-little-devil sins, the amusing bad habits, the less overwhelming virtues, the overall presentation of oneself as house-trained above the stealthy meannesses, dirty vanities, and two-a-penny lusts.

Hogan does not offer me a censored version of himself. There is the manuscript, rubic and blot, gilt and scribble, no erasures. He does not play down his unfashionable nobilities and saint-like tolerance any more than he puts a gloss upon his carnality and venality, his fears and weaknesses. Since he neither admires nor pities himself I can play back matching tempers with love and safety for he also neither pities nor admires me as I neither admire nor pity myself. I sigh a little to recall, now, that all those years ago he is thought the protective and stronger older man, I the frothy one. In truth, I am the steel-nerved one, the puritan, the surgeon, the painter-cutter, the unforgiving, and he the tortured, indecisive one, tethered by many threads, scarred by many scalpels, as forgiving as Christ. Our public Mutt and Jeff appearance as *toujours gai* blokes are authentic enough. Behind the scenes we have already, in a corner of the Baltic Club or the Greek Club, bandaged afresh with grog and horse-sense such of his wounds as are weeping again—remembrance of the death of his baby daughter Marie, Jack-in-the-box wraiths of Roman Catholic remorse, trouble with Helen his wife, trouble with his non-commercial painting, problems of love without lust, and of lust without love. He does not pick these wounds awake. He bleeds easily. I have few problems and no bleedings of my own to swap with him—indeed, the only one that is not piddling is that of the novel.

I am writing very little, too little. My passion and need to write have not abated. I am, however, giddy and drunken with a fresher passion for the city. This, I tell myself with an infuriated sincerity, will *not* do, this new love. At night, I brutally drag myself away by the scruff from the polished streets, and the late taxi-cabs hissing along them with fixed eyes, I steal like a convict past Abramson's caviare, and climb up and up, fighting a desire to turn back to the unfinished wonders. My room smells of night, or is it planets? I write. My hand moves, the pen moves, the ink knits a few lines and a few slower lines more of Williamstown and its ten years of familiar faces advertising trivialities, its ten years of familiar disorders and delights, and known tomorrows. Here, at the task of knitting with ink, lies my duty to the leprosy. The hand and the pen must keep moving. They falter. How vulnerable one is when on heat for— for whomever, for whatever, for the city's tablets of stone. My hand and I cannot hear and see but can sense, layers of rooms below, the hissing taxi-cabs, the fixed golden eyes, the city with its unfamiliar disorders and delights, and its unknown tomorrows. I put away my knitting.

This—I begin a slick litany as I prepare for bed—this will wait. Soon you will go home to the country, to the peace of the country, the black nights of the country, the lamp breathing for you on the kitchen table. Then you'll write hour after hour after hour. . . . Explore the city thoroughly. First. Do it now. *First*. Dive below the surface. Time and tide wait for no man. You've netted Williamstown. Net Melbourne. Opportunity knocks only once.

I attempt thus to strive, as though striving feebly with the Holy Ghost, with the problem of consummating a new love while still bearing the child of the old. It is too light a problem to do anything but put me to sleep, a sleep I hurry through so that I shall miss as little as possible of the tomorrow the clock has not yet manufactured. My eyes close. I need no more than this bed, this dark, this scrapbook of plotless dreams, to travel the brief distance to morning, and May shouting at the door, "Ups-a-daisy, Snowy! Get this into you!"

I get it into me, and leave all Miss Beveridge's monogrammed silver-plated vessels empty—teapot, milk jug, hot-water pot, toast dish—and screw back the lid on the marmalade jar, and twist the napkin, rolled like a diploma, into the ivory ring. I put aside the port wine, if it be a port wine morning, to sip after showering and shaving. As I sip, whatever my window tells me of hail or wind or sun, my mind noses about like mice seeking an exit. Where today? When the mice stop their nonsense, which is only something to do while the port is beginning to transform itself into something else, I lock the door, and go downstairs. I must go downstairs but—why?—cannot ever recall doing so. I do, clearly, remember many goings-up, club-footed drunk, talking to a lover-to-be in the clear tones of brother telling sister nothing important for Miss Beveridge's ears, two steps at a time because I am coming down again, weary and witless from listening to Abramson dusting dusting dusting the horrible *objets d'art* on the shelf of Europe, 1937.

If I do not recall the descents, I do recall opening the plate-glass door and stepping, immediately—and *immediately* never once gets dusty—into the heart of glory, into The City.

In the same way as history has none of the salt of reality, and is merely a technicolor banquet to trick the eye, so Melbourne, The City of 1937, the first city I *live* in, now, set out in memory, displays no gritty bits, no tear stains, no blood clots. If there were something nasty in that woodshed it is now no more than a shape of ambergris or amber. However often I lay out the cards, they are all there, kings and queens and knaves and aces, the spades and clubs are black, the diamonds are red, the hearts are still red. I remember everything, yet there must be something I forget. There must be one element common to all the separate things I recall that has faded as the scent of poison fades from the empty phial leaving it a jewel of glass that could have held chypre or Chanel Cinq. Otherwise how could the city of that year, and the people in it, still burn, flames within a flame, with such pure intensity?

Perhaps the clock of pain has stopped.

Perhaps, because I will not agonize or even fret about my own flaws and laxities and poverty, will not diminish myself by suffering for myself, or pervert myself and swindle others by pretending that I can suffer for others, I have put a stop to the tick-tocking, torn off the talking hands, so that there remains only the gagged and inscrutable disc encircled by its out-of-work figures, insignia of sufferings not to be recorded except as beautiful marks, as indelible designs rimming a perfect shape.

My ten to fifteen hours a week of imitation work at Arcadia Displaye Specialistes makes me a little money and much time.

Time, if one has it, can be cut into keys for many doors.

I have, in 1937, a supply of keys as invisible as keys cut from time must be, many invisible keys. The city has many doors. I forbid myself none. If forbidden any, I am unaware of the forbiddings.

The doors?

They swing apart on people I can never be: shells containing lives that waste away unused; scarecrows hung with the cast-off rags of false crusaders; attitudes in a chain-mail of evasion, and a visor of secrecy; people who ring like telephones in empty rooms; people who open like fans to the eye that peers through the Judas-trap of my heart. Some open just so much, shy and sly, so much and no more. Some open fully—swish!— but the truth of the decoration on the fan is lost in the twirling and flutter-flutter, the snapping-to, the flicking-open. Is it a viper, dark with bile, knotted to the shape of a rose? Is it a dark rose itself with a core of bitter snow? Is it the footprint of the hunter? Is it the very heart, desiccated to tinder, yet painted to resemble the blood-plump original?

The doors?

It is a rainy night. In the depthless city roads the city lights plunge down trembling anchors to hook their flukes in illusion. The wind whines a cold *Nachtmusik* between its teeth. This is a night I am nearly certain to find Audrey sitting like a citified Anna Christie in the steam of the Broadway Café. My trench coat flapping and sodden, a *Journey's End* officer, I come to the long street-window of the Broadway Café, Russell Street. The window is lead-lighted, its art noveau poppies buckle inwards, buckle outwards. A more manly wind than the wet whiner could punch the grimy glass petals of the poppies out of the twisted lead, could wrench them from their shepherd's-crook stems, and shower them like bloody slices of trespass into the laps of the prostitutes, into Audrey's lap, into the tea-cups of the taxi-drivers sitting at the grey-marble-topped tables in the steam. It is steam of tea. I smell it as the door, groaning from its sciatica, opens and closes behind me.

Audrey is not there.

"Audrey's not here," says one of the other prostitutes sitting there like an elegant mother. It is the cultured one. Cultured? Well, crossword-cultured, quiz-cultured, anthology-cultured. She asks me "literary" questions so inquisitional that I backtrack some to this day because the recollection of not being able to pick up the answer, which must still be lying in the grass somewhere, now and then comes back to me.

"Tea-with?" says the cultured one—Mavis? Merle? Marie? It is something starting with M. Tea-with is tea with brandy. The Broadway Café is a night-people's cubby-hole at night, and provides for them, at its price, in thick ironstone china cups of respectable white with a rim of respectable maroon, such posset-like comforts as tea-with.

"Broke!" I say. "I'll just get myself a glass of hot milk. I've got a zack."

"Would you *like* tea-with? Don't be coy: I'm flush. Anyway I asked you. Have a tea-with."

She is tatting away at a maidenly adornment for a piece of furniture, a runner of some sort. She puts down the work on the silk scarf it lives virginally in. She opens her red harlot's handbag, takes out a note, holds it up, calls out, "Macca!" at the waiter who sits drowsily mumbling between his sideburns to two taxi-drivers drinking undefiled tea. He looks up. She mouths the order for him to lip-read. She hands me the note, and takes up her tatting.

"You pay," she says. "No tip. He got one last time. And now . . ."

I dread what is coming.

"And now, I'm glad you turned up tonight. When I was near the Bijou Theatre, and this bloody rain started, and kept on and on, on and on, I saw a poor old creature with a walking-stick crossing Bourke Street. Who wrote:

> *The woman was old and weary and grey,*
> *And bent with the chill of a winter's day?*

Now, who wrote that?"

Her eyes probe me like a stern nun's. Will she next say, "And you can't have your drink until you answer."?

I am able, this time, thank God or whoever taught me, to answer. I can drink my tea-with without shame for, in much the same way as I give my ear to Abramson in payment for caviare so I give my tongue coloured with the words of others for the tea-with. Made mercenary by this tiny success which pleases M. out of all proportion, I produce enough Clerihews to allow myself guiltlessly to accept another drink. She is mad about Clerihews and Humbert Wolfe. I shut off the engine of the part of the mind daring to move towards the question, "What was he like, the man for whom this woman, tatting and talking here, simulated passion, got up, pulled down her dress, smoothed the quilt, indicated the bowl of water and Condy's Crystals, and took the note that bought the drink that bought the Clerihews?"

I still owe her, the prostitute with the name beginning with M., with the tatting in the silk scarf, with the bunch of violets pinned upside down above her heart, some answers for some drinks.

Does she still need those answers?

Is she still asking,

83

"Who wrote:

She was wearing the coral and taffeta trousers,
That someone had brought her from Ispahan?

Who wrote that, and what's the rest of it?"?
Is there still a voice somewhere saying, "Who wrote:

My father was a jockey, a jockey, a jockey,
My father was a jockey, and a jockey was he,
And when he went a-riding, a-riding, a-riding,
And when he went a-riding, he always took me."?

The friendship with M. and other street-walkers is Audrey's doing, as is my acceptance into the choosy Broadway circle of prostitutes, taxi-drivers, minor dry-crimers, and less polished confidence men. It is possible that what seems to me to be an orderly and happy family is more sinister than that. I'll never know what lies behind the tea-urn, the coming and going in the steam, the dreamy whisperings. To me they and the veiled moon that is the centre of their long night are fascinating. Their gods are different and as young as children; their lies are more charged with truth; their truth is charred but recognizable; their platitudes sound like exotic sagacity; they wear their infantile fears like rosettes.

Audrey.

At State School 1409, in 1928, when I am seventeen, I watch Grade Eight rehearsing its item for the annual school concert. It is to finish up as a song-with-gestures number with the girls and boys as fancy-dressed Dutchies—cardboard sabots, draughts-board skirts, patched sateen trousers, hemp plaits. As I turn the music pages for Miss Whoever-it-is, the accompanist who is bashing out again and again the tune of "Little Mr Baggy Breeches", I can scarcely credit the evidence of my senses. That pretty-as-a-picture girl of fourteen in the front row of Dutchies cannot be winking at me, just *can*not, as she trills

Little Mr Baggy Breeches, I love you.
If you'll be my Sunday fellow,
I'll patch 'em in purple, in pink, and in yellow. . . .

Has she a tic? She has not. She *is* winking at me. She winks

84

again. Just in time to forestall an expression of ploughboy astonishment or Junior Teacher outrage, I arrange an unseeing one. I endeavour to age myself, on the spot ("Over, please," says Miss Whoever-it-is), from seventeen to some sterner age safe from insult, twenty-four, say. Am I blushing? I try to induce pallor as well as age, sightlessness, and an Abraham Lincoln sternness.

The winker with the tilted nose is Audrey.

It is Audrey, nine years later, swinging her handbag among the moths under the ten o'clock plane-trees outside the Occidental Hotel, ten o'clock of a tawny evening no warmer than blood, who as it were winks at me again. As I come towards her I know what she is. The silhouette of woman who fish a street as posh as Collins Street is a loitering silhouette, the silhouette of a scented flame that is nervously on the alert to lick sideways and softly fuse with—with whomever can buy the silhouette of flame and reduce it to a horizontally inverted Y of flesh.

I am ready with a polite, "Not tonight thanks, dear," to her fife-clear murmur, "Lonely tonight, dear?"

I am not ready for the "Mr Porter!"

I stop. In my tracks, that is the expression. I hear the powdered wings of the moths.

"You are *from* Williamstown?"

She lingers there, delicate and young and painted, swinging her handbag, and I haven't a notion who she is.

I'm sorry, I say, that I don't recognize her.

She is wearing a fragile elegy of a hat of some glittering black material, and a nose-length veil sparkling with black spangles. She lifts it above her eyes, and brings those eyes nearer to me, offering them like a visiting-card. I read sleepiness and fearlessness.

"Williamstown," she says. "The state school in Melbourne Road. Remember now?" and she winks. I remember. She sees that I remember before I speak. I tell her who she is. She agrees with me.

"Are you doing anything tonight?" she says. Oh, dear!

P. J. Green and his point-to-point stick, Madam and her

85

jabot, the ex-A.I.F. teachers, the Junior Teachers, Miss Glew and Miss Benson and the twin Misses Macdonald and Miss Lynch and Miss Sangster and Miss Furphy and Miss Sarvaas, all suddenly line up in my mind. I see a blackboard on which is chalked in copperplate *Practise what you preach* and *Never keep in one girl only after school.*

I see that Audrey perceives what this moral chorus does to my expression. Cat's-paws of indefinable doubts are doubtless running across the surface of my face. The night becomes cooler than blood.

"I don't mean *that*," she says, her veil again twinkling between her eyes and me. "I only mean that if you're doing nothing, come and have a drink with me. I used to be pretty keen on you when I was a girl. I feel a bit low. I need a pick-me-up. There's no catch. Come and have a drink."

She takes me to the Broadway. She does not stroll loiteringly but minces along beside me like a girl friend, her high heels peck-pecking through the pretty night, her voice spinning out the virtuous drivel of a fiancée.

We become friends. Her friends—women who spend lives like street corners, petty criminals dressed to the nines, people with the tender pale hands of those who despise labour— become mine. Drifting in and out of the dimension they occupy, a dimension in which sin is so serious an occupation that one does not expect smiles and chyacking and charm, I find the charm and chyacking and smiles hypnotic. I wander drugged in the forbidden territory where poignancy and treachery and despair seem swathed in a gossamer of indifference and resignation.

Audrey tells me, on that first session of Broadway teas-with, that she has been a prostitute for six years, since she was seventeen. She tells it dazedly as though of someone else, some semi-transparent girl from a ballad. Days pass before I realize I've placidly listened to a sordid story, a crime. She goes on, sipping tinily from the ironstone china cup, to inform me how it all begins.

Her mother dies when Audrey is twelve. At thirteen she is seduced by her father, the widower, carpenter, and a forty-five-year-old lay preacher. At first she loathes the business but

86

not, she says, her father. "He was," she says, demi-drowsing above her cup, "a very good dad, really, and very generous. He was a bit of a wowser. Religious, y' see. I suppose he was a hypocrite, but he was very good-looking and very sexy. I got to like it after a while. I could always tell when he was going to have me. He used to come home whistling. He was very particular though. He'd have a bath first, a real good scrub. And he'd suck peppermints." When she is sixteen, and turning her attention to boys of her own age, to dances and picture-shows, her father becomes jealous. There are frightful rows. Once he beats her. First time, last time. "That," she says, "was the stone end. I just packed my glad rags, and took off. I write to him about once a month, but I don't go near him. It wouldn't be right now." The light flakes of her voice carelessly fall like warm snow, so that the jagged branches of words such as hypocrisy, incest, child-corruption, immorality, and crimin-ality are coated and blurred. Words like right and wrong have the same mild shape. Without a pause or a change in tone she goes on to talk about State School 1409. Do I remember this and that and the other? Do I remember "Little Mr Baggy Breeches"?

She begins to sing quietly, stirring the air one-two-three with a forefinger, smiling at me under her trembling veil of spangles which are now seen to be not black but midnight-blue, smiling at me blindly because she is also smiling matern-ally back at herself, her father's fourteen-year-old mistress, in cardboard sabots and a Dutch bonnet:

"*I'll patch 'em in purple, in pink, and in yellow;*
And folks will sa-ay, as he leans on the old sea-wall:
'Lena's been patching her Jacob's
Till he's got no breeches at all!
Patches big, patches small, ja, ja, ja-a,
Till he's got no breeches at all!'"

Later in our acquaintanceship I take her to dinner at the Latin Café to meet Dargie. Is there some talk of using her, a dyed-in-the-wool street-woman, as model for one of the char-acters in the conversation pieces Dargie is then painting? I for-get. There is no portrait of her, nothing to record the prettiness at once vague and sharp, senseless and sensitive. I see, ten years later, in the newspaper *Truth*, the photograph of a woman being charged for the twentieth time with vagrancy. It shows a face from which sensitivity has been trodden out, a face bestial and defiant as an orchid. It is Audrey's. It is one of Audrey's. For me she still sits at the grey marble table, singing a schoolgirl's song into the steam of the tea-with, still unde-flowered by time. The lead-light poppies of dirty glass still flourish behind her on the door of the Broadway Café, torn down these many years.

The doors of 1937, when one had the keys of time!

There is the door to Kingsley Hall. It is a solid, kicked-at looking door with a lion's-mask knocker. It opens on to a hall-way that contains nothing except a bandy-legged pedestal on which stands a piece of Italian Statuary of a little girl holding up her skirts. Someone has crayoned on her a curly moustache and a pair of spectacles and a squint. Beyond the hallway fur-nished like a nightmare lie the rooms and flatettes and bed-sitters of a tribe new to me, and consequently tempting.

Kingsley Hall is a stucco terrace of four two-storeyed houses, and is in a one-block-only street behind St Patrick's Cathedral and the Eastern Hill Fire Brigade building. The street is generally called the Street of Leaning Trees because its plane-tree avenue, striving skywards, has become so "pic-turesquely" skew-whiff that, rain or shine, a beret-topped middle-aged artist and a middle-aged easel can be seen stradd-ling together at the end of the street.

Kingsley Hall, built *circa* 1870, to house four middle-class families—ma and pa, children, nursemaid, cook, and tweeny—goes through this period for twenty years. Doorways are then cut through the three inner walls to make one establishment which is, first of all, a private hotel for gentlewomen—retired governesses and deaconesses, Anglo-Indian widows, the spin-ster daughters of archbishops and admirals. These menless women with their mourning millinery, Benger's Food, copies of Miss Braddon's novels, bee brooches, and Perry Davis' Veget-able Pain Killer are replaced, during the reign of Edward the Seventh, by the women they could have been: Kingsley Hall becomes a discreetly opulent brothel smelling of Havana cigars, oyster suppers, and Jockey Club. It leaves as heritage a number of looking-glasses set high, and tilted at an angle, between the flower-blotched wallpaper and the ceiling with its gasolier depending from the centre of a wheel of gilded plaster acanthus leaves. It is next a ragtime sausages-and-mash boarding-house for entertainers of the barnstorming sort: bell-ringers, contortionists, Shakespearian monologuists looking like Liszt in old age, raddled soubrettes, buck-and-wing dancers, tattooed ladies, itinerants of all sorts whose unravelling theatrical baskets can hold anything from a ventriloquist's doll as battered as its master to a brace of world-weary carpet snakes with blasé eyes. In 1937 it houses those huddling on the fringes of the arts and the outskirts of spivvery—empty-bellied music students, piece-work commercial artists, door-to-door salesmen from photo-enlarging firms, chorus boys rooming in petulant couples, makers of china masks, amateur confidence men. Most of them work only when the world is sodden with sunlight.

I come to know them as well as one can know the half-opaque, half-honest, and half-awake. My own part-time world much resembles theirs except that my address is less raffish, my desires less amoral and deconsecrated, and the blueprint of my intentions for the future more meticulously drawn.

I am first taken to the place by Esther, a young woman whose career as a musician has been clawed to death by poverty, the Depression, and the need to support a weakling husband, and the child she bore, alone and half-starved, on the floor of an attic. It is my friend Leon Hogan who introduces me to Esther at the moment where she needs a black dress to get a job as a waitress. I pawn a camel-hair overcoat to get money to buy the dress; the gesture is less magnificent than it might appear because, no sooner have I bought the coat from Henry Buck's than I realize that not only has an error in taste been made but also an error in intrusion on the uniform of others—camel-hair coats, peccary hogskin gloves, Paisley scarves, suède shoes, and a handkerchief protruding from the cuff of the left sleeve are all part of the conventional costume of the Melbourne homosexual of the nineteen-thirties. I pawn the coat, therefore, without a twinge and never redeem it. Esther gets her black dress, and becomes a waitress, and goes to live at Kingsley Hall, high up, just under the slates and the stars, in what must have been a box room.

All of those who live in Kingsley Hall are not on the bread-line, nor are all of them scouting along the dangerous frontier Audrey and her Broadway Café friends have stepped over into a country of another climate. Enough of them, however, do seem—even to me—to have put into peril their intelligence. Tomorrow is always coming. As they traipse, fresh from prolonged hot baths, and smelling of talcum powder, up and down the narrow stairways and along the corridor-carpets thin as dust, seeking with whom they will drink cheap coffee or cheap and scalding wine; as they watch themselves buffing their fingernails or making love in the canted looking-glasses framed in violet plush; as they loll in pairs or trios, looking down from the windows like Rapunzels and carpet-knights, while they eat bruised apricots, tomorrow is always on their lips as honey to come. Today never is. They cannot speak such quartz. Although I am myself, at this time, also procrastinating, and have also stepped for a while off the nine-to-five chart, although their articulate and feckless and sex-bedevilled existence mesmerizes me, the calvinistic one in the innermost gallery of my nature despises them. For what, since their warmth and wit are so engaging, is not perfectly sharp to me even now. One does not despise the aquarium fish, sequined and striped, with fins of chiffon. These are no more than merely aquarium males and females who do not care to fight a cold current, and though the current of the Depression has, in 1937, already thawed, it is still not tropical enough for them.

An autobiographical writer, one who rides a horse to catch a horse, rounds up in half a century of jog-trotting, cantering, and outright galloping a limitless host of characters. He is compelled, therefore, severely to limit the number of them he lets out at one time from the overcrowded concentration camp crowning the ridge of his mind, from that Ark straining at the seams like a lunatic asylum or bargain-sale department store on the Ararat of memory. Were he to attempt to let all free, the avalanche would dance and roar over him, mouthing the un-mouthable, scorching him to flinders, mashing him to silence and nothing beneath a torrent of flaming soles. Out of control, the cascade of square-open mouths and hyper-eager eyes, of hair streaming like a storm of oriflammes, of billows of ardent flesh and hot hearts, would hurtle operatically into the quicksands below, carrying optimism and cowardice, modesty and flattery, honour and menace, guilt and grace, forever out of hearing, forever out of sight.

The outlet must be kept narrow; a few figures beckoned into the flood-lit outer world; the gate slammed—oh, quickly. Even so he finds himself reeling back a little from the power of life left in these long-time internees, finds himself drawn into a frieze of posturing profiles, hemmed in by the inhabitants of that Wagnerianly bloated cliché, a Cavalcade of Humanity. Hemmed in, nose to nose, it is difficult to see beyond the warts.

Thus it is with those sipping and conspiring in the fly-blown Venusberg, the diluted Alsatia, of the Broadway Café. Thus it is with those pigging it with mangled social ritual, middle class to the last cup without a handle, in the wastepaper basket of Kingsley Hall.

Audrey, and such of her friends as I get to know fairly well, are the easier subjects. Animated by a need for confession, and controlled only by social rules I cannot pinpoint, they do reveal a little of the outline of their souls.

A whore who sits tatting a rectangular garment for a refectory table or wireless cabinet reveals more than an ability to tat. She unwraps other layers from the legacy of herself when she says, with no more pique than one talking of a mild headache, that she's pretty sure she's got clap again from some yobbie and, in the next breath, this time girlishly teasing and full of pride, "I'll bet you a tea-with that you don't know who wrote:

> '*I know her little foot,*' *grey carpet said.*
> '*Who but I should know her light tread?*'
> '*She shall come in,*' *answered the open door.*
> '*And not,*' *said the room,* '*go out any more.*' "

Her body will never be the land-mine stumbled over by princes or presidents, and will never stir up intrigues, rifles, emerald chokers, and scandalous downfalls. It is a poor field

91

never fallow, a trite body for the use of trite men. Why doesn't she let it credibly say, " 'V'ya heard the one about the poofter cardinal?" instead of pleading, incredibly and insinuatingly, on behalf of some cherished vision of itself, "Come on, write down the rest of

> *Night will not see thirty again . . .*
> *How old is Spring, Miranda?"?*

The Kingsley Hall subjects, whose surface social antics I recognize to the last deft somersault, are more difficult to see wholly. As they pick away the petals from the hours in the Street of Leaning Trees they grow more obscure—self-mock-ery mists them over; they move behind a smoke-screen of tom-foolery and fashionable jargon; the smallest upset and the most shocking cataclysm are served up with the same dressing, are equally *shame-making, too utterly ghastly, terribly off-putting, quite too bogus,* and *maddening.* The designs on the wide-open fans of their natures are too serpentine and iridescent to be read as no-hoper, layabout, scrounger, bludger, or even as un-fortunate-victim-of-the-Depression. If it be advantageous to find them a little ennobled by a veiled self-pride but otherwise as shallow and winning as sunset-reflecting puddles, it is because I lack the advantage of discovering them to be as deep as lakes. The door of Kingsley Hall opens, and there they are, talking of tomorrow, shampooing hair or puffing at an affected church-warden from Altson's or drinking two-bob-a-gallon muscat as though it were Château Yquem, and talking of tomorrow.

Another door, then.

Twenty-eight Collins Street and twenty-six Collins Street are controlled by Miss Beveridge and, so far as I know, entirely looked after by the muscular, port-swilling May. Perhaps there is a devil or old-age pensioner in the basement who gets rid of Schultzie's chicken carcasses and Abramson's caviare pots, and who stokes the furnace that makes boiling water stammer and blather to itself in the walls and ceilings. I do not remember ever seeing him or hearing of him. Twenty-four Collins Street, the next building, has no May with a silver salver of breakfast, no Miss Beveridge to keep an eye sharp as a sapphire on the social, if not the moral, aura of one's visitors, and no tangled and chatterbox world of hot-water-inhabited pipes. Its back rooms and attics are rented for a song. Here lives Loudon Saint-hill, a young man who is—as Dargie the young man is—later to become famous. Loudon occupies a polyangular *vie-de-Bohème* attic largely furnished, memory seems to say, with Spanish oil-jars, a low and choppy divan, and hangings of war silk which he has handblocked—there are lithe niggers with sugar-loaf coiffures and decorative laplaps who fluidly cavort while other niggers punch at bongo drums or gum-gums. He seems, himself, too lethargic a stripling to have had the force to do these seeming miles of handblocking, or to have withstood without loss of languor the Antarctic sleet of Tasmania, his birthplace. His somnolence and the somnolence of his eyes are deceiving. His tongue and mind are alert; he has chosen a path to suit his feet, and knows where the path will take him—theatrical London, New York, Europe, the Old World.

He and I, descending from our aeries, often meet outside the dictatorial façades of pilastered and extravagantly carved stone consoles and balconies that conceal our scungy bed-chambers, and stroll downslope under the twilight plane-trees of Collins Street until we turn to enter Little Collins Street and the Café Petrushka. The Cavalcade of Humanity which flows in and out of the door of the Café Petrushka, a glass-panelled door streaming like a butcher's shop-window with the con-densed breaths of Melbourne's 1937 intelligentsia—writers, musicians, painters, actors, dancers, and their hangers-on, is another one altogether to the Cavalcade that flows in and out of the door of the Broadway.

The Petrushka is a Russian café-restaurant run by two young women, Minka, who is Australian-born of Russian-Jewish par-ents, and Jessie, who is hedge-rose-pink-and-suet-white English and, in appearance, rather resembles the early Gracie Fields. With the help of a part-time assistant cook, Minka and Jessie prepare the food in a ten-foot-square kitchen separated from the dining-room by green curtains. Since they are also the wait-resses, pantry-maids, hostesses, and charwomen, and must arise at unseemly hours to buy meat and vegetables at the Prahran and Victoria Markets, they are slaves to their enterprise, which is a popular one because the food is authentic, cheap, and good.

93

In the nineteen-thirties foreign food has not become modish with Depression Australians, and seems to interest only city dwellers, intellectuals, and the most venturesome of the frivolous, who do the rounds of the Melbourne restaurants—Italian, French, Greek, Viennese, Chinese, German, Japanese—which provide it.

At the Café Petrushka I pay, when I can, for *kotletki* or *golubtzi* or *lenivy shchi*. When I cannot, Minka is willing to give me poppy-seed rolls and a large bowl of *borsch* for lettering out menus in Cyrillic script, which is one of the scripts, like Greek and Fraktur, I have picked up in the same way as one picks up and puts aside pieces of string and discarded door-hinges in a this-might-come-in-handy-one-day manner. Once I earn a series of *borsch*-to-*halva* meals by painting a picture to join the paintings already hung on the sweating green walls. These have been done either by artists with an affection for Minka and Jessie or by others, like me, bartering on behalf of a hollow belly. Some of the works are grimly abstract or murkily Message-ridden as though to prove, right there and then, amid the laughter and melodious tea-spoons and the smell of coffee and cabbage, that twentieth-century art is no more than a branch of revolutionary politics. Some, like my friend Hogan's, are frivolous. Mine is an attempt to kill two birds with one stone, to make a gay decoration while at the same time making a gesture of a sort against those of the diners who are Marxists, Friends of the Soviet Union, fellow-travellers, members of the Writers' League, Gorki fans and Lorca-lovers. The decoration is very Old Russia with Cossacks flinging out their legs and grasshoppering about, with apple-cheeked peasant wives carrying roosters in baskets, with balalaika-strummers, and a plethora of cupolas like striped onions. Doubtless the inspiration for this chromatic essay in poster paints belonging to Arcadia Display Specialistes comes from my visits, in the company of Dargie and Roy Hodgkinson, to sketch behind the scenes during performances by the Colonel de Basil Ballet Company—Woizokowski's balletic paroxysms as Petrushka in Benois's setting are in my 1937 sketchbook. Woizokowski is, that year, no chicken but is still an agile dancer as well as a vain man. Although ballet is among the types of entertainment I find least enthralling, I do find his entrance as the Slave in *Sheherazade* electrifying, more so seen from the wings than from the stalls. He chucks Dargie and Hodgkinson and me, as he attitudinizes for us in the light from the stage, one supremely false and snow-white sliver of smile, rubs his points in the rosin-tray, crosses himself, grows preposterously younger in a flash, and leaps—a-a-a-a-ah!—on to the stage.

When I have eaten Old Russia and the skip-jack and musical-comedy Don Cossacks, and am back again to a last sixpence, I buy a tumbler of Russian tea, count my cigarettes to plan the intervals needed between smoking them if they are to last the evening, and settle down to learn what extra I can about myself by learning about others. Some of what I learn during those yakata-yakata nights at the Café Petrushka is, at the time, so disconcerting that, after 1937, I steer clear of Australian writers for about fifteen years. I am disconcerted because, naïvely, I've not expected to find so many leftists among the writers. What is more disconcerting is that they are *dernier cri* leftists—their dogma-inlaid opera-glasses are directed at the world's latest blood-and-thunder production, the Spanish Civil War. What is most disconcerting, then and now, is the impossibility of my conceiving the formula of a compound which turns the litmus paper of their minds to red. I can get no further than assuming it includes much self-secreted acid; and must accept that, in relation, one is oneself more metaphorically alkaline, more corrosive, less sour.

If I am disconcerted, that is all, except that my anti-leftism sets like cement. At the age of twenty-six a sloppy middle course is not to be thought of. Moreover, no matter how much time I have, there is never enough, and never will be enough, to be wasted in unnecessarily changing seats on the express train to death. Facing the engine or back to the engine makes no difference. At the appointed second one will arrive. God knows who will be there to meet or not to meet, He knows; but, empty platform and eternal blackout, or pandemonium in an unimaginable dimension—fourth, forty-fourth, or four thousandth, whatever and whenever, the journey is too short to be spent in trying out other seats on the recommendation of those whose ideas of comfort—equality, wealth, peace, pro-

95

gress, religion, Uncle Tom Cobleigh and all—differ from one's own.

It is less extraordinary than might appear that not one person has, before I am twenty-six, suggested that seats labelled atheism and communism are worth trying: I lack the disadvantage of a university education, my mind has not been de-loused by the sheep-dip of philosophies, my hungry curiosity has not been side-tracked by sandwiches of chaff. At the Café Petrushka, however, for the first time in my life, suggestions that I change my seat come quick and fast. I listen to the touts, agog and somehow insulted, but carried away most by the lines of discontent bracketing their mouths, the out-of-this-warm-world expression which gives their eyes the glaze of mermen's, and their intelligence-cramping political Volapük with its mingy vocabulary as crystalline as mud.

I know that the creative human being is more likely than the less afflicted human being to be pixy-led by systems of universal reform, and to be snowblinded by the glare beating off such banners as Social Consciousness. Born to be perpetually outmoded, younger in 1937 than I am, that is younger in the sense of being more naïve, I am nevertheless old enough and not naïve enough to be taken in by banners. The words flashing on them—Perfection, Equality, Internationalism, Peace, Liberty, et cetera—have no clear meaning to me. The evils of peace, for example, equal those of war. I believe this, in those days, because war has been presented to me by history teachers, Grandfather Porter, the Bible, Shakespeare, and even the Lorca-lovers, as too good not to be evil. The evils of peace I am seeing for myself. It is along these lines I talk ungratefully back to the Petrushka writers who are trying to snowblind me with their banners. I go on to point out that the words are particularly meaningless because they do not embroider themselves on the banner. Nor does the banner carry itself. Down below, puffing and panting, are the banner-makers and banner-bearers. It is easy for me, I say, I lie, nibbling at a slice of tea-soggy lemon, to spot the bearers as victims of a dry-rot of the emotions, caring little for living people but impassioned by the *idea* of future people. This mind-lust for the idea is a love-making from which the emotion of love has volatilized, the love-making of those

96

unhinged by abstractions. Everything the banner-bearers touch has the one flavour, everything the one price, the same.

"Fascist!" snarl the contributors to leftist magazines with restaurant *borsch*-stains on the beer-stains on their crimson ties. "You are a fascist!" This merely means, "We are something else!"

The name-calling does not inflame me. If it be time for a next self-rationed cigarette, I light it and, as happily as one slipping into a dressing-gown, slip into a little fable which, then, I have word-perfect. It is a fable picked up in some forgotten magazine; e. e. cummings is, I think, the author. It goes somewhat thus:

One wants to catch the bus (train?) to Utopia, the Perfect State. Examining one's resources, one finds that the only coin handy for the ticket is marked Communism on one side, Fascism on the other, and that the coin is therefore Dictatorship. What to do if Dictatorship is a coin one will not use? One walks. Ah! but what if it rains? "Fortunately," I say, in e. e. cummings's words, "there still exist persons for whom living means something more complex than keeping out of the rain."

"Cummings!" they say. "He's a bloody fascist too!"

Meantime, on the mignonette-green table by the fireplace with its tramp's bonanza of cigarette butts heaped on the hearth, the portable gramophone is being constantly rewound to sore-throatedly exhale "Stormy Weather", "Die Dorf Musik", Paul Robeson singing "Ah Still Suits Me", and Josephine Baker singing "J'ai Deux Amours". Ah, those evenings of November 1937, when every second woman is dressed in cyclamen, with cyclamen-painted lips, and a tricorn of cyclamen silk tilted over the left eyebrow! That left eyebrow is, as all female eyebrows of the period are, plucked thin as a pen-stroke. Eyelids gleam with Vaseline. Those who are not thus wearing a Jean Harlow mask, a Thelma Todd mask, the cryptic egg-face of the talking-picture *femme fatale*, have arranged a shining beige face inside the lappets of their shining page-boy haircuts, and wear the shoulders of their garments padded square, and the gauntlets of their gloves fringed. The tail-feather of pheasant or rooster quiveringly nods above their Tirolean hats. They smoke the cigarettes one can then buy in glossy tins,

97

cigarettes of baby blue, primrose, pink, and *café au lait*, oval cigarettes, cigarettes tipped with silk—scarlet, fuchsia, hunter's green, cigarettes ivory-tipped and gold-tipped, or tipped with delicate holders of—is it goose-quill?

Meantime, the glass-panelled door of the Café Petrushka opens and shuts on the entrances and exits of Melbourne's intelligentsia and decadentsia, leftists and gourmets, journalists and broadcasters, potters and actresses, lesbians and advocates of trial marriages, and high-school English teachers on the ran-tan ready and willing to buy tumblers of tea and scalenes of *halva* for any out-of-pocket intellectual who will bicker or agree with them on the Marx Brothers, Ernest Hemingway, Eisenstein, Grosz, Aldous Huxley, Walt Disney, Lytton Strachey, Liam O'Flaherty, Picasso, Delysia, Marie Dressler, any of the season's conversational counters.

There is no record of the famous, near-famous, flash-in-the-pan famous, or famous-to-be men and women who walked up the narrow incline of Little Collins Street, and opened the door of weeping glass, and dined at the small green tables, and yelled above Josephine Baker singing "Le Petit Tonkinese", and the garrulous never-to-be-famous, and those most dangerous of all talking animals, the non-creative intellectuals. It seems reasonable, therefore, to record some of the diners or sippers of Russian tea I recall as being there during my few months' use of the place. There is Fay Compton nibbling a piece of *halva* with Michael Wilding as they are on their way downhill to the King's Theatre and *Victoria Regina*. There is Woizokowski, discreetly painted, making an entrance with his daughter Sonia and, trailing them, circumspectly a-twitter as a school crocodile, all eyes and legs, the *corps de ballet*. There is Loudon Sainthill eyeing the glass panel on which there will, late as ever, appear the white face of—is her name Diane?—a fey young musician dressed in black like a romantic midinette, with fog in her black hair, and a roll of music in her black-gloved hand. She will come. They all will, sooner or later. Helene Kirsova with her hair in pale braids, with pale eyes and flaming cheeks. Albert Tucker performing his squeaky baby-talk act for George Bell and a group of his students. Theodore Fink, driven by a chauffeur, and weighed down by wealth and a hundred-

98

weight of rich overcoat. James Flett and a portfolio of water-colour pirates and self-portraits. Dr John Dale and Max Mel-drum. Dargie and the beautiful Kath Howitt he is later to marry. Hayward Veal who is later to marry Minka and take her, and his paintings of Melbourne streets opalescently slimy with rain, to London. Tom Challen who has given up being a boy-prodigy violinist to grow into a plump and witty cartoon-ist for *Table Talk*, and is on his way to leaving his Collins Street attic and the ikon over his bed-head to be the cartoonist Tac on a Fleet Street newspaper. They are all on the way to some-where else, to money or fame, to notoriety or nowhere, or to drowning in the whirlpool of talk-plans about their Great-Opus-to-Come, or in alcohol or the undercurrents of indiscip-line or the sloughs of sex or the shallows of egoism.

If I am not playing Mr Gallagher to Leon Hogan's Mr Sheen, or pitting my country-bred conservatism and amateurism against city-slicker professional leftism, I pass the evening in the inspiriting brew of cigarette smoke and hullabaloo with Bob Close and Alan Marshall. We are a loquacious trio happily bound by the loquacity and by the fact that each of us is wear-ing, brazenly as sandwich-men, our first published short stories —periodicals such as *Flame* and the *Bulletin* have taken us up.

Close, an intense and excitable consumptive, the most vigor-ously good-looking of the trio, is being pointed out as author of a *Lower Depths* sort of story called "Sputum Sam", a story founded on his observations in a hospital for tubercular pati-ents. It is published in, I think, a leftist magazine called *Point* in which I also have published a story called "Frieze of Victims". This first-and-last contribution to a publication inclining left is intended as a satire on socially conscious writers. I suspect the satire of failing but, not having seen the story for over a quarter of a century, cannot tell. My intention to mock—would it be Gorki?—is probably lost in the cataloguing of things for which, as the Japanese do, I have a feeling that amounts to animism. Since "Frieze of Victims" is set in the long North Melbourne street I walk along to Arcadia Display Specialistes, doubtless the catalogue is also long, and late-Depression seedy —mont-de-piétés, wine saloons, fish-and-chip shops, second-hand bicycle marts, greasy Greek restaurant after greasy

99

Greek restaurant advertising Three Course Meals For Seven-pence, a street of unwashed foreigners, and broken-down perambulators, and oranges with a decay of green velvet on them, and hand-pushed ice-cream carts with weather-rotted awnings, and barber-shops with faded yellow-and-blue-striped veranda posts, and whiffy hamburger-shops, and the Gladstone Palace—once the Oriental Coffee Palace—offering bed-and-breakfast for three-and-six, offering a hundred bedrooms with curtains as tattered as Miss Havisham's bridal veil, a draughts-board foyer of black and white marble defiled by smudges of dirty mopping, and a façade of wind-chewed bricks and cast-iron sill-fences painted chocolate.

Bob Close has written a novel, not yet published in 1937, called *Love Me, Sailor*, and, his Borsalino rakishly set on the battleship-grey undulations of his hair, reads to us, while the portable gramophone sings "Mean to Me" dimly from a record grey from years of rotations, the more censorable episodes. Alan Marshall has also written his novel. It is about life in a shoe factory and it, too, is not yet published. He reads the more gruelling episodes of this. I have written so little of mine that I keep my mouth zippered. It is all I can do to shut myself away from the many-doored, many-planed city long enough to sleep and, once in a while, to write a short story. These are set in the country because I have found out that it is unwise to write of a place while still in it, or of people and paraphernalia not separated from me by space or time. Hence I write of Japan in Western Australia, of Western Australia in Victoria, of Victoria in London and Rome, of cities in the country, of the country in the city. In fact, it becomes clear, as I listen to Close and Marshall and what they have done, that it will soon be time to move on again—Melbourne is not far away from Williams-town, the seagulls skimming the slate-tiled fairy-tale turrets and curlicued weather-vanes of the Melbourne fish market are the same ones that mince sideways along the wet and moiré sands of Williamstown Beach. I do not want to leave the blue-stone pinnacles and Corinthian stucco. The writer has to, but I keep him a month or two more in the city by letting the artist take over for a while to prepare some work for an exhibition at the Athenaeum Gallery to be opened by Fay Compton.

The other young people exhibiting work at the same show are painters in oils from the George Bell School—Albert Tucker, Nairn Butchart, Colin Macgowan, Maidie McWhirter, Clothilde Atyeo, and Frank Morgan. Their portraits and still-lifes are buttered thickly with paint, the portraits rather angular and inflamed in the shadows, the still-lifes bleak with crumpled table napkins stiff as newspaper, and apples of belly-ache green. Allan Lowe with his off-white and oyster-grey pottery suitable for a Mrs Somerset Maugham décor, and I, are odd-men-out. My illustrations to Edgar Allan Poe are nearly-Harry-Clarke, the costume designs for Maeterlinck's *Blue Bird* are too-too Bakst. Although, astoundingly, four of these are bought—by whom? and where are they now?—they are the last purposeful drawings I do for twenty-seven years, and they are only done to clap a self-indulgent hand over the mouth of the writer canvassing me to return to the country and work solidly on the Williamstown novel, and to encourage the delusion that, as Art of Life behaviour, it is reasonable to linger on and on in Melbourne, listening to whores, spivs, dilettantes, Little Audrey yarns and, at the Petrushka, to well-heeled communists and to artists such as Roy Dalgarno, William Constable, Max Meldrum, as well as to Bob Close and Alan Marshall.

Although my admiration for Alan Marshall is, at that time, tempered, and my affection for him is outweighed by the he's-my-china-plate affection for Leon Hogan, the admiration is there. This is not because Marshall has been crippled by infantile paralysis, and doubly crippled because he has been thrown from a horse, and is "brave" about it, but because he is a sensitive, alight and centralized human being. He does, however, as the first physically crippled man I get to know, teach me something strange. It is the same thing that one learns from a beautiful woman. Cripples and lovely women, somewhere along the highway, both tire of being looked at as though they had but one quality, tire of being picketed by observation. Each learns, therefore, to return a deeper look, a clearer look, against the mere stare-stare-monkey-bear look. Once upon a time Marshall's problem may have been—but I don't really know—when he was younger, a youth, a boy, a problem possessing the refinements of difficulty it needs refinements of acting-a-part to level out. To stand with ease and nonchalance on the deadly straight line between appearing tragic and appearing wilfully brave is a feat of social balance so complex I should not like to have to rake in the solitary dark for the super-organization of spirit necessary to accomplish it. I prefer idly to be fond of people or, if they are not my cup of tea, selfishly to be passer-by indifferent to them, rather than to be dazzled into sit-about respect and admiration. Marshall is, however, one of a mere handful of men and women I admire and respect to the point of love, that treacherous and rabies-ridden emotion.

Ah, well! The glass-panelled door opens and shuts, and the *chanakhi*-eaters and dream-tellers and *Esquire*-conners of 1937 drift away into the midnight fog leaving to languish and grow shabby in the succulent mugginess of the Café Petrushka the ghosts they have called up—Peter de Vries and his poems, Auden, Horatio Alger, Havelock Ellis, Pietro di Donato and his "Christ in Concrete", Saroyan and *The Daring Young Man on the Flying Trapeze*, Scott Fitzgerald, Manuel Komroff, Hemingway and "Hills Like White Elephants", Marcel Proust, James Joyce and "Anna Livia Plurabelle", D. H. Lawrence and *The Virgin and the Gipsy*. . . .

While these garden-fresh ghosts mildew to out-of-dateness, and the Café Petrushka is torn down to make room for the hindquarters of a post-office, the diners are blown about the world—Challen to draw in Fleet Street, Veal to paint in England, Tucker in Provence, Dalgarno in India, Sainthill and Constable in the West End of London, Close to grill on the shores of the Mediterranean, Marshall to bring back mammoths' tusks from Russia and fly-whisks from Samarkand.

The few Petrushka-ites here recalled, and so many more of us who sizzled out our cigarettes—Vice-Regal, De Reszke, Du Maurier, Spud—on the drowned lemon slices in the fluted glass saucers, how much of the world we have, in the free-booting Australian manner, nomadized over since the glass-panelled door last closes behind our younger backs! At least none of us, so far as my knowledge goes, has attempted to shrink the world until it fits no one. This sort of satanic boyish-ness is the obsession of scientists who lust to make the moon an airport, and to dehydrate the truth of appearances into the lie of fact. The poet in Man, that deathless giant, holds the moon like a crystal ball in his bare hands and, with naked eyes, sees in it the one flaw—the scientist in Man scrabbling with gloved feelers on the sterile dust of the moon, and staring at the non-human signature thus made through the false eyes of the apparatus encasing him.

In November 1937, becoming suddenly fed-up with shilly-shallying, I take myself uncompassionately in hand. It is all too obvious that the novel, of which only one-and-a-half of the twenty-four chapters are written, will never be finished in the city. Moreover, I shall need money to support me in the country while writing—this has not struck me earlier. Struck and awake, I cold-bloodedly plan. If I am to work and save for about three months, outside the city, and in the kind of place that will not encourage me to fritter, the Education Department is—for me—the easiest solution. I arrange to take on, in February 1938, the head-teachership of a one-teacher school on the ridge of the Strzelecki Ranges. Secondly, I move from 28 Collins Street to a seven-shillings-a-week room at 9 Mackenzie Street, on the rim of the city, and nearly a mile nearer to Arcadia Displaye Specialistes where, thirdly, I reveal a willing-ness to work thirty hours a week. Money in the bank, hitherto eschewed as unnecessary, is the aim—enough to keep me when the Strzelecki job is over and I can return to my childhood home, the lamp and I together at the hub of midnight silence and country blackness. Ultimately, this jigsaw plan does inter-lock but, by the time the novel is finished, the expected penny-plain design is more twopence-coloured than Joseph's coat.

Nine Mackenzie Street is a two-storeyed bluestone building, originally an inn, built in 1861, and time-out-of-mind de-licensed. It is run as a general store and rooming-house by the Misses Gregory, three old spinsters of the sort who are mur-dered for the hoard of bank-notes they legendarily secrete under hearth-stones and in the kapok of mattresses. The years have scoured them for so long with the same abrasives that, at a quick glance, they could be triplets. They are of a height, short and meagre, and each has hooded eyes with pink stains under them, bundles of hair patently dyed the colour of rose-

103

wood, right-angled shoulders, and each wears—except on Sundays—a grey dress and a bibbed apron of starched white. On Sundays, all in black, with rufous strips of fur hung boa-like about their necks, the apparent triplets, in step, their furled umbrellas also in step, stride off to church. Closer attention to them reveals that, despite the many resemblances, there are more differences.

The Miss Gregory with the hare-lip is older, coarser, truculent, almost brutal. She dominates the shop and, although the other two also take turns there, it is as underlings.

The Miss Gregory who is imperceptively the most talkative, youngest and meekest, is the downstairs housekeeper and cook.

The third Miss Gregory is the upstairs chambermaid, washerwoman and rouseabout. She is the last woman in Australia I see shaking mops and dusters out of windows. As washerwoman she has, whether of her own or under orders from her hare-lipped sister, an obsession with the cleanliness of bed linen. Every day except Sunday the copper in the bluestone washhouse is boiling; the first daytime sound is of Miss Gregory morosely smashing crates to feed the fire. Every day except Sunday the clothes-lines swing or flap with blue-rinsed sheets and pillow-cases and the Misses Gregory's blindingly white aprons. Every day except Sunday one has the luxury of fresh bed linen, the special and fragrant freshness of hand-washed linen dried in the open air and put on the bed unironed, linen that has not been soiled by more than one night's sleep.

Nine Mackenzie Street has other qualities. Since I have arrived but to depart, and am consciously impermanent, and nostalgic in advance, these qualities are seen to tone in and be tinged with regret.

The days are fugitive, and faint with summer; the bed nightly utters a human sigh, the soul of old pine breathes a syllable of regret from the depths of the wardrobe; from behind the surface of the looking-glass above the dressing-table the lips and eyes of past roomers attempt to indicate some sweet-and-sour verity; when it rains the eaves weep with the inexorable gentleness of Alice in Wonderland. Unheard, minified among hulks of Victorian furniture, the three sisters occupy the ground floor in an unimaginable after-closing relationship. Upstairs, the other roomers, none of whom, because of my fancy hours, I ever see, tonguelessly indulge in unimaginable relationships with solitariness, with the seductive rack of the iron bedstead, the false depths of the leather armchair. Upstairs? The inside stairs are never used. A nursery-gate, left over from a past of upstairs children, is nailed shut at the stair-head.

We roomers, rain or shine, night or day, descend and ascend by a ladder-like outside stairway flush along the side wall. It is of wood weathered so silver and fragile that its skeleton quivers underfoot. The balustrade has already gone. One climbs up and down with one's hand on the bluestone, stove-hot or body-warm from sun, or blood-wet from rain. Off the outside landing of aged planks a never-locked double door opens on to the central corridor of brown linoleum so polished that, like a canal, it reflects the closed doors and their transom windows covered with floral transparencies, and their handles of golden glass like fist-sized cairngorms. Who lives behind the doors I do not know, and never shall. I hear no quarrellings, conversations, snorings, no whimpers of passion or pain. The daily changing of bed-linen cancels out the possibility of opium den, Blue-beard's larder, or forger's lair. The roomers are probably merely poor people, as I am, poor but quieter. Once or twice I hear, from the lavatory at the far end of the corridor, the sound of water cascading to find its own level. Once, from the bathroom opposite the lavatory, the sound of the shower beating on an unknown body is heard and, once, from one of the rooms, a gramophone—Galli-Curci reedily singing "Lo, Hear the Gentle Lark!" Since I see no one, no one sees me: I come and go in my own dream as no more to them than a foot on the trembling ladder, a hand that turns the heavy iron key in another door, a mysterious someone always whistling "Memory Lane" or singing "I've Got My Love to Keep Me Warm".

This secretive colony of never-touching, never-seeing, this half-world without echoes, exists only above the Misses Greg-ory's ceiling. Daytime, down below, the copper is always bubbling or the backyard in full sail with sheets; the cook sister, lamenting like a bird through old songs such as "After the Ball" and "The Luggage-van Ahead", is at work on meat pies, Corn-ish pasties, vanilla slices and apple turnovers for the hare-lipped sister to sell; the little iron bell on its helix of steel over the nine-paned, lace-curtained window of the shop door is never silent as the people come and go with their purchases—comic papers, butterscotch, blue-lined envelopes, red ink and violet ink, packets of pins, bars of soap, slices of sweating cheese, cheap cups, onions, fireworks, tobacco, black sausages, celluloid baby dolls, canary seed, liquorice pipes, bottles of ginger tonic, eggs, combs, moth-balls, newspapers, Beecham's Pills, and waxed-paper daffodils and chrysanthemums.

Since there is no May at the door each morning with her salver of breakfast, I eat fruit bought at the Victoria Market on my way to Arcadia Displaye Specialistes. I should like, as a general gesture, and also as a special one because of the un-orthodox luxury of the bed linen, to be a customer in my land-ladies' shop which still has beflowered china beer-pulling handles on the ex-bar counter. I try the cook-sister's pies. Once is enough. Among the countless things with which the shop is packed to the ceiling there is no commodity I need except cigarettes and matches. In three months I am able to buy noth-ing else other than a bottle of fountain-pen ink and a pair of shoe laces. I sense some disapproval of my seeming meanness but am not certain of it until, one day, and with the intention of em-barrassing me, for she chooses a time when the shop is full, the hare-lipped Miss Gregory fixes me with a forked look from under her pink lids, and says, "Oo-eye oh oo eye awe ooze-ay-er o ee?" It is impossible to say briefly why I don't. She has to listen while I explain that I don't buy newspapers because I am not interested in a daily collection of information about crimes, divorces, accidents, strikes, beauty contests, objects lost and found, the sailing times of ships, the rough-cast chicanery of half-illiterate politicians, the alabaster-smooth guess-work of literate leader-writers, the marriages of men and women, and the results of horse races, boxing matches, and sand-building competitions. I do not go on to explain why I am not inter-ested in newspaper accounts of these things because I don't know why. As well I don't know why I should be expected to have an interest in them. Anyway, the square fact is that I've no more got the gift of newspaper or detective-story reading than I have the gift of understanding absolute music or abstract painting. So far as I am concerned a journalist's account of a rape or a murder is pearls before swine, is playing a harp to an ox, quoting Shakespeare to a Samoyed.

Swine or ox or Samoyed, I feel the Old Year take from me as it goes some intangible quality—the last tatters of boyishness? —I feel the far-off tearing away, yet there is no pain, merely the faint gone-for-ever sense of loss.

January 1938 bowls past like a hoop of flames, and falls down, and burns out.

Here comes February and the school on the spine of Strzelecki Ranges.

I begin to disburden myself by giving away what will certainly not be needed there—Helen Ogilvie lino-cuts, Lionel Lindsay woodcuts, Frances Burke and Loudon Sainthill hand-printed materials, Shirlow etchings, the Williamstown Portman decanter and others picked up in secondhand shops, Medici prints, chessmen, wine-glasses, and books, books, books. Now and again I encounter one of these once-cherished objects in the house of an old friend. It sits there with something of the air of a pickled appendix one has forgotten one had removed. I give away partly because the desire to possess things is weak, but mostly because of a premonition that, with the pot-bound decade of Williamstown behind me, I am to be henceforth a wanderer, and in no need of furnishings for a stockade. The premonition is correct. I *am* a Thursday's child with far to go. The premonition does not warn me how far nor by what devious paths.

I know that the whole of the last evening in Melbourne is spent with Leon Hogan on a farewell tour of places and people —Audrey, Esther, the Café Petrushka, Kingsley Hall—but safe memory of this cuts out at sunset in 9 Mackenzie Street. He has helped me finish packing, and lower the level of whisky in a bottle. At sunset we are leaning from the window to look into the large backyard with its high bluestone wall topped by broken glass, and its stables which the Misses Gregory, earning more money to be murdered for, rent to itinerants such as clothes-prop sellers and scissors-grinders and tinkers, the last of their tribe. Looked down on, the yard is a cistern of tangerine-coloured luminescence in which the washerwoman sister wades about unpegging the last tangerine-dyed sheets as though, I demi-drunkenly feel, she is unpegging the last hours of my Melbourne life. In the farthest corner a little hunch-backed man whose long and graceful shadow climbs the wall behind him feeds and waters a tangerine horse. To this day I wonder, just as I wonder then, what merchandise lies beneath the tarpaulin of his cart. Then, that sunset, Leon says he will go down and ask, but he doesn't. We drink more whisky, and I do not remember any more of my friend until I meet him eleven years later when I am a manager in the George Hotel, St Kilda, and he and Henrietta Drake-Brockman come for after-hour drinks.

In the early morning, home again from the forgettable round of farewells to lie drunk between the sun-scented sheets of the dottiest Miss Gregory, I hear the vegetable carts clip-clopping along Mackenzie Street towards the Victoria Market. In 1938 there are, of course, also motor-vehicles but there are still enough horse-drawn carts with their hurricane lamps swaying to provide that noise, so incomprehensibly consoling to one of my generation, of iron hoofs clip-clopping on bone-hard roadways with other clip-cloppings in counterpoint. I try to fight drunken sleep to listen as long as I can but the clip-clop-ping itself, as much as the whisky and fatigue, wear apart the threads tying me to consciousness.

It is the last time I hear this sound, hundreds of years old, of hoofs in the dawn, of cart-horses on the way to market.

It is the last time, so far as my relationship with Melbourne is concerned, for other things. Next time I am in Melbourne it is as a married man, a crippled man, and a man who has written a novel about a place called Williamstown, and given away the manuscript and all interest in it in much the same mood as he gives away woodcuts and wine-glasses.

I catch the eight-thirty train to Gippsland, to Traralgon, a tatterdemalion nineteenth-century country town smelling sickly-sourish of paper mills. Here, the bus to the Strzelecki Ranges is to be boarded. As the train flounces earnestly along chattering to itself, and now and then exultantly keening under its headdress of smoke, whatever correct premonitions I have about an uprooted self and a weathercock future, there are none about the landscape submerged in summer, none about the hamlets fixed in a web of post-and-rails, the provincial one-storeyed towns panting under the peppercorn trees, or the whistle-stop railway stations where on the gravelled platform are always the sun-browned postmistress, the grinning heeler, the bruised milk-cans, the line-up of red fire-buckets, the middle-aged geranium bushes, and the outbursts of agapanthus, all backed by pine trees poking out indolent green plush paws from their own simmering dens of shadow. No premonitions at all—I have travelled up and down this line so often since the first time in 1917 that the thought of any but the most minor additions to or subtractions from what is always there, and apparently eternal, never enters my head. I am, nevertheless, to see this landscape of beloved miles as it has always been just one more time only. The next time, years later, it has become something else, has become modernized with such speed and delirious savagery that nothing, not even time, can mollify what has been done. The hawthorn-edged fields of lucerne and oats are car factories fenced like prison camps. The tall timber of the Haunted Hills is as down as Jericho. The sweet Auburns of Moe and Morwell with their elm-lined streets, honeysuckle, pubs with ferneries and wide verandas and tame cockatoos, their sleepy tea-rooms and banks and general stores, have become first-class horror towns adorned by all the advantages of progress—used-car dumps, hoardings, treeless streets, neon advertisements, jerry-built motels, petrol stations, secondhand car compounds, drive-in theatres, garages with checkerboard doors, traffic signs, cubic weatherboard houses painted lilac or pink or forget-me-not blue with gardens of Woolworth annuals growing inside truck tyres, and landscape-windows through which it is impossible not to see, behind the landscape-windows opposite, the same arrangement of stick-figure furniture and television set and sun-burst clock and plastic flowers in a white amphora that sits, like the shop-window display of a conveyor-belt furnisher's, behind every landscape window.

In February 1938, however, I can still look out of the carriage window on towns not planned to satisfy the habits of motor-cars, on a landscape of hedges and wind-breaks, of creeks and dams overhung by weeping willows, of barns and haystacks, of wading cows, sheep at siestas, horses using their fly-whisks and geese sieving the ochreous mud of waterholes. I slide up the window to breathe, to drink thirstily, the Gippsland air in which, already, are some of the ingredients, some of the flavour and scent, of that blend of air enclosing my home town, Bairnsdale. A few ingredients are missing—the river odour, sensual and melancholy, the scent of salt lakes, and the taste of the ocean in winds that come from the south, but the fumes of eucalypt are there, intertwined with fumes of blond grass, and sassafras and musk in the gullies, and boxthorn and pine-needles baking in the oven of mid-morning.

Experiences and convictions are, like God, portable. They travel with me, whatever I am. Each hangs neatly on its own hook. There are uncountable hooks, millions of them—each day of the ten years at State School 1409 hangs there; all my errors in judgment and taste and control are there; the destroyed poems; the unavailing franknesses; the hours of sunbaking on the beach; the silly discussions at the Café Petrushka; the lustful solicitations of this or that mistaken voluptuary— the lawyer's wife, the Brownlow Medallist footballer, the theatre-manager's mistress; the walks by moonlight and starlight; the millions of words heard and read; the circular waltzes in suburban town halls; the lies to others and the lies from others; the cynicisms and disdains fought against; the values emotionally or intuitively acquired which are beyond the realm of mere knowledge, and far beyond logical analysis. Because a person is largely a series of mental happenings, however minute, connected to a shape of bones and flesh, I am composed of what hangs on the millions of hooks—Audrey's wink, Esther's black dress, Stella's forgiveness, Mrs Bachaus's broken vase, Mrs McArdle's paintings, P.J.G.'s truisms, Alan Marshall's crutches, Leon Hogan's mocking laugh, Mrs Kellow's tale-bearing, Tommo's forbearance, the newspaper dancing at dawn in a suburb of sleepers, the roomers of 9 Mackenzie Street whose hands I never see and am never to see turning the cairngorm handles I see and am never to see again.

I am, by and large, give or take a small-fry monster or four, fortunate in the human beings run across up till February 1938, fortunate in their offhand trustworthiness, their travel-stained nobilities, the refreshment offered and accepted gratefully from the chipped cups of their hearts. As in my own nature there is slush so there is in their natures, and I witness frowsy moral behaviour, and displays of spleen, cupidity, boorishness, rancour, malice, jealousy, improbity and impurity but nothing sufficiently evil to do anything more than disgust me until I am—as quickly as possible—out of range. My own sins are the only ones difficult for me to get out of range of. Several deeds committed by others on others have shocked me deeply enough but, as in the case of Audrey and her father, the shock is not immediate and, arriving late departs early. Anyway I am neither a father, incestuous or not, nor a thirteen-year-old female child and, having no imagination, cannot put myself anywhere near reproducing their bygone feelings so as to be able to taste the full flavour of the crime. It is merely a tale told drowsily by a friendly pretty whore. Nor can I suffer truly for Audrey's later Mask of Suffering photograph in *Truth*. If I do decide to suffer on its behalf how shall I know that the suffering runs parallel to the suffering imagined to bestialize her face? Immorality is, after all, the business of the immoral. Since I've no imagination, my vision of people is limited by a belief in the value of the qualities they openly tender, is impaired by the clarity with which I see the exact size of what they tender. This is a great deal, as the widow's mite is a great deal. It is years after 1938 before I become involved with a group of studiously evil people, my first evil people.

It is noon when the train reaches Traralgon. It is hot with the vertical, callous, palpitating heat I love. The outlets of the town are quaking vistas. The ends of roads lie swamped with mirages, with illusions of looking-glass shallows. I drop my luggage at the bus depot, and eat, a lone diner, in a hotel dining-room.

The Venetian blinds are lowered, and noon flourishes incandescently beyond the slats. High up, the propeller blades of the ceiling fans rotate and hum. Far off, on the gunnera-green wallpaper, hang Marcus Stone reproductions, passive trysts in old gardens, tender renunciations under old trees. The slippered waitress is lank and languid, and materializes and dematerializes like an apparition. The damask table-cloth and bishop's mitre napkins are starched to enamel. The cloth is an Oxford Circus traffic jam of electroplate—trumpet vase, water-jug, cheese-cover, butter dish, salt cellars, pepper pots, ashtrays, bread-container, sugar bowl, menu-holder, and sauce-bottle support-ers. Multiplied, miniature and distorted in reflections, I see myself drink a cold-misted bottle of lager, and work my way through vegetable soup, river-bream, roast lamb, and lemon sago. The bowls and plates seem of the same maroon-banded ironstone china of the Broadway Café. To make sure I order tea. When the cup and saucer arrive, along with three extra mirror-surfaces of electroplate—teapot, hot-water pot, and milk jug—I perceive that they are the shape and size of the Broad-way cups and saucers. It is impossible to resist ordering a glass of brandy to add to the cup of tea. Then—nostalgic fool—I toast whatever remains of those months as a city-dweller. It is little enough, a vestige, a wisp, and it burns away to nothing in the midday furnace outside. I drink the last cup of tea-with I am ever to drink, and that is that. It is not revealed that I have eaten the last satisfactory meal I am to have for three months.

At two-thirty I catch the bus, a small mail-and-passenger one to hold about a dozen passengers. I am the only one except a front-seat girl-friend, an aggrieved bitch with a sharp-beaked profile that, mile after mile, woodpecks away at the driver's unwincing calm. He shows no blood: *she* is the one in the prickly patch. He is blond, a *Heldentenor* of a bloke, a dinkum-Aussie in the mould of Siegfried, his ruddy blacksmith arms filmed by a pelt of golden hairs. Now and then, as we climb up and away from the ground-swell of breast-high grasses on the plains vibrating with heat, he stops the bus opposite the milk-can platforms and white gates of farms, and delivers something from the conglomeration on the floor and front seats—mailbags, wet batteries, sugarbags of vegetables, cartons of groceries and bread, a child's tricycle, a bundle of horror comics. Newspapers he shies out with bull's-eye nonchalance as we move. Each turn of the road, always ascending, winds deeper into the foothills. Looking downward and across the interfitted valleys thousands upon thousands of killed trees are to be seen, bleached trunks of lofty trees seeming no more than finger-bones, match-sticks, white nails, quills. Miles of fences are thrown like a mesh over the undulations. The steeper walls of gullies are beaten into terraces of pathways by the hoofs of sheep. At last, the crest is reached, Strzelecki Ridge, and my future for three months.

I descend from the bus and, as I walk from it with my luggage, there is the almost physical sense of sloughing off a long tail, a tail of curry-coloured gravel spiralling round and round the convolutions of the foothills and the minor summits of the ranges. That is behind, in the basements of heat. This is the fin, ultimate and cool. Here are half a dozen raw weatherboard houses, the school surrounded by pines, and the post-office-and-general-store. No other buildings. There seems no one to meet me. I wait until the *Heldentenor* finishes his business with the postmistress, and spend the time watching the girl-friend who remains in the bus painting her bitter mouth, and viciously powdering her beak, sharpening it for the return descent. When the bus starts, I speak to the postmistress. I realize, almost immediately, that she is sizing me up, and that she is not going to be run down by a la-di-dah voice, inconsequential gaiety, and quick-as-a-flash directness. Who do I think I am with my city airs and graces?

She answers slowly, wrapping up each word so that its outline loses sharpness.

That's right, no one to meet me.

Oh yes, they know I'm coming.

I am to stay at Tretheway's. Tim Tretheway's.

No, he doesn't live in one of those houses across the road. They belong to the timber-cutters.

Tretheway's place is up the road a bit.

It's no good trying to ring them. No phone. They know I'm coming. I can leave my luggage at the post-office. Tim Tretheway hasn't got a car but someone will drop it at his place later. Or tomorrow.

My mind, too long used to snip-snap and hurry-up suburban and city ways, to electric trains and cable trams and taxi-cabs and telephones, suddenly stops whirling like a roulette wheel. Dead-still, it informs me that I am not only in the bush, but high up in the bush. This is hill-billy country and I am, so far, a foreigner. Here I am, higher above sea-level than I've ever been, a foreigner on the knife-edge of a mountain. Far far below, and twenty miles south, is an ocean convulsed by Antarctic currents. Far far below, and north, lie the endless miles and count-less acres of the inner land. There isn't a taxi-cab in sight.

"Right," I say. "I'd better take off for Tretheway's. Which way?"

She points with her thumb.

"How far?"

She says three miles at the most. She says I can't miss the turn-off—it's the only one. On the left.

I buy forty cigarettes, get my sponge-bag out of a suitcase, and take off for Tretheway's. It is not three but five miles and, every working day for the time I am there I walk the ten miles. The walk is scenically dramatic, a travel-poster colonnade of trees rooted in rock.

The trees are mountain-ash over two hundred feet tall, almost the highest trees in the world. As in most Australian trees the trunks are not secondary pedestals supporting a great globe of foliage, but dominant pillars, imperial columns on the tops of which a minimum of leaves the texture of morocco sickle the upper air, and glitter near the sun. The road to Tretheway's turn-off, of gravel slimy with green from the perpetual damp and shadow, is no more than a meandering cleft between abnor-mal verticalities, between the vegetable skyscrapers. I have the sense of walking the bed of an earthquake crack in a botanic brain centuries old. Though split, the brain still lives—I hear the mimicking of unseen lyrebirds on either hand, the activity of sly animals in the undergrowth of ferns, the splashing of deli-cate waterfalls and, a long way off, the coughing of timber-cutters' axes and the echoes of the coughing. There is no per-spective. As it twists and turns, the road contracts immediately in front, contracts immediately behind. One is unaware of the sky. Once only, just before the turn-off, there appears a vertical panel of heaven. Some colossal paw of weather has scooped in the bastion of pillars a loophole through which one can look down on leagues and hundredweights of treetops and, stretch-ing for miles far below and beyond them, the sheep properties and dairy farms of South Gippsland, and an involved filigree of roads and hedges and fences. Beyond all is the ocean.

The turn-off road into the valley of the Tretheway farm is a penurious farmer's road, a horse-and-cart track. This is instantly to be assumed because the track is two ridges of grass and three earthy grooves. Two of these grooves are wheel-made, the central one is hoof-made. Car tracks, on the other hand, have merely one central ridge of grass, and two grooves. Tretheway's track—jostled by bracken, thistles, gorse, and fences fractured from wrestling like Laocoön and Sons with victorious briers, blackberries and wild raspberries—is not the sole testimony that he is an impecunious and dirty farmer. On every hand are paddocks of ragwort and charlock, dodder-strangled trees, rusted harrows and scarifiers, shicker gates, falling sheds just kept together by dinner-plate scabs of lichen, and giant apple and pear trees bearing tons of degenerate fruit —bottle-green, hard as golfballs, bitter and useless as wealth. Much is Tretheway's fault. He has inherited a prosperous mountain farm which, in its heyday, must have been self-supporting, easy to run, comfortable to live in, and even beautiful.

Tretheway is about forty-five, and somewhat resembles in sluggishness, improvidence, and appearance—run-to-seed hand-some—the husband of the Gem Pier Café landlady, except that the bristles in his ears and nostrils, and on his cheek-bones, have run wild. His hair is long, and as black as the miniature pom-pons in his earholes. A left-over habit of his tomcatting days is the lavish use of Californian Poppy hair oil. Since, as one of Mrs Tretheway's slatternly domestic practices, a side of bacon hangs over the enamel washbasin in the bathroom at the end of the back veranda, and since he leans his head on the bacon while washing his hands, I do not eat bacon.

Mrs Tretheway is a little younger than he, and is the smudged copy of a fine-looking woman, a Pola Negri with the springs broken. She, no less than her husband, is to blame for the all-round dilapidation. She does keep my room tidy, but the rest of the house with its imperishable Victorian and Edwardian furniture, its brass beds, and side-boards, and ornate kerosene lamps, and whatnots burdened with china shepherds and shep-herdesses, china shoes and boots, and china poodles, is squalid. The front room hearth is filled to the hobs with soot. Fluff shifts about under the chairs. Behind curtains of decomposing lace the unopenable windows are green-paned from a sort of alga. This room is tiled from ceiling to dado with photographs of the dead, unwinking, unsmiling, and linked each to each by cobwebs. Aunts, nephews, old maids, young clodhoppers, they stand by pedestals or sit stark upright on stark upright chairs with their macassared hair parted in the middle, their waxed moustaches, Alexandra fringes, leg-o'-mutton sleeves, watch-chains, twenty-buttoned gloves, their Hapsburg jaws, their buttonhole roses like curls of mutton-fat, their unmoving sullen stares.

It is difficult for me, then as much as today, to pin a final price-ticket on Mr and Mrs Tretheway. They are lazy, filthy, and unintelligent. They are also, in an apathetic way, contented —or seem to be—with little. Since I am also content with little, it is odd that I feel there is something defective about their contentedness. Perhaps it is that one instinctively springs, beneath the sluttishness of the one and the bone-laziness of the other, a desire for possessions—a car, a wireless, a pianola, a re-frigerator, electric light—a desire that is strong but not muscular enough to overcome their sloth and animalities. At night it is impossible not to overhear the exercise of their frequent matings. They are a moronic and draggle-tailed version of the Kingsley Hall people, afternoon farmers, child-adults playing blindly in the mud because there is no overseer.

Mr Tretheway is never out of bed before ten or eleven, and haphazardly cultivates about one acre only of the several hundred acres, growing the crops of the shiftless—potatoes, swedes, broad beans. There are a few pigs, fowls and geese, a cow, an old horse and a small flock of Border Leicesters whose long idiot masks, dissipated and scornful, watch through the dried docks and fennel and the spider-webs beaded with seed-pearl drops as I wade the morning mists on my way to the road, and the miles of trees with their crowns plunged in mountain fog, and the school.

At the school where, on the first day, I kill two snakes lying in the sun by the lavender bushes, there are fourteen pupils. They are timber-cutters' children from the houses opposite the post-office, or children from nearby farms. The oldest is twelve, the youngest six, and they are all docile, ingenuous, and of average intelligence. It is pointless giving them the oppor-tunity to be anything more than sweet-natured, well-behaved, and diligent. After years at the noisy, full-steam-ahead Williamstown school where no class has fewer than thirty pupils, it is less than easy to teach the same curriculum to the small group of mountain-children, to carry out the same ritual. On Monday, there the bare-footed bush children stand under the flag, right hand on left breast, reciting, "I love God and my country. I honour the flag. I will serve the King, and cheerfully obey my parents, teachers and the laws." I try to work out how many thousands of times I've heard how many thousands of children recite that since I was a suburban schoolboy reciting it myself. The sum defeats me. On Friday, in this one-roomed school on a mountain crest so high that the building sometimes sits in the centre of a cloud, the same working-week machinery runs down in the same dawdling and sedative manner as it has since I was a boy, and the fourteen children do the traditional paper-folding, plasticine-modelling, free reading, basket-making, and chip-carving, and wash the inkwells, and empty the vases, and pipe out "Now the Day is Over", and return like puppy minotaurs to the labyrinths of tree-ferns, to the weatherboard houses, the smoking chimneys, the gates made of old iron bed-ends, the backyards littered with rusted furphies, forty-gallon oil-drums, worn-out tyres, and shattered dray-wheels wreathed in bindweed. Monday to Friday, Monday to Friday, I earn more money—is it £4 10s. a week?—than ever before for doing less than ever before. Beyond board and lodging, cigarettes, and fruit, there is nothing to spend this on. There are no cinemas, pubs, wine saloons, bathing enclosures, or bookshops, and no cafés or restaurants—Latin, Petrushka, Wild Cherry, Greek Club, Wentworth, Italian Society, Hoisan, Chung Wah, Broadway, Navaretti's, Mario's, Twenty-nine, Cavalier—in which to adjust one's mask to go with chopsticks or spaghetti or angels-on-horseback or ouzo or tea-with. I climb the road of ancient trees, doorless, neon-less, signless, watching the snakes flow across like stripes of oil, hearing the lyrebirds imitating the woodcutters' axes, eating blackberries under the barrister-like disapproval of Border Leicesters, and reach home. Home? Home is where the bed is. Here one can annihilate the universe with one's eyelids.

Except on one occasion, which seems real and tragically real, my relation with Mr and Mrs Tretheway is without reality because it is without friction. It is no more than a we-are-used-by-those-we-use relationship. There is no meeting-point beyond. An inch ahead is pitch blackness. They are no more monosyllabic with me than with each other. It is like living with two de-fanged and slipshod animals, and it is, the first step having been taken, an easy-going life, for animals are never vulgar. By 1938 my experiences with many human beings and a number of landladies (that is, a number of households) have gentled me towards being quite unrattled by the Tretheways. Historically, so far as *my* slap-happy history is concerned, they are the end of the line. Not until years later, in Ceylon and India, does the line reappear for me. The Indian mind, affected by heaven-knows-what hereditary traits as well as a sensual, ego-smothering religion, is a mind with little humour because it has little humanity, and is one that avoids the clash between good and evil. Thus, in their own hill-billy way, the Tretheways. Mrs Tretheway, cooking in a slummocky trance, prepares meals of bog-Irish-cabin crudity. I eat what I can of them, excusing myself from other dishes besides hair-oil-scented bacon. Fortunately there are eggs, milk, butter in plenty. At the school I keep a case each of apples and oranges brought up from Traralgon by the *Heldentenor* bus-driver who turns out to be, as I am, a Kipling fan. What would, six years earlier, before my round trip of others' households begins, have dismayed me into calling a Yellow Cab, is no longer permitted to dismay. Anyway, even if I were dismayed to the point of delirium and escape, there is no taxi-cab, and nowhere else on the Ridge to take it to. The Tretheways are the only ones poor enough, shameless or indifferent enough, and with room enough, to accept a boarder. The schoolie always stays with them. A succession of schoolteachers have worked up nervous breakdowns on the Ridge, doubtless tossing and turning, and nibbling their fingernails to the quick, or whatever it is nervous breakdown subjects do, in the bedroom with its bashed rosewood furnishings, and a squawking concave bed on which the linen is changed fortnightly. There is nothing now to quibble about in this—the Misses Gregory's capricious luxury of daily clean linen is a balancing memory.

118

All in all, the place has wonderful advantages. A preference
—I still have it—for writing by kerosene-lamplight in the immaculate and natural silence of a country night is the easiest of
preferences to gratify. The man and his wife spend the last of
their blurred and gentle monosyllables for the guest in the
house, and their natures can be felt to grope primevally nearer
together, to fuse. They wane away from me, and move early to
bed. I am left with the lamp, the cessation, the inevitable night.
I am, at this stage, young and garrulous enough to be a copious
letter-writer. It is, once again, a last-time frivolity largely kept
up with Alan Marshall. Our letters to each other are long and
frequent. I am also writing short stories about the city, and
about places and people distant from the Ridge. Of these, four
are preserved in publication—"And Nothing More", "Café
Samovar", "The Two Bachelors", and "At Aunt Sophia's". I
send none of these stories anywhere because there is nowhere
in Australia to send them. The *Bulletin* publishes them twenty-
odd years later, but it needs only a brief study of the other
stories it publishes in the nineteen-thirties to see that it will be
uninterested then in any work of mine that does not follow its
pattern. Sometimes, accidentally, one does, and is sent and published. Otherwise, having no interest in rejection slips, I put the
stories aside until there is the foreseen change in policy, editor,
or fashion. Magazines, like women's skirts, are always raising
and lowering their hem-lines. Because I am essentially uninno-
cent—as well as having decided that writers of my sort have no
right to consider that their leprosy should be looked on as
sacred stigmata—it has not dismayed me suddenly to realize
that publishers are businessmen baiting their hooks with people
to catch people, and that the older established Australian writers I was in touch with six or seven years earlier are so suspect
innocent that wariness is called for. Take two samples.

Norman Lindsay, a young man's sort of deity in 1932, extols
my short stories which, in the stupid manner of the unweaned,
I have sent to him for "honest criticism"—the "honest" under-
lined thrice. They are stories, baroque to a degree, and populated by fauna I've never seen—czars, archbishops, duchesses,
peony-breasted courtesans—all lusting, agonizing, and invariably dying, in a no-world of settings filched from Piranesi,

Emil Jannings films, d'Annunzio, and Ibañez. While waiting for Norman Lindsay's reply, I grill myself in the last corner of the last corridor of my mind, and am forced to admit that I *know*, without another opinion, that the stories are experimental, unsellable, almost unreadable, and decidedly unextollable. The receipt, on top of this, of gracious eulogies from the established Lindsay therefore makes me wary. Does he, lolling like a demigod up there on the billows of cumulus with his fleshy nymphs, sleek panthers, urchin satyrs, and platters of grapes, tell tarradiddles to tiroes? P. R. Stephensen, to whom Lindsay has passed on some of my poems—Masefield-and-syrup or out-Sitwelled Sitwell—is another overenthusiastic notability, another innocent, and makes me warier still. He dashes off letters on the startling orange writing-paper of *The Australian Mercury*, a one-number-only publication, telling me that my work is "ideally suited to a *real* literary magazine." And have I £200 to finance such a magazine? I abandon my czars and carnal countesses, and begin again, this time to write about the common-or-garden people all around, the year enclosing me, the streets I walk through, places as multi-dimensional as Strzelecki Ridge.

Two recollections of the Ridge stand forward from the others. One is Mrs Tretheway's behaviour about the letters. The other is the behaviour of the elements.

Exhibitions of Nature in a fury have the air of being very convincingly directed and stage-managed. I have often, at Williamstown or along the Ninety Mile Beach, walked the edge of a ravishing storm but, no matter how buffeted and saturated, do not feel so much a participant as a sightseer who can retreat from danger. On Strzelecki, often storm-overtaken in the defile of trees, in a situation there is no retreat from, it is interesting to find oneself still a spectator, an actor-spectator, even though the thunder is so close to one's elbow that its explosions and the lightning happen together. Thunder, and the echoes of thunder violently volley-balling in the gulches and canyons, are so terrifying that terror disappears, one's frail shell switches to a shape of air through which the bolts hurl themselves. The lightning turns one incandescent. The branches cutting down in the perpendicular falls of rain have the inconsequence of twigs as they *just*—the stage-crew is spot-on—miss slicing one's head off, or felling one into the rivulet the road has become. From the gap made by some past vendetta of weather in the Great Wall of trees, I look down on the giant trunks far below as they surge together like mere rushes, part like grass stirred by a soldier's wind. Behind this ocean of timber and tempest lies the real ocean, distant jade and sunlight and dead calm and, between the two oceans, a miniscule town where people standing in the windless sunshine say, "Storm in the hills!"

Mrs Tretheway and the letters?

I keep the letters of Alan Marshall and others in a top drawer of the tall-boy in the bedroom. The eye of those who are pernickety about the disposition of objects in a drawer does, I'm sure, carry away a snapshot record of the disposition. It is not long after settling in with the Tretheways that it strikes me that the letters have been disarranged during my absences. I give the matter almost no thought, am not swear-on-the-Bible certain of disarrangement, and decidedly am not moved to set cunning little traps even to test the clarity of the morning snapshot. About a week before I am due to leave the Ridge for Bairnsdale and the remaining twenty-two chapters of the novel, there is an unforeseen afternoon holiday at school. I return to the house hours earlier than usual and, for no reason, approach it by way of the orchard outside my bedroom window. Through the pane, just a second before she sees me, I see Mrs Tretheway reading a letter by the open drawer. By the time I enter the kitchen from the back veranda she is standing by the stove in an empty-handed, where-can-I-hide posture. She does not look at me or speak as I walk through to my room, open the drawer, see the letter half-out of the envelope, and with it in my hand return to the kitchen. Why, why, why? She has not moved. Using the clipped accent and higher tone and theatrical phrasing one is inclined to use—icy is it?—in such circumstances, "Mrs Treth-eway," I say, "I do so hope you'll not consider me irrational but I'd really rather you didn't read my private correspondence."

Do so hope! Really rather! Consider me irrational! Private correspondence! The very choice and grouping of the words is bogus, contrived, snide.

This affected, cruel, absurd, cheap, immature, selfish, clumsy, unthinking, unnecessary, destructive sentence is near the top of the list of sentences in my life I should like not to have said. Its effect is immediate and shocking. Mrs Tretheway's face becomes contused as a flush of magenta-coloured shame rises in it. She moans, once, briefly. Her eyes try to escape, and fill with a liquid. Confronting me is the countenance of nude shame itself, and I see with horror that I have struck too suddenly and savagely at some defenceless part of a defenceless animal. What does it matter if a simple woman read the letters I have already enjoyed and put aside? And I, of all people, who have no qualms about playing Machiavelli for hours for the sake of one paltry adjective, why should I be stacking on this act of outrage? I don't really care a straw who reads whose letters. The woman has done nothing.

From her dark and muddied well of distress she fumbles out some words, and drops them with bewilderment: "You're always having showers; always cleaning your teeth."

This cannot be the non sequitur it sounds. My translation of her sentence has the tints of tragedy, and is one of the reasons why I cannot clap on her the sort of price-ticket I can clap on others more civilized, transparent, and articulate. Her sentence is, surely, a muddled plea for understanding, for give-and-take. Although there are overflowing tanks of water—the mountain is a magnet to mists and downpours—she and her husband rarely bathe, and scarcely do more, daily, than the automatic hand-washing of farm people. Yet, there am I singing under the shower every morning, scrubbing at my teeth at least twice a day, always—from her primitive point of view—in the bathroom. She has said nothing about this habit which, by implication, can almost be read (is read?) as a rebuking comment. She takes it, and is silent. Why couldn't I take the reading of the letters, and be silent? Why couldn't I remember Stella and her forgiveness?

Yes.

I have transformed into a near-crime a mere yokel curiosity about an exotic world, a curiosity about how her boarder, free to move and gad about, is addressed by friends still in the city he has come from, and to which, in forty years, she has never been. She never leaves the farm; has never been in a train. During the last week I try all the charm possible in what I know are unavailing attempts to apologize tangentially. It is too late to pat the whipped dog, offer beads to the natives. She never once looks at me. Are her eyes turned dumbly inwards on un-healing wounds of shame? On the last day the Kipling-loving *Heldentenor* with whom I have become very palsy-walsy arrives at the farm to pick me up. She is nowhere to be found to say good-bye to. Since, as it were, we met once only, and exchanged two parallel sentences only, both of them hail-and-farewell, and final, it is foolish of me to be calling out, "Mrs Tretheway! Mrs Tretheway, I'm going. Mrs Tretheway, where are you?"

In the tall weeds, behind a rotting sulky, in a lichened shed, she hides until the bus starts, and takes me and my insensitive tongue down the tri-tracked cart-road, down the road of green gravel through the canyon of trees, down the mountain, in and out of the foothills, to Traralgon, and the railway station, and the train to Bairnsdale.

Bairnsdale has altered little since I left it, a country stripling, eleven years before. On the gravelled slope outside the station Mr Bailey's horse-drawn cabs are no longer lined up with their sole-polished back steps pierced like fish slices, their walls of black waterproofed material as *craquelé* as a clay-pan, horse-hair seats, and panels of ruby glass etched with raspberry vines aspiring from Grecian urns. Mr Bailey, however, successfully disguised as a taxi-driver, sits there in a taxi-cab.

There are many more motor-cars in the town, and the Shire Council has seized their presence as an excuse for as much municipal vandalism as possible, and has pollarded or uprooted a number of street-trees, and chopped down street plantations. Everywhere wireless aerials are poking up, sapling ones like elongated clothes-props. One neon sign with a tic rears above the roof of Bairnsdale's first fish-and-chip shop. An unshaven Greek in a grimy apron runs it and, behind it, a restaurant which serves such drunk's fodder as steak and eggs, fried whiting in batter, crayfish, and oysters, all to be washed down with navvy's tea or coffee-essence coffee.

For the rest, visually, Bairnsdale is so little changed that I am reassured of its physical past, of the correctness of my memories, and the validity of my own physical past. If I have returned with the empty shelves of my 1927 self half-filled with jewels and rubbish, old convictions reburnished and baby-new disdains, the litter does not affect the degree of love with which my eyes continue to see what they used to see—the notices advertising bazaars, clearance sales, funerals, and tennis club dances tacked on the nail-head-speckled telegraph post at Cook's Corner; the ringbarked red-gums gesticulating Dantesquely on the outskirts of the town; the wooden foot-bridges over the brick drains in back-streets weedy with Shepherd's Purse and Fat Hen; the Drevermann drinking-fountain of pink granite; the Boer War and Great War memorials; Mt Lookout and Mt Taylor lying in the north like blue pet beasts; the grain-stores and out-of-use stables with new years of the past—1913, 1919, 1924—tarred on them by past New Year revellers; and the high corrugated iron fence, wistaria-topped, which surrounds the tangled garden of Miss Read (Reed? Reid? Reede? Reade? Reide?) and on which Edwardian larrikins, now as respectable as Wordsworth's poems, have painted in red:

> In 1904, the Scotchies went to war;
> They had no drums, so used their . . . .

What happened to cause the long-dried dribble of paint? A helmeted bobby with a truncheon? An angry shout from across the road? Or a sudden delicate remorse?

The country town of my boyhood and youth is still there, and the street-lights still go out at midnight, and—smack!—there is the undefiled dark I worked to buy, night absolutely neat, uncharted, waiting for me to work in.

I write the Williamstown novel. When I read it, it is not the Great Australian Novel at all. I have spawned nothing more than a first novel—wordy, affected, self-conscious, a creature to be strangled at birth, and buried in the back garden. I give the manuscript away, some here, some there, to friends of that year. Because I've not seen these friends since, I've no idea if the manuscript is still on earth. I hope not.

The days pass and the months pass in writing, in Proust and

Pirandello and pruning roses and planting beans, in gathering mushrooms and visiting Mother's grave, in swimming in and out through the weeping willow curtains along the river, in a thousand tranquil and solitary pursuits. That is not all. My nature is not a shandy one, half-and-half, middle-of-the-road, and in subfusc tone. It is white This. Or black That. Here I am solitary, happy as Larry, singing to myself, and busy as a weaver. Here I am, on the other hand, gregarious, chattering like a magpie to whomever seems to be listening, and doing nothing at all except drink illegally. I have become one of the town's after-hour topers, one of the classless band of hard drinkers whose selection of pubs extends from those on the rim of the Dargo snow-plains to those on the rim of the ocean.

My companions on these law-breaking and hilarious pub-crawls or Bairnsdale grog-sessions until the early hours of the morning are, socially and intellectually, a mixed bunch. Most are a little older than I, and are men and women who, in the Gippsland version of the Roaring 'Twenties, were the defiant ones, the gay ones, the Jazz Babies and Flaming Youth of the provinces. At certain stages of intoxication, one or other vamps out "Don't Bring Lulu" or "I Wonder Where My Baby Is To-night?" and the Charleston is danced. Drinking is, however, the main task in hand, drinking and gossip and affectionate duels of insult and the singing of sentimental songs of the "You Were Meant For Me" sort. There is the Australian unwritten-law avoidance of the topics of politics, religion and, except for risqué stories, sex. We are drinking to get drunk with each other, publicly, while keeping to the rules of being non-boring, non-argumentative, sardonic, and reckless. We all know most of Omar Khayyám by heart, and every word of "Night and Day".

At this time the hotel bars in the State of Victoria are compelled by law to close at six in the evening. This leads to the illegal drinking which, because of the kink for defiance we have in common, is infinitely more enjoyable than the legal drinking we rarely do.

It seems proper, right here and now, to attempt to state what I feel about alcohol. It seems to me—like plastic, tobacco, television, space-ships—to rank high on the list of unnecessary inventions. It has an unpleasant taste, and its use by those incapable of self-discipline is dangerous. My view is not a moral one. I don't care how many alcoholics there are any more than I don't care how many gluttons, misers, lechers, opium addicts, or heroin-takers there are. I am merely incapable of understanding those who cannot do without alcohol—or tea, or gambling, or books, or—well, any luxury. I have loved, however, a number of drinkers of one degree or other, from blue-ribbon alcoholics to one-pot screamers, and have myself been drunk in places the world over, and have twice finished the evening in lock-ups—once in Darlinghurst, Sydney, once in Bow Street, London—both of them mid-Victorian, white-tiled, smelling pleasantly of disinfectant, and marred only by the din of the more selfish detainees kicking at cell doors and screeching out obscenities. I drink because I like drinkers more than non-drinkers. I drink deep when I do drink because half-way house is nowhere. At my present age I should not fret if all the alcohol in the world turned in a twink to soft, sweet, cold water. However, in 1938 and 1939, living again in Bairnsdale, it is exhilarating to balance the white (or black) half of my solitary writing life with the black (or white) half of gregariousness and making whoopee, during which I learn not only a great deal more about Bairnsdale and its people but a great deal more about myself.

Not having been such a committed one-of-the-mob drinkers before, I am fascinated by the unexpressed but definite obligations, and the suavity and propriety that lie under the noisy laughter, the sentimental singing, the perilous drives through the starlit bush to a lake-side pub or a pub in a town thirty miles off. I perceive strengths of great delicacy in these rip-roaring high-flyers, and sweetness of great strength. What have they to do with the disappointed Aldous Huxley, the angry Juvenal, the misanthropic Swift?

Only rarely do these booze-ups (which we call orgies) end in anything except tomfoolery of the all-good-friends sort, or demi-uninhibited behaviour of a punctilious nature. For example, during one spell of hot weather when parts of Gippsland are blazing with bushfires, swimming in the nude is the rage with us. That we euphemistically say "swimming in the nud-ee" indicates our respectability, our tender consciences. Moreover, the entire business is carried out in a manner which suggests that we are under the lorgnette of an all-seeing spinster even more parochial than we. The men undress in one clump of bushes, the women in another. There is also the rule, based on the notion that women are not as interested in seeing undressed men as men are in seeing undressed women, that the women enter the water first. Only after the women are clothed to the chin in the glinting and star-sown garments of the Mitchell River or Jones's Bay or the Southern Ocean do the men caper, as awkwardly as the unclothed must caper, from their bushes into the water. This modesty or decency or whatever it is does not, at the time, strike me as untoward. Years are to pass before I find myself having flatly to refuse an invitation to take part in a nude swimming party, in a well-lit swimming pool, in which, it is indicated, swimming is not the point at all but that group fornication is. I am, by this time, too old to be shocked but not too old to be insulted enough to ask, "What makes you think this is my cup of tea?" My moral sense is not outraged. I am somewhat outraged at being misread. Among this group of overeducated people, who have philosophized themselves into putting so many stakes on sex that it has become a cerebral and degenerate game, I become instantly déclassé.

Nights-out with my country friends may sometimes end in a fusion of two bodies but that is strictly the business of those two bodies, privately, after the curtain has been rung down. More often the nights end with car trouble on the loneliest and most inconvenient sections of bush roads. Kangaroos bound on to windscreens. Trees remove mudguards. Fences crumple radiators. Tyres puncture themselves in two-o'clock-in-the-morning sleet and mud. Inanimate nature takes upon itself an irksome mischieviousness.

Most of us finish up at one time or another with cracked ribs or, more showily, with the scars of sewn-up cuts. Whether these scars got in nearly killing ourselves are less or more worthy than those got by soldiers killing soldiers, boxers punching boxers, jockeys steeple-chasing against jockeys, Jews circumcising Jews, or mountaineers climbing mountains, is not a problem I can solve.

I speak only for myself in saying that, as much as I relish life, I do not relish the idea of death less, and should not have regretted—how could I? why should I?—being killed on the way back from one of those amusing beanos. The others? I think that their what-the-hell attitude to the absurdity and un-avoidability of life includes a what-the-hell attitude to the unavoidability and absurdity of death. Already some of their lovable grog-pink masks are toothy white bone.

At the time, these carryings-on are especially valuable to me because they seem to clear up a doubt I then have about myself—have I grown away from the country town? It comforts me that I have not, that I am not only Australian but localized Austra-lian. In later years, no matter how I happily kick up my travel-worn heels in foreign places—Auckland, Honolulu, Teheran, New York, Kyoto, Glasgow, Cairo, wherever—it is the dance of a weightless man among weightless people, a shadow among shadows. It is nothing more than an encounter of bodies and words. The weight of memories, experiences, years, and loyal-ties is missing.

When I return to Bairnsdale in 1938, requiring and expecting nothing from it except a peaceful corner to write in, I forget to foresee being undone and enthralled by details I've forgotten to remember: the scent of fog-grass and taste of river water and sound of the angelus, the owls and bats at night, the butterflies and buttercups, the voice of the midnight train answering itself from the hills, the dry kisses of billiard balls in the weather-board frontier-town saloon, the Main Street shops that close for an hour at noon, the tides of sheep complaining through outrider streets on their way to the sale-yards.

One turns the pages of the book closed for so long, and the plates are not foxed, there are no wormholes. Hibernating emotions wake up, emotions through which the past intertwists. These blend with the emotions newly born of one's acceptance into an adult under-life not shown in the book of childhood and adolescence where night is largely illustrated as a sleeping town, erased by a blackness in which the cows and the postman and the black-eyed Susans and the water in the water tower, the stale statues on the Roman Catholic church, the Chinese greengrocer's horse, and the bell in the State School tower are all dead to the world.

There have been no plates to show me that, here and there in the silence and blackness, are buried these boxes of smoky light, these treasure chests of wideawake flesh and blood, these lairs of laughter and din, the concertina playing "Red Sails in the Sunset", the beer-glasses filling and emptying and filling, the law-breakers—*my* cobbers—disguising themselves as hearty sinners just as, in the daylight, they disguise themselves as efficient everyday people—as hospital matron, barber, ladies' hair-dresser, school-mistress, bank clerk, housewife, estate agent, draper, shop-girl, squatter's daughter, timber-cutter, truck-driver.

These double-yolked but light-hearted ones present me with their own happiness, a brand of easy-come, easy-go happiness that grafts easily on to my own inbuilt and indestructible kind. The value of this gift may be smaller than it appears to me— or greater. It is, however, a gift, and it is always, at rock-bottom, a little difficult to forgive the givers of gifts. One has been put in the position of having an inexpungeable obligation.

Inexpungeable!

Had I not been such a willing and frequent passenger on their rollicking line with its wickerwork of branch lines I should never have met Olivia, the woman I am to marry.

It is June 1939.

Since leaving Strzelecki Ridge I have done what was to be done, have satisfied the writer by writing the novel, some poems, and some short stories. One of these wins a prize in the Sydney Sesqui-Centenary Celebrations literary competition, a godsend cheque enabling me to extend my out-of-work dalliance among the home-things familiar since I was a barefooted child in a khaki sou'-wester who goes fishing for bream with a sugarbag, a boot-box of shrimps in damp sawdust, a nid-nodding bamboo rod, and an egg-shaped red-and-white floater. Because my sister, as housekeeper for my father, follows my mother's household observances, I am lapped in an unrepealed domestic past while already on the mark for a hit-run future.

It is the last time, in the house where I grew up, that the old scents and sounds are to be as whole as they once were—the salad-dressing odour when the furniture is being polished with vinegar, olive oil, and turpentine; the enormous iron kettle singing with a marble in its throat; the guelder roses mildly thumping at the breakfast-room window in a sea breeze; the smell of linseed oil drying out of the jarrah boards of the front porch on hot afternoons; the sound of rain advancing across acres of corrugated iron roofs; the mingled smell of fresh white-wash in the shed and the bush of cherry-pie outside it.

I sense that my time for these things is running out.

I do not sense how soon it is to run out.

Because I do not read newspapers or listen to news broad-casts on the wireless, and because none of my friends discusses the tribulations of the Old World, I have no idea that another Great War is three months away. My last milky impression of affairs in the portion of the globe north of the Equator, the portion said to be civilized, sophisticated and cultured, has come from reading Hemingway, out of whose fake masculinity and Yankee sentimentality I cannot pick clear outlines, and from listening to the communists of the Café Petrushka, the in-the-swim homocommunists cut to the template of their world-over kind in the nineteen-thirties. The impression is of romantic—and because romantic, humourless—skulduggery in Spain. From the minute platform of earth I have, by 1939, moved not very far on, and not once off, an area about two hundred miles by fifty, the Civil War is as remote and romantic as any remote and romantic war, be it Pelopennesian, Hundred Years, Opium, Maori, Jacobite, Ashantee, or Boer. Certainly I have read *All Quiet on the Western Front*, and Siegfried Sassoon and Stephen Crane and Henri Barbusse and Guy de Maupassant and *Vanity Fair*, and have seen *The Birth of a Nation*, *The Big Parade*, *What Price Glory?*, *A Kiss for Cinderella*, and *Cavalcade* on films, and Frank Lawton in *Journey's End* at the Athanaeum Theatre in Melbourne. The war shelf of the littered shelves of my mind is pretty full—Napoleon in a funny hat, Nelson saying "Kiss me, Hardy!", dolls dressed as Red Cross nurses, Karl Dane and George K. Arthur, popguns, Horatius on the bridge, the Black Hole of Calcutta, Lady Butler's and Grand-father Porter's paintings, "When Did You Last See Your Father?", Florence Nightingale, Boadicea, the Wars of the

130

Roses, the Massacre at Glencoe, Tobler cards of *Navires de Guerre*, wooden swords, tin soldiers, the Relief of Mafeking, the Motherly and Auspicious Dowager-Empress and her Boxers, *The Burial of Sir John Moore at Corunna*, *The Charge of the Light Brigade*, and the photographs of dead uncles and cousins, wearing puttees or leather leggings, in special frames on top of which are the crossed Australian flag and the Union Jack, and a wriggly ribbon, two-fanged at each end, on which is printed FOR GOD, KING, AND COUNTRY. Among the first songs I am taught at school in 1917 are "Anzac" and "Men of Harlech"; they lie at the back of the shelf with "Just as the Sun Went Down"; "Goodbye, Dolly Grey"; "Just Before the Battle, Mother"; "Roses of Picardy"; "Over There"; "The Rose of No Man's Land"; and "Mademoiselle from Armentières". I know every word of the Harfleur speech and the St Crispin's Day one. They too are on the shelf with Mata Hari, Wolfe, Kitchener, Lord Bobs, Bonnie Prince Charlie, Old Bill, Lord Cardigan, and all the Philistines and Huns, galleons and Spartans, submarines and Medes and Persians, all the losers, all the winners, all remote, all romantic. So many skulls glinting like infinitesimal beads in the embroidery that weighs down the dirty and glorious cloak of history.

It is June, 1939, a winter evening. With no knowledge of the civilized Old World's martial ambitions, and no thought of a wife four hours off, no pricking of the thumbs at all, I bounce lightly as an indiarubber ball, from friend to friend.

It is Friday night, late shopping night.

The stars indicate with immaculate clarity the intentions of the air.

Tomorrow morning there will be a white frost.

At six-thirty I return the copy of *Ulysses* borrowed from Mrs Tulliver, an intelligent and fast-talking school-mistress blonder than the Knave of Spades, or any of the blond Knaves. Her husband, a man of matador good looks and dark humours, an ever-smouldering male, once—and once only—upsets the good-clean-fun pattern of an open-air drinking bout at Eagle Point Park by accusing his wife and a sonk of a bank clerk of unchaste designs on each other. Admonished by all, he further disorders the pattern by driving off, apparently still in a mood of devil's jealousy for he merely hell-drives to the Tulliver house, gets a rifle, and blows out his brains in the garage. Mrs Tulliver has not yet, June 1939, married again. We sit in the Oriental Hotel while trying to work out why James Joyce's *Ulysses* is so esteemed by academics, but several drinks get us no further than deciding that academics have been trained to relish pretentiousness and perceive the value of pornography.

At seven-thirty I depart from Mrs Tulliver to keep an appointment with Miss Maclean and Mr Tudor at the Commercial Hotel. Miss Maclean and Mr Tudor, neither of whom is married to anyone else, and who are not married to each other, have lived together for years. He is a well-read agnostic who collects old books, and steel engravings of the eighteenth century. She collects such Australian painters as William Frater, Hans Heysen, and Elioth Gruner. As well, when in her cups, she does a species of cancan.

While we drink together we are joined by a young Roman Catholic priest and a dapper barber, night-owls as we are, and I decide to go with these two to make a call on Sister Mollie Framlingham and Sister Violet Framlingham at the private hospital they conduct in a spacious brick house belonging to one of Bairnsdale's rich merchants.

The barber takes a bottle of gin for Sister Violet, his lady-love of the moment. I take three bottles of beer for anyone at all. One never knows who is going to be in the vast kitchen at the back of the house besides several new-born babies asleep in bassinets before the kitchen range. The priest takes nothing. He is going to collect a green pullover Sister Mollie has knitted for him.

When we arrive, Sister Violet is off duty, so is Jessie the cook. Sister Mollie is bedding down the patients. Barber, priest, nurse, cook, and—?—and I, drink in the kitchen among the kidney-bowls. Jessie makes us sandwiches of roast lamb and chutney.

The two sisters, Roman Catholic women who have invested a substantial inheritance from their sheep-farming father in the hospital, fascinate me.

Sister Violet keeps what she calls a Fornication Chain, a record of each time she goes to bed with a man, a link added for each consummation. The chain is long. The barber and the gin will doubtless, this June night of stars already icily foretelling frost, be responsible for a link or two.

Sister Mollie's spoonerisms and malapropisms, perhaps a result of the drugs it is later discovered the two sisters take, are funny enough to be deliberate. A like malapropism infects their charity, and their capricious largesse. It astounds me to be given, arbitrarily, a pair of Austin Reed pyjamas, silk, loud, expensive, for which I have done no more than enjoy the sisters' company. Others, I learn, have found themselves, without warning, on days sacred to nothing but the whims of Sister Mollie, being presented with crystal water-sets, brocade dressing-gowns, musical cigarette boxes, and imitation Della Robbia wall-plaques of Madonnas and Holy Infants. Battered and boozy old-age pensioners bearing names like Danny or Pat or Murph have, in specified hours, entrée to the kitchen, the materialized centre of Sister Mollie's slopping-over heart, where they are fed on sick-room delicacies—chicken broth, turkey, egg custard, and port wine jelly in which slices of banana are embedded. No temperamental cook protests at the soup-kitchen atmosphere behind the hospital's more practical front of expensively looking after those who are conventionally getting better or conventionally dying in rooms hung with pictures of the Blessed Virgin uplifting immense un-bloodshot eyes, or of Christ revealing, through an aperture in his sternum, a vermilion and gilt heart like a St Valentine's Day Postcard. There are no protests because most of the domestic staff—cook, wardsmaid, washerwoman, general char—are people no one else cares to employ, or are unmarried mothers. There is often an illegitimate toddler being played with on the back lawn by six-year-old Susso, a Dickensian waif of a Tiny-Tim-faced boy the sisters have adopted.

Of these people, so alive and lively, who adorn the last three hours of convinced bachelordom left to me, few are still alive and lively. Time-out-of-mind ago the seeds that are to blossom into their deaths in an inescapable time, place, and manner infest the texture of the universe. Aeons before the brontosaurus and Babylon, cancer is there for Mrs Tulliver, diabetes for the priest, heart-failure in a butcher's shop for Miss Maclean, something else for Sister Mollie. Just as, time-out-of-mind ago, I have been committed to outliving them, to preserving the fragment of their lives and the fragment of their deaths I contain, so I am committed, at nine-thirty, to take to my heels, to leave the hospital kitchen and its smell of methylated spirits and night-cap cocoa, to leave the barber and Sister Violet to gin and each other, to leave the priest in his new green pullover drinking beer, and talking racehorses and football with Sister Mollie. I have promised to pick up Mrs Scott, a ladies' hairdresser, with whom I am to attend a drinking-session in the Main Hotel, a preliminary canter to a later session at a roadside hotel at Swan Reach.

When I reach the hairdressing salon Mrs Scott is still at work in one of the cubicles. From behind the dove-grey and dusty-pink poplin curtain she says, in a voice that shows she has something held between her lips, "Go through. There's another bottle of whisky in the cup cupboard if those old harpies have knocked off the first."

Old harpies?

Half-a-dozen paces through the nasty reek of setting lotion and cooked hair, half-a-dozen paces along the grey-and-pink carpet, and I am in the back room, and a victim of love at first sight.

There are the sink, the ball of Castile soap, the nail-brushes, the horseshoe-shaped flower troughs filled by crumpled wire-netting, the empty soda siphons and whisky bottles under the sink, the out-of-action posters advertising hair-nets and lipsticks no woman would now be seen dead in, the electric jug with the broken lid, the laundry basket filled with used pink and grey cloths, the umbrellas and coats hanging on nails behind the door, and the several old armchairs of jazz-patterned moquette.

In one of them sits Olivia.

Who climbs high, falls fast and hard.

For ten years I have been designedly climbing up and up out of the reach of the wife-woman. At the age of twenty-eight, it seems to me that I am out of reach.

Twenty-eight! A babe in arms! The fool, the fool one meets i' the forest!

It has not, of course, been a difficult climb because my eyes have been searching for anything and everything but a wife. Women, okay. Wives, napoo. Almost constantly "in love" with this woman or that woman, for this reason or that reason, I have been able to climb higher on these "loves", my skin thickening rung by rung. This series of barley-water crushes has none of the intensity and mind-scalding quality of, for instance, my passion, while still in high-school knickerbockers, for a schoolgirl called Olwen. After Olwen, the charming playmates, the charming animals, are no more than women for other men to marry, women to marry other men. How skilled I become in spotting the works of authors—Strindberg, you beauty!—who present me with phials of ready-mixed and concentrated anti-wife tonic to sustain me while I climb.

I do not know why I fall. I cannot tell, at this moment, why. Instinct? Yes and no. And instinct, what is instinct? Preordained, as all is preordained? Of course, of course. Even to pick up the trail leading to Olivia from as recently as when I first crawl on a floor makes a journey of many hours, many miles, many doublings-back as one advances, many crossings and recrossings as one takes many steps forward, many inevitabilities that no self-deceit can cancel out. After instinct and preordainment, after so elaborately simple a journey, why ask "Why?"? The answer will be the answer will be the answer, as always: "It is the same world, the same rose. The sun is round. The night is dark."

At the time I ask no questions, but move on, blinded, aware for the first time that moving blindly on, however wide-open-eyed and however many eyes there are in the back of one's head, is all one ever does. To lose one's heart is to lose one's entirety. Losing one's heart, one loses one's head. Losing one's head, one loses one's eyes, and arrives at the signpost one cannot read—Love Is Blind.

There seems, then, nothing to be blind to.

For me Olivia is beautiful as I've not known a flesh-and-blood woman to be. I've not the power to put into words the beauty—physical, mental, spiritual—I find her to have, nor shall I ever possess that power. I cannot even define beauty. There remains nothing to do but outline, no more than outline, the course of our love before it turned, as love will, into something else, and one can see again, traced on the dust, written on the wind, scored on the moon: "It is the same world, the same rose. The sun is round. The night is dark."

It seems usual to the nature of a beautiful woman to wear a less beautiful woman as a foil, as a protective sister, as a buttress to the weaknesses that go with beauty. Olivia, tall, galvanic, elegant, has travelled from Melbourne to Bairnsdale with a short, plump confidante, the classic companion of beauty of the *Commedia dell' Arte*, the Pasquella or Corallina, the stooge and go-between, pert, quick-as-a-flash, ceaselessly amusing in a giddily brittle manner. Olivia's Corallina, a childless married woman, is called Maida and, true to the stage pattern, provides comic relief, unappreciated loyalty, and disregarded advice in a situation which almost immediately leaves the rails of civilized convention. Love, like its opposite, hate, is hardly a civilized emotion although it can, like hate, be a civilizing agent. I remember Maida as seemingly always wearing, even over her nightgown, a coat of glistening brown fur with a brocaded lining, as she makes fetching-and-carrying exits and entrances to Olivia's room. She and Maida are staying at the Main Hotel where Mrs Scott also stays.

My presence in Olivia's bed on Saturday morning causes merely a minor flurry—two breakfast trays instead of one. I am, at first, no more than something left over from Friday night's party. At first is, however, no more than just that. By Monday, so speed-of-light efficient is the bush telegraph of a provincial town that everyone who knows me has heard that I am carrying on with a city woman, that I have sent home for my sponge-bag and fresh clothes, and that Kate, the publican, has overnight turned into a heart-of-gold fairy godmother ready to mow down anyone who censures us.

Kate's girlishly enthusiastic sanction, indubitably a result of Olivia's charm, is more amazing to the rabble than our lack of discretion, for Kate, a tiny, ferocious, hard-drinking woman of sixty-odd, trained in the tough pubs of Carlton, then one of Melbourne's seedier and shadier inner working-class suburbs, and capable of physically throwing out troublesome bar louts without the aid of bruisers, is also a woman of the strictest

136

moral standards. Any line she draws is one not to be stepped over. I can only think that she sees Olivia and me cinematically. This is not, I am to learn, how my father sees us. Kate is too moral, unsentimental, and worldly to see us as anything less than wanderers on a Milky Way by Metro-Goldwyn-Mayer. Father is too immoral, sentimental, and unworldly to see us as anything more than layabouts in the mud, the mud by Balzac.

We two, of course, are beyond the virtues of practicality for a while—at least I am. Perhaps women scarcely ever are. However, imagining that we are being as practical as buckets, we decide, if not on the Friday night then on the Saturday, that we shall marry.

It is three o'clock in the morning and, from the first-floor window of the room, we are looking out on the campanile of St Joseph's Cathedral rearing up opposite the hotel above the scarps of the slate roof luminous with young frost, above the ice-and-snow statues of St Joseph and St Patrick in their lofty niches. Yes, we shall marry, but not immediately, not for some months. We must both be pragmatic; we must plan sensibly; I must get a good job.

Idiots!

Meantime, let's Omar Khayyám on, unborn-tomorrow-and-dead-yesterdaying, let's play out the next two weeks like characters from a provincialized Scott Fitzgerald novel.

Idiots! Dupes of nature and novels and popular songs and our own inner untruths! Already Omar's caravan has started for the dawn of nothing; already the frost on the slates is older; already it is tomorrow, the one day less; already yesterday is the one day more.

It becomes Friday again.

I am completely unable to recall the exquisitely subtle stages by which we abandon the notion of marrying later on or, indeed, the arabesque of emotions that has us deciding, at five-thirty, in the Main Street, outside Kyle's Bakery, where a display of wedding-cake ornaments having the same fusty character as china grave-roses emit no electrical ray of warning, that we shall be married that night, at nine-thirty, exactly a week after our meeting.

Four hours to go.

As always, a decision made, I start slashing at the briers. The minister is the first one for the bill-hook.

He is young, professionally sympathetic, has a hyphenated surname, and sounds English.

"D'you maind if Ai put on a paipe?" he says.

He puts one on.

Olivia and I put on cigarettes.

As he puffs at the pipe—it is a cherry-wood—his eyes, professionally alert now, the eyes of a man, a priest, and the Church of England, rifle us of dishonesty. We are in, for me, a me-haunted room, a younger ghost, wiser, less innocent, less likely to dicker centrality away. To this room, ten years before, I come with a feeling of unreality more real than reality to tell a former priest of my mother's death. Now, to the same room, with much the same feeling, I come to have a priest tell me what must be done about the death of a bachelor. The church knows. He telephones the bishop. The bishop knows too. He grants a special dispensation. The woman and I are to be married that night. We talk a little about some writer—Galsworthy? Eleanor Dark? Do we drink a dry sherry together, the man who is to marry, the two who are to be married?

There are more briers—the minister's fee, the wedding ring. I borrow from Olivia or Maida or a barman or someone.

At nine-fifteen we are outside St John's Church of England, the church of my boyhood and numberless recitings of the Apostles' Creed, the church with its royal blue carpet scattered with dandelion-coloured fleurs-de-lis, and its lancet windows with diamond panes of aesthetic tints—greeny-yallery, mauve, weak pink. Here, we remember to notice that while Olivia, dressed to the nines, has her attendants, Maida and Mrs Scott also dressed to kill in garden-party hats and white gloves, I have no one to hand me the ring. Leaving the three women singing "Under the Spreading Chestnut Tree" and smoking a last cigarette beneath the plane-tree outside the Sunday School, I race back along Main Street. Already it is deserted, the shops shut. I am on my way to the pubs, in search of the soberest, most decorously habited friend I can find to press-gang into being best man, when one open shop—it is a Jew's—comes in sight. There seems nothing for it but to try him on the basis of

138

any port in a storm. Since he is merely an acquaintance, an optician with whom I have nothing at all in common except the cancellable certainty that we are both bipeds, it is necessary to use all the blarney of a vacuum-cleaner salesman on his national reluctance, conventional disapproval, and possible dislike of me.

The wedding, so hastily arranged, takes place.

The choir stalls, communion rail, sanctuary steps and high altar blaze stereoscopically at the end of the nave. The church, otherwise, imitates an abbey vastness in the demi-gloom.

Maida, temporarily demoted from a gay-gay-gay Corallina to a subdued matron, gives the bride away.

The ring is handed to me by what appears, out of the corner of my eye, to be a sawn-off Danny Kaye, a Russian-Jewish acquaintance on the lenses of whose gold-rimmed spectacles the candle-flames and the glittering altar cross minutely mop and mow.

The wedding over, the attendant females weep gently and foolishly, as females will, for whatever has been slain.

The wedding breakfast for five people more ill-assorted than they know takes place in Spiros the Greek's restaurant with its palsied neon. It is too early for the midnight drunks to be there with their gift of din in which to be private. In the empty restaurant, four of us are exposed to each other as fatigued by the hours of denaturalized behaviour, as chastened by anti-climax, and in need of stiff drinks. We are further depressed by the inexplicable and salt-in-the-wound liveliness of the Jewish optician whose idea the meal is, and whose set of party tricks is so alien to our senses of humour that we must politely overact fits of merriment. After what seems a year we are free of the well-meaning foreigner who refuses, as we know he will, to return with us to the Main Hotel—Mr and Mrs Porter and two conspirators anxious to find out what lies on the other side of anti-climax. We find out immediately we reveal what we've been up to.

Kate's imperceptibly altered attitude to us is nonetheless altered. An elusive disappointment is in it. By becoming man and wife we are no longer living kicking versions of Loretta Young and Ray Milland. Not only have we lost our gilt, we have looked a gift horse in the mouth. Kate's fairy godmother period is over, a waste of sponsorship. On the other side of anti-climax lies the fact that married couples are twopence a dozen.

Several days later I take Olivia to meet my father, who has not married again since my mother's death ten years before. He has a widow friend who is certainly quarter-caste Chinese, if not half-caste, and is, I think, an ex-barmaid. It is to her he goes every evening while my sister, taken from school to be his housekeeper, brings up his four other children.

I know country towns well enough to be aware that my father will be more up to date on the details of the association between Olivia and me than we are ourselves. He will have the illuminated manuscript with the scandalous addenda. What I expect from him I do not know for, even though inheritance has landed me with many of his characteristics, it has not landed me the means of guessing what his next move will be.

He is standing by the wireless when I introduce Olivia.

He says, "How do you do?"

He turns to the machine, and twirls up the volume, not too much, a mere shade.

That is all.

I shall never know what his feelings are at that moment and, years later, many years later, when he and I are friendly, do not ask. I accept then, as I accept now, that the feelings are strong ones. There is—this I do know—nothing to be said or done to chip his silence or change the situation. The wireless plays "Freckle Face". My father lifts the Zane Grey from the top of the set. It is *Riders of the Purple Sage*. Olivia and I leave the house. I show her the garden. She picks me a yellow rose which I keep for years. Does he turn down the volume, not too much, just a shade? And go on reading with his blue eyes which are my blue eyes? I do not know, ever, what he will do when I am there, and cannot know what he will do when I am not. My father is never, like landladies and women, predictable as yesterdays.

Olivia, when she returns to the city, is not to tell her family she is married. I forget why, but it is probably because she deems it better to break the news when I am working, when I am something more than an unknown writer on the loose. When I do come to Melbourne to meet her people it is merely as a man she loves, a man in love.

Her father?

He, too, says little more than, "How do you do?" He is huge, with a deep voice, a cigar-smoking club man. At that time, and for a little longer, I am six feet tall, but feel shorter before his merchant bulk, his preoccupied sonorities. He is, however, visually and socially inconsequential in the company of his wife and four daughters. Individually they have presence to burn; the impact from the five women together is considerable.

The mother, brought up in India, is puppet-small, eyes like a Parisian's, inky, flashing with intensities. She is ravaged to fragility by malaria but, sustaining the fragility and the almost febrile feminity, one is aware of power. The generator is never turned off. She is, when I meet her, on some hobby-horse connected with *The Golden Bough*. She is riding it with the concentration of a Grand National jockey, and at the same time behaving with the exquisite obliquity of a maharanee among her lofty daughters.

Olivia's three sisters are as tall as she and, in varying degrees, have the same sort of theatrical loveliness—or what seems to me to be loveliness. One is, in fact, an ex-beauty-queen who has become an actress, one is a pianist in the middle of practising to play in Sir Thomas Beecham's orchestra in the Melbourne Town Hall, the other is a married woman.

There is no doubt that the heat of my heart at this period, like breath on a pane, mists over the glass. I observe in the four sisters nothing that is not glamorous, highly polished, cut like a jewel to catch whatever light there is in others and to fling its intensification back. To the universe of fools there might seem an overcultivation of self, a surface too sleek to be anything but skin-thin. Not so to me. The surface to my own depth of placidity has too often been mistaken for indifference—I recognize therefore that there are muscular currents and fathomless tides at work beneath their surfaces, beneath the decorative behaviour, the panache, beneath the trappings of orchids and diamonds and expensive gewgaws and unctuous head waiters and wealthy playboy escorts and clothes from Schiaparelli. They are, by reason of their natural endowments, conspicuous. Being intelligent as well, they have become skilled in the fastidious arts, are urban and cosmopolitan, and have perfected every gesture and intonation so that unavoidable conspicuousness is not marred by the most hairline of faults. Yet, since each opulent and eye-catching shell contains a simpler woman, the more sombre glance of this enclosed being glows behind the brilliant public glances, a wearier and steadier glance expressing regret at undervalued merit.

I am not yet sobered by the fact that I am married to a beauty with beauties for sisters, but am a little sobered by the secrecy Olivia and I are keeping about the marriage. Love likes to display itself. Dissimulation is fatiguing. Aware that an attitude about this, something male and perverse, is stirring, I am not in the sac of enchantment long enough for the attitude to be bred.

The sac is torn violently from me.

I have taken a small upstairs flat in an 1880 terrace house in Victoria Parade, East Melbourne. It is directly opposite St Vincent's Hospital, is temporary, and I loathe it. I have persuaded one of the commercial broadcasting stations to commission me to write a series of plays on historic assassinations. Julius Caesar, Marat, Abraham Lincoln, the Archduke Ferdinand, and Paul the First of Russia are, I recall, some of the subjects. My days are spent in research at the Melbourne Public Library.

On September the first I have worked there throughout the afternoon, and have become so engrossed in the stranger-than-fiction characters and outriders in the Abraham Lincoln assassination plot that it is nine o'clock before hunger reminds me that I am two hours late for a Friday night out on the tiles with Olivia and a gaggle of theatre women and vigneron playboys.

When I arrive at Mario's where the walls of the restaurant are hung with paintings of blurred oyster-coloured roses by Mario's wife, Madame Vigano, the others have dined, and have settled down to drinking champagne, or to swinging and trucking on the table-sized dance floor. Everyone has reached the tally-ho stage of intoxication which the orchestra encourages by playing "The Lambeth Walk", the stage of intoxication which, when one is hungry, mentally cross-eyed, and more than sober, makes one's most consequential and beloved friends seem to be inconsequential, to have buckled minds, and a crack-pot sense of humour. I have several dances to such atrabilious melodies as "Deep Purple" and "Moon of Manakura", melodies which now have a highly coloured poignancy for me because they accompany the last dances I am ever to have with Olivia. As well, it is to these tunes I last dance as a six-foot man with legs of equal length. When the grilled rump steak and the bottle of beer I have ordered arrive, I settle down to them. The others are now at brandy.

Suddenly it is ten o'clock and a police raid.

The others, further exhilarated by this appearance of men in uniform, decide to go on elsewhere, to some licensed club like the German Club, to some sly-groggery like Frau Roder's. I beg out, partly because I am tired, more because there is no chance of catching up on the mood of the others. I am to be dropped off.

We pack into two or three cars.

In Victoria Parade the car I am in draws up to disgorge me, outside St Vincent's Hospital, opposite the flat. I wish them happy drinking, and start across the road laden with what Olivia has bought for me during the day—a dozen oranges, a dozen lemons, a pineapple, a ream of foolscap, and a parcel of chemist goods including a bottle of Aqua Velva, an after-shave lotion. With my library notebooks plus a bunch of wallflowers given me by one of the actressy young women in Mario's, my arms are full.

I see headlights coming at me.

Retreat?

Go on?

That minute faltering is dangerous. More dangerous is the fact that when I do go on, hurling myself forward, I do not throw away the hampering and balance-impairing parcels. The mudguard of the car strikes my hip. I feel the ball part of the hipbone plunge through the socket, feel the bones of the pelvis smash. There I am, flat on my back on the road, still holding the wallflowers. They have the wrong smell, and this is the first of a number of disconcerting and disillusioning things to happen in the next hour. The wrong wallflower smell is that of Aqua Velva from the smashed bottle and, this first problem in a new milieu solved, others present themselves.

The main one is the problem of correct behaviour under the scrutiny of the hedge of people that has sprung up around me in a neat oval—one woman has unusual lime-green gloves, one man has a twinkling fly-button undone.

Shall I say, "You there, bend down. I want to whisper. You've got a medal showing."?

What to say, since I cannot move? A smile? It will, doubtless, be sickly, and misunderstood.

This is not only an embarrassing situation not experienced before, it is also one not witnessed before—and not witnessed to this day—of a human skittled by a piece of heavy machinery. Even the films let me down. And suppose I am dying, what shall I say? My mother's dying words were artless, and are certainly not for me. Plays, novels, films—their death-bed speeches are too high-flown or sloppily long-winded or arch. Only the girl in *The Story of an African Farm* watching herself dying alone on the veldt with a looking-glass in her hand seems authentic. However good an idea, hardly correct, the looking-glass in front of these vertical bystanders who have sprung out of the ground. Anyway, death seems far off. I have never felt so relaxed before. The bitumen could be a goose-feather bed; the stars, I observe, are not sprinkled on the sky's surface at all but embedded in it at various depths; and, disillusionment above all, there is absolutely no pain, nothing for me to centralize an act of manly grit and silent suffering on. It is bewildering. If I could get up and stroll off I should get up and stroll off, but body has told mind, and mind now tells body, "No!"

Olivia, whose car has not had time to move off before I have spoiled the rest of their evening, is my salvation. She is what I call beautiful, and what Somerset Maugham calls "exquisitely gowned", will raise my stocks, and is my wife, and knows what to say to me. She makes her perfect entrance among the immediately inferior onlookers. I know she will not let me down. She doesn't.

"Darling," she says, "this is too ridiculous. Wallflowers!"

"There were no orchids left." Ah! I can speak!

"I told you that florist had no morals."

"Florists don't need morals."

This absurd exchange, impromptu burlesque of Noël Coward, provides the bracer we need in an absurd contretempts among strangers who, by behaving with human simplicity, seem to put themselves into absurd Alice-in-Wonderland focus. They play their parts with conviction, picking up oranges and lemons and dusting them, helping the woman who has run me down be sick under one of the trees in the central plantation of the road. One has said, "Stand back and give him air." One has gone, as into the neighbour's to borrow a cup of salt, to St Vincent's to get an ambulance. It is all very convenient.

I see Olivia's hands being deliberately precise and untrembling as she lights two cigarettes. We are waiting for something to happen. The hedge gets thicker by a tram-load of audience.

"Do men," I say, "have pelvises?"

"Certainly not. Only child-bearing women."

"Well, it's very confusing. I think what men have instead of pelvises is broken."

"*Pas devant les domestiques*! There is no need to be coarse."

Half panther, half tuberose, she is sitting on the road beside me. Half panther, half tuberose, what do I mean by thinking this? Am I delirious? She puts the cigarette between my lips.

One puff, and another illusion goes. In countless films I have seen the dishevelled buddy put the lit cigarette between the lips of the wounded soldier, the machine-gunned gangster. It seems always to be just what is wanted to bring on "Thanks, pal," and a wan smile. For me, the one puff is one puff too much even though the cigarette is Army Club, my favourite of the moment. I make an ugh noise. The hedge perks up, eyes alert, ears pricked for grimmer entertainment.

"Army Club! My dear young woman, I'd sooner smoke hashish."

She understands what I mean, and her face, hitherto controlled, goes haggard at some thought I'm not aware of.

The ambulance arrives from next door, the neighbour Joe Blows in white coats, the stretcher, the worn grey blankets edged with red stitching. Accepting my word that the pelvis is fractured, they slide me on to the stretcher. I feel a kind of visual pain, the key-in-the-broken-lock movement of loose bones, an intimation of pain to come, but no pain itself.

Pain, incidentally, is something I know less about than, at the age of twenty-eight, I should. Even the conventional pains— headache, toothache, belly-ache, earache—have been denied me. My experience goes no further than a cut or two, momentary, superficial. Lack of information increases my curiosity. I feel once again the suggestion of pain to come as I am off-loaded on to a casualty-ward bed which has wooden sides so that I lie like a mannikin in a shallow box.

The doctor comes in, young, petulant, dissipated-looking.

Unaware of the etiquette the situation apparently requires, I drop an outsider's brick by saying, "I'm awfully sorry, dear boy, but I think I've fractured my pelvis."

"I'll tell *you*," says the doctor. "And don't call me dear boy."

At this the accident really begins. I see that I am no longer my own man. Olivia and I exchange a glance indicating that, without raising them, we have raised our eyebrows. The doctor examines me briefly, and presses his hand on my hip. Pain? I tell him no pain, and increase his dislike of me by saying, "But, dear boy—sorry, *doctor*—but, doctor, there are intimations of pain. There's a sort of visual pain somewhere."

How else, poor word-crazy fool, can I explain what I can't explain? It is how I talk anyway. He looks at me as if I am a heroin addict. I give up.

The dead calm of a stubbornness I recognize as inherited from Father comes over me, and a weary scorn of the doctor whose fingernails are chewed, the points of whose collar are curled up like the corners of railway-buffet sandwiches.

To this day I do not know why he leaves me, like a ventriloquist's dummy without a master, in the shallow box until nine o'clock next morning. I can, he says, use the bed for my—he pauses to make a *moue*—bruises until it is needed by someone else.

At one o'clock I send Olivia home. She is beginning to suffer.

Left to myself, I try to organize what I can of the powers of self-command. I refuse, first of all, to allow myself to throw a net over the thought crossing and re-crossing my mind that the doctor's unmistakable dislike of me has to do with what I know is offhand treatment. He is young, nervy, fallible, a mug doctor. Leave it at that. If I die, I die. Meantime, how to occupy myself until something happens for, I know, something will happen? I wish I had remembered to ask Olivia for her handbag-mirror to study my expressions now that pain is starting to put its nose out of the hole it lives in until it is useful. The hours pass, and my first contention with increasing physical distress calls into the arena aspects of myself that interest me a great deal. I should, for example, be pressing the bell-button by the bed, or yelling like a banshee. Instead, I cultivate a silence useful to no one, least of all to me. The electric light blazes throughout, and is still blazing when another young doctor comes with the gift of nine o'clock, and release from my own obstinacy.

"Still here?" he says.

Ah! Something has been said in one of those white corridors. I know who has said it, and I make my effort of defiance.

"Yes, *dear boy*, still here. I'm awfully sorry to be so tiresome but I've fractured my pelvis."

This is cheap, but reassures me that I am still I.

The next second I am something else.

The doctor moves the leg I have not moved since being lifted into the box. I scream, and continue to scream. Never having made such an uninhibited din I am impressed by my technique and power.

Now, I have split into two creatures.

One is the watching creature who sees the doctor's face fall before it settles itself into a workaday mask, sees Olivia, anguished and pale, sees nuns in white, one of whom pulls my shirt down over my nakedness after my trousers have been slid off and my underpants cut off, sees the corridor walls sweeping by on the way to the X-ray room, sees two carpenters putting up a scaffolding of fresh wood about the bed I am in, and the chloroform mask descending on me like a candle-snuffer.

The other creature is the screamer, the one who has wasted silent self-command hour after hour, and is now playing—almost deliberately—with the effect of various fluctuations in

147

the volume of sound, making a twerp's chant of pain. The word *keening* pops into his mind. It goes on and on. Pain, eh? Ah well!

Now, under the candle-snuffer, a drunken voice—surely not mine?—is chattering on, purposely in stage-cockney, "Twenny-noine, firty, firty-one, fir-ty-two, fir-ty-free. . . ."

I am engulfed.

Now I am the idiot mumbling, "Pig-trotters rolling down a hill, down a hill."

I do not understand the meaning of the mumble until absolutely clear of the chloroform, when I can work out the association of ideas: high in front of me my piggishly swollen toes protrude from their plaster bandages at the top of an incline of sheeting. I am every way confined in mid-air. My right leg, stretched rigid by a weighted cord passing over a pulley, sticks up like a jib-boom. Weighted cords attached to each corner of a square of sailcloth, and passing over four pulleys, form a sort of hammock for my pelvic regions. In this Heath Robinson device I am trapped like a pudding in a pudding-cloth for a couple of months. I do not enjoy them, but the writer is satisfied by the experiences as he is by the later successive stages of bathchair, crutches, walking-stick, and a contraption of steel and springs buckled on the leg. Perhaps more grotesque than any of these aids towards walking unaided are the stays, flesh-pink, which enclose me for a long period. Early nineteenth-century cartoons of antique beaux, and Edwardian postcards of gross mothers-in-law being brutally laced into stays of almost similar design to mine incite me to seem as ridiculous to myself as I indubitably am in the valet-less struggle with the pink tapes every morning.

My inborn desire not to be manacled by possessions, money, ambition, love, anything, is so aggravated by this period of physical circumscription that, the moment I am patched up and vertical, I take off with such speed and vigour that my burden of information-gained seems lighter than a loofah. The most discomposing paradox in my luggage of new information is that I prefer to live alone because I am too fond of those I love.

One wants to be alone, fundamentally, not to escape others but to escape oneself, the versions of self compelled into existence by others. It is safer for me to be mere wood than to be wood painted to look like wood.

My experiences in a Roman Catholic hospital are only unusual to me because I am Church of England with no clear conception of nuns. Apart from one boyhood encounter with a nun who taught my mother in the convent she was educated in, I've not met a nun. They are classless, sinless Brides of Christ, infinitely mysterious in their strange costumes. Suspended in my bed which, with scaffolding and block-and-tackle, resembles some hybrid between gallows and bosun's-chair, it is fascinating to hear these white-robed non-women exchanging weather chat and female platitudes in working-class Australian accents, to have them pouring Guinness's Stout for me with the skill of barmaids, to hear one say "Blast!", to be attended at one stage by a young nun, pretty in a waxen way, who so manifestly can't bear me that she brings me hot urine-bottles. I think of the Spanish Inquisition. They are skilful nurses, and much more to my taste for the unusual that invisibly occupies the usual than the teddibly refained Special Sister I have during the first three weeks when I am in some danger. She is almost a caricature of the fusspot, stage-convention nurse—"End hah-oo are we this braight morning?" She has such a mania for the appearances that, to avoid the close-shaving she requires me to do at dawn, and to protest as best I can, I grow a beard which gives me some resemblance to a Holman Hunt Christ. Once, while combing this sandy tangle into more Christ-like design, I am caught out by Archbishop Mannix on a visiting round, sumptuously rustling in several shades of fuchsia, and flanked by two candle-bearing nuns, black-robed, both with faces of such vivid roses-and-cream that they appear made up. He drops a sentence of cheer in holy brogue.

For the rest, I go through the routine of learning to be unembarrassed by what initially embarrasses me, and have my first tussles with insomnia. It disappears when I have come to the conclusion that sleepnesses is a useful donation of time in which to work our story plots.

I also have my first nightmare. I am hanging there in my cat's-cradle in a grey dawn which fills the sick-room with flickerings as in an early silent film. A little terrier, yellow, with a

Cheshire Cat grin, is creeping slowly but inexorably down my bowsprit leg towards my face. It is old knowledge that my legs are useless, and horrifying new knowledge that my arms will not move and beat off the creeping dog, which is patently up to no good at all. I begin to call for a nun. I wake up, saturated in sweat, and the nun is there, brought by my wailings. This, my one nightmare, has occurred again, about a dozen times in the last twenty-seven years, invariably in a room I've not occupied before. I cannot see why this should be so, but the nightmare, unpleasant as it is, is also a familiar one. The yellow terrier never gets farther than my chest.

I am many months and hundreds of miles away from St Vincent's before I let myself face the knowledge already there, the guilty knowledge that during my step-by-step return to health and self-sufficiency Olivia has, step-by-step, and as a result of my demands on her, become exhausted, physically and emotionally. I am, years later, a docile patient capable of taking hospital routine in my stride. In 1939, unfamiliar both with hospitals, and myself as a patient, completely unrehearsed, I am a temperamental and demanding patient.

A wife is like a wall of bricks; take one brick off, there is always another underneath.

In fulfilling my demands, capricious, careless, imperious, many bricks are removed from the structure of Olivia's nature. Not once is the exposed next brick an imperfect one. No irritation, moodiness, resentment, tartness, no estrangement of any kind. Nothing but gentle patience, sympathy, unending loyalty, and for hours every day, week after week, a complete absence of self-nature. The debt I owe, absolutely unpayable, must go with me to the grave. That she is forgiven for later ruthlessnesses and brutalities means little. She is forgiven before she acts, has been forgiven for ever. The debt is still not paid: forgiveness is not enough, and never can be. Love is not enough. The resources are not there. I am too imperfect. My very placidity, a form of non-interference, will not allow me to interfere with my placidity. How else could the knowledge of my ingratitude circulate like acid within, and not cease to circulate, while I shrug my shoulders and say, "We are born. We die. All are the same—Genghis Khan, the woman in the empty house, Marie Antoinette, John the Baptist, the cat and the fiddle."

If whispers of regret do sound like thunder in the ears of heaven, and dark secret wickednesses stab like lightning in the eyes of the gods, they do also in one's own ears and eyes. One is not, one is certainly not, however, deafened or blinded. What has Christ or Buddha to give in exchange for the unrattled insouciance with which, undeafened and unblinded, still regretful and still secretly wicked, one can go skipping on ahead of oneself?

I cannot, in 1940, go skipping where I will.

The accident on September the first, 1939, by lopping off abilities useful to soldiers, prevents me from taking part in the World War which begins on September the third, and is well on its 1940 way while I am being pushed about in a wheelchair, or recline listening to "Boomps-a-daisy", "We're Gonna Hang out our Washing on the Siegfried Line", and "Roll out the Barrel", in the pink stays, on a chaise-longue of cane and sennit. Skipping war-wards is out. As a writer more than as a man, but also as a man, I regret losing the opportunity to experience war directly. Maybe, to lose in this manner is to win. For me it does not seem so. A slice of the century is missing from my total. I shall remain incomplete while others are fulfilled—schooldays friends, my baby brother, cousins, frail children I have taught, all experience what I never shall, and keep the secret. The war years include some of the gayest of my life.

Very well, no blood and guts, and boredom, and horror, and despair for me. As well, on the second thoughts that come while I am strung up like a garrulous ham in St Vincent's, the new-husband, wife-inspired notion of writing for a commercial wireless station becomes repugnant. I see once more that writing is not to earn money with. It is, like virtue, its own reward. The most pleasant job—short hours, long holidays, dead-easy work—is teaching. I shall teach again but not, this time, in a government school, and not in Victoria. There are other sorts of schools, other parts of Australia. Let me skip outside the rectangle of earth two hundred miles by fifty that I have been stuck on for nearly three decades.

I apply for a position as Senior English Master in an Adelaide private school. First, however, having read Evelyn Waugh's *Decline and Fall*, I investigate the school's reputation. It has, I am told, a good one.

The Headmaster comes from Adelaide to Melbourne to interview me.

Misgivings scratch faintly behind the wainscot when the interview takes place in the hotel the Headmaster has booked into. The extrovert stucco façade of soaring pilasters and columns, of Volumnia-like statues and lofty embrasured windows, all shabby and pigeon-beset, enchants me, as do its grand staircase guarded by amazons of bronze standing on the newel posts, its public rooms lined by ill-fed palms, and its domed tower topped by a light like a dark-blue planet. Its reputation is less enchanting. At the time, it caters much, and unwinkingly, cash on arrival, for a sozzled stream of Mr and Mrs John Smiths who arrive late, without luggage, together, and leave early, and separately.

The misgivings are a shade less faint when the Headmaster is seen to be wearing his wristlet watch on a white band. This hotel and the white wrist-band notwithstanding, I accept the position. Are the pigeons on the consoles outside the Headmaster's window, and the seagulls I can hear distantly at the Fish Market, complaining, "Decline and fall! Decline and fall!"? They should be. I am on my way to my own *Decline and Fall*.

I talk over with Olivia the wisdom of my testing the status of the Adelaide school, and of investigating accommodation for us, before she come to me. She falls in with this apparently level-headed idea. After the months of entertaining, coddling, and supporting me through hospital tantrums and selfishnesses, a temperamental convalescence, and my snowballing anxiety to move on, move on, move on, she is badly in need of a period of coddling and convalescence herself. I shall move on. She will rest, wait, and follow in time.

Time! That is the lie. What has time to do with it?

I buy an academic gown. I refresh my wardrobe at Henry Buck's. I pack my cases, and paste the lists of contents inside the lids—1. Manuscripts 2. Shoe-trees 3. Light Dressing Gown 4. Slippers, and so on.

I am on Spencer Street station, the interstate platform.

Outside, in an early night already fulfilling its preconceptions, the fag-end of the city does nothing but wait for nothing. Olivia and her three sisters are there on the platform, and could —for my eyes are filmed with tears of champagne—be visitant goddesses with pure voices and shadowed eyes.

Now I am in the carriage with the scent and warmth of Olivia's kiss on my lips.

Now, as the train begins slowly to glide away like a swan, I see that the goddesses are no more than four stately women, tall, soigné, with lit smiles, and eyes that contain their own secret and dark sadness.

Olivia stands a little in front of the others.

Good-bye, darling! And good-bye.

It is nearly ten years before I see her again, by which time the scent and warmth are gone, and she has divorced her second husband, and I am that bureaucratic freak, a civilian-with-officer-status, on the eve of catching a Lancaster to fly to Manila and Japan.

Who runs late and alone, runs far.

It has not entered my head that, in voyaging asleep through the night, north-westward for about five hundred miles, I am to wake up in a part of Australia where everything is different, much or little, strikingly or subtly, from everything observed in the fraction of Australia I've known. The landscape seen through the sleeping compartment window an hour or so after sunrise galvanizes me. There are hills. Immeasurably ancient, abraded low and smooth, they seem young, boneless, pagan, sprawling like adolescent creoles in a languor of passion, but passion undeveloped and never to develop. Floating just above and across the sun-browned limbs, thighs, navels and half-ripened breasts of land, are shoals of blue-violet, colour disembodied, separated from matter, and unattached to the body of earth it feeds on, a weed in flower which, I am to learn, is called Salvation Jane. The hills are not stitched to the sky. There is no seam of horizon. The sky is seen to curve up from far far behind the hills as if the hills, the earth, are centrally

153

contained in a globe of glass hanging plumb and steady from the rafters of infinity.

This first glimpse of a landscape less Anglicized and ordered than what I have been used to, more animal and flamboyant, arouses an excitement with this part of Australia which increases, and abates little, during my six years there. I am perpetually stimulated by dissimilarities and variations—climate, the quality of light, architecture, accent, vocabulary, vegetation, customs, sensibilities, and regional convictions. It is an Australia that is nothing but Australian but is tonally unlike the Australia I've known, Mediterranean and yet class-conscious almost à l'anglais, seductively half-somnolent and yet provincially wide-awake.

Part of the stimulation, but part only, is due to my age: the first half of his thirties is a pleasant plateau of years for an unhampered man to frolic confidently and zestfully across. Part is due to the sense of physical exhilaration, the sense of fizzing good health and independence that follows more than a year of pain-ridden limitation and dependence. I am, as well, absorbed in and animated by the enclosed and intricate world, new to me, of the private school, the church school.

I have been better prepared to slip with ease into this microcosm than seems possible, but it is ram-jam full of characters and situations familiar to me for twenty years, situations and characters from the English magazines and books which have given me my grounding. What has been osmotically absorbed from the pages of *Chums*, *The Boy's Own Paper*, *Magnet* and *Triumph* in earlier boyhood has been more consciously added to by reading *Tom Brown's Schooldays*, *The Hill*, *Stalky and Co.*, and, finally and most recently, *Decline and Fall*. The school in this book, give or take a little, has much in common with the school—call it Duke's College—towards which I advance from the Adelaide railway station through a morning of such crystalline heat that I am intoxicated by it as by the freshly picked gerberas in the nickel-plated wall-vases of the taxi-cab; by the apricot-coloured sandstone houses enclosed in sandstone walls sometimes topped by a barbaric jewellery of broken glass, and overhung by grapevines; by the parklands and olive-trees which surround the square city; by the width and immaculate cleanliness of the roads edged with elms and kurra-jongs; by the gardens filled with rosemary and poinsettia, plumbago and oleander, hibiscus and pomegranates.

I approach Duke's College happy in the anticipation of in-creased happiness and augmented knowledge. Whatever it turns out to be, and that is quite as odd as Eton or Harrow, my anti-cipations are fulfilled. Not that that is a difficult task. My de-sires, then, are simple. Words like Rome or Athens or Cairo have not, in those home-paddock days, turned either into dirty words or words with a purely artificial charm. They still have their Chimborazo-Popocatapetl appeal. I don't know then that Bombay stinks, and sells living human flesh in its Grant Road cages.

I am not yet in search of a nameless city in an unbaptized continent with no boundary. Adelaide is city enough. It is in another state, another year, is over a border. As combined place of employment and boarding-house, Duke's College is enough.

It too is over a border, physically, and over the border lying between reality and the literature of *Decline and Fall*.

I can indicate and almost sum up the nature of the two years spent at Duke's College by writing that, once, before the nineteen-forties, it was a well-esteemed preparatory school. Small, dedicated, pleasantly situated, it trained not only the little boys of rich South Australian parents but, such was its standing, the young sons of rich parents hundreds of miles away in other states.

These first two earnest acts are, however, over before I get there, and the third act, the decline and fall one, is well on.

The school has been acquired by the young Headmaster wearing the white wrist-band. Its name has been changed from the original Duke's School to Duke's College, its curriculum from purely preparatory to one covering everything from preparatory to matriculation. Here is finite man with his infinite desires self-trapped with an outsize project in too small a build-ing with not enough staff. Tradition goes awry. Ideals get dusty. I am to spend nearly ten years working and eating and sleeping in institutions—church school, Babylonian hotel, army officers' mess—and learn to pick up every nuance of their enclosed and feverish climate. In retrospect, the brief period at Duke's College is less grotesque than it seems at the time but it is grotesque, alive with hilarious incidents and scruffy make-shifts, littered by the squeaking victims, unfatally wounded, of petty skirmishes between Good and Evil. Let us suppose that the schoolboys pass examinations, are coached in cricket by an ex-Test cricketer, elocuted at by bishops, and that the school closes down a few years later, leaving its products peppered over the country—diplomats and dipsomaniacs, temperamental tennis professionals, barristers, sub-deans, graziers, shire engin-eers, actors, turners-and-fitters, counter-jumpers, truck-drivers, car salesmen, doctors, little-businessmen, and the operators of shady enterprises. This may all be safely supposed. What else goes on?

Since school and boarding-house are so small—the boarding-house is no more than a converted middle-class house on one floor—there are only three resident masters. One is a mathe-matics man of German heredity from one of South Australia's Teutonic and Lutheran hinterland wine-and-wheat townships. He is a natty dresser who leaves the bathroom misty with tal-cum powder, and is courting a nurse he is soon to marry. The other, with the defined eyeballs of Queen Victoria, teaches in Middle School, accompanies morning hymns on the piano, and is one afternoon arrested for errors of homosexual judgment in a public urinal. I, Senior English and French, am the too-many-parties-and-too-many-pals one. Whatever the comforts of for-getting, the certainties of remembering assure me that often, at three o'clock in the morning, there I am, after being driven home in a car with a charcoal-burning contraption it wears like a rucksack, tiptoeing in the blackout, above which search-lights creep and fumble along the sky in search of the raiders who never come, tiptoeing under the arbutus overhanging the front gate, under the almond-trees stretching over from the garden next door, with my dress-shirt crumpled and my white tie undone. There are so many sleeping bodies laid out cheek by jowl in the house that I must tiptoe until I reach my room, long, high, narrow, a sort of mortuary vault with spinach-green walls. At the bottom of the vault is the iron bedstead two inches short, a boy's bed, in its horsehair mattress the impression of a

156

curled-up boy, the one shape of countless boys now middle-aged or bones. These horsehair mattresses on which we all lie are so indestructible that it entertains to wonder how many of the names on the school's honour rolls and tarnished cricket shields and electroplated cups won on forgotten afternoons, and urns now for dried blowflies, belong to those who ground foetal hollows into the mattresses.

Resident masters and boarders, especially in a small building already saturated by emanations from other generations of confined sharers, develop an almost cave-man alliance, an alliance beyond their waking differences, when they share the same little roof and the same close walls in the ancient community of fatigue and dreams.

A solitary woman, at Duke's College, sleeps in the boarding-house with us—Matron. I recall three but think there are four Matrons who come and go in the two years. It is the sort of school, nearing the bottom of the downward slope, to which masters and Matrons only come to go. Come and go. Come and go. It is this fact, in my mostly happy memories of Duke's, that is the sour ingredient, the only congealing what should only be the nostalgic melancholy of *Alles ist weg, weg, weg* into the hard flatness of, "What else to be done but get out while the going's good."

When I first stand on the front veranda at Duke's College Boarding House—there is a brass plate stating this on the rattle-trap timber gate—the misgivings aroused by the white wrist-band and the hotel in Melbourne, despite my elation with the entrancing city I have just been driven through as through a suburb of Paradise, scratch again behind the wainscot. Their revival has something to do with the unpruned ferocity of the rose that climbs the veranda post, its chocolate-coloured thorns the size of shark-teeth, the black-red of the roses themselves, and the burnt-paper petals littering the tiles of the veranda floor—the streets have been immaculate, the entrance to this unknown cave is forebodingly untidy.

I harrow my hair neat, take off my dark spectacles, and tug at the white china bell-knob.

The Matron who opens the door wears her starched uniform with such an air of conviction, and is so recognizably no-nonsense tough, so recognizably a "lady", with a face flayed by living but also controlled by a knowledge of the done things, that the misgivings retract their minute claws.

The boys call her Slut, not because she is sluttish, but because her authority is bitchily expressed, her warmth official and switchable-on, her maternal brutality unadorned by the female silliness of mothers and dotings of aunts. She does not see, as I do, in the burnt-paper petals crowded into the veranda corners, an indication that all is not just-so elsewhere. Her competence is a wall she does not look over the top of. She performs her duties with ruthless skill, and is never in error. Now and then I am invited to drink a sherry in her quarters—a good dry sherry poured from a decanter. The decanter is Waterford, and she knows it. She talks of her friends Sir John This and Lady That but reveals no more vulnerability to their titles than a need, when in her own chintz den with her own silver-framed photographs—one of them is of her mother or sister or best friend wearing presented-at-court ostrich feathers—to do just enough name-dropping to make sure one is not left to the uncertainty of surmise. I retain an impression that she trained under someone who trained under Florence Nightingale. She has *cachet*, and adds *cachet* to the boarding-house.

She takes it with her when she goes.

Almost immediately the stuffed hawks and the unglittering geological specimens in their glass cases seem to lose, the one, tautness, the other, any reason for existing at all; there is an outbreak of measles among the boarders and, ripples from the war, the introduction of identity cards, ration books for sugar and butter and clothing, matchboxes with one striking surface instead of two, blackout curtains, air raid wardens, slit trenches, and white edgings to steps and kerbstones. Pork disappears from butchers' shops and menus.

The next Matron, an almost spherical cabbage rose of a woman with a terrified grin, curranty Welsh eyes, and Fragonard ankles, bounces ineffectually about the boarding-house for a week, has an epileptic fit in the dining-room, and goes her way.

School matrons are more often than not, even in the better Public Schools, and almost always in the minor ones, women

158

with more than a touch of the adventuress in their psyche, dominating women in a world of fenced-in males, the sort of high-priestess women who seem to be always having ritualistic baths at midnight. The epileptic Matron's successor is a dyed-in-the-wool adventuress, not of the jet-bodice sort with a mother-of-pearl-handled dagger in her garter, but a dinkum-Aussie sort, a woman of Rodinesque build who drinks, not upper-middle-class dry sherry poured from a decanter into a sherry glass, but poor-man's sweet sherry, cooking-sherry sloshed out lavishly from its flagon into a beer-tumbler with *Stolen from Mac's Hotel* engraved on it.

Not only is the war on, it is too late now for the recovery of *cachet*, and the school cannot afford to buy it. The staff is a bargain-price one.

The new Matron, with her rough-as-bags air of a sundowner, does try to resemble whatever she thinks a someone in her position should resemble. Although not a trained nursing sister, she affects an approximation of a sister's uniform, white dress, shoes, and veil. The shoes are of the cheap sort known as wedgies, and resemble whitewashed hoofs at the bottom of Matron's varicose-veined harrier's legs; the veil, ever askew and creased, is attached by too many too visible bobby-pins to hair dyed ink-black. Beneath this, between her large leatherette ears with their clip-on ear-rings of white china, is the pioneer face she has painted another one on in an old-fashioned way—triangular dabs of rouge on the cheeks powdered clown-white, dark-red lipstick drawn in a cupid's bow. Her teeth are blatantly false with vermilion gums. To match this attempt at a mask she has a special visitor's accent, a classy telephone voice, "Juke's Coll-edge heah. May-tron speaking."

Poor adventuress!

After years of it, of being a stewardess on a South American coastal steamer, of housekeeping for a bachelor near Alice Springs, of mothering Central Australian aboriginal girls with pipestem legs and flat blobs of feet, of suburban slavery with arthritic women and drooling Mongolian adolescents, she has come to relative haven in a place so down-at-heel that the fly-wire screens are as ragged as the Bayeux tapestry, an institution in which even the aim of perfection is an intention constantly postponed. Any dream she may have had of lady-like use of re-laxation is an exploded one. The boys, foxy and cruel, take every advantage of her heart and ignorance, both too large. We see her lugging the bucket that is the sick-room commode, agitating bottles of the purges her superstitions and former experiences suggest are important, compounding gargles of kerosene, binding mumps in red flannel, rubbing camphor on the chicken chests of little wheezing boys, handing out nut-megs for adolescents to nibble as a pimple-abating remedy. Disorganized, systemless, harried, she is flat-out all day, every day. Sometimes, late at night, I encounter her groping tooth-less and drunken to the lavatory she has to share with the resi-dent masters.

It seems a pity to me that she and Cook, who has her quar-ters in the back regions of the Headmaster's house slap-bang next door, do not console each other with feet-up, hair-down, woman-to-woman tippling. Cook is also a sweet-sherry-drinker who toured when young as a bathing belle in Annette Keller-man's troupe, and used to eat a banana under water in a glass tank on vaudeville stages. Cook's and Matron's here-today-gone-tomorrow lives have left them without intimates. Perhaps they do not draw together for Dr Fell reasons. I sense more in it than that. Difference in status cannot be as easily put aside by women as by men, and Bathing Belle and Tugboat Annie keep to their separate polite orbits even though each is solitary in a hive of males, of boys acting *Boys will be Boys* with hysterical and boring fervour, a shrewdish rabble with its own two-up protocol, conventional as cannibals, secretive as stool-pigeons, and as transparently meretricious as Christmas stockings.

What happens at Duke's is not, in essence, unlike what hap-pens in all boarding-schools of its design, large or small, fashion-able or shabby, social-climbing or true blue. The upholstery differs but the framework is out of stock.

The tide-wave rises and sinks punctually; terms open, terms close; lessons begin, lessons end; cricket matches are played on pitches a chain long, Latin is inexorably Latin, and "For Those in Peril on the Sea" has the same tune.

The bells ring for morning showers, for breakfast eggs in the school-crested egg-cups of hotel-ware china, for prayers, for the midday meal of burnt sausages made no more savoury by gravy and *Benedictus, benedicat,* for detention, for compline, for prep, for lights-out in dormitories. The cadets march, the Boy Scouts make clove-hitches, the cane rises and falls, the cricket pitch is rolled, the Bishop pontificates, Cook's drunk again, the scales stumble along and back along the sallow piano keys, straw boaters bring in summer and sandy bathing-trunks and grapes rotting in desks and the smoke from mosquito-repelling tablets scribbling shadows of comments on the Common Room walls, chilblains and macintoshes restore winter and mallee-root fires and stamp albums and bed-time cocoa and inclinations to be in someone else's bed with someone. It is all small-time.

Someone steals, and is found out. Someone steals, and is not found out. Russell Secundus, hope of the football team, breaks his leg. Mighall, on a midnight feast in the rafters, put his foot through the music-room ceiling. Or through *a* ceiling because, at Duke's, music-room, assembly hall and partial class-room have the one ceiling. The Headmaster, a humourless man, beneath this ceiling, after "The Old Hundredth", investigates the loss of Stow's bicycle pump. "Does anyone," he says holding on to the glazed ribbons of his gown, "know anything about Pump's stow . . . about Po's stump . . .? Does *anyone* know about . . ." He pauses to get it right. ". . . about Stump's po?" Callaghan, in an emotional dither, runs away from school—but no farther than home. Two policemen, dressed as men, come to take the homosexual master to the lock-up—but the scandal is muffled: the man with all his noisy hymn-playing might never have been heard, or heard of.

Sin is only spilt lemonade: wipe it up before anyone sees, write a hundred lines, miss an *exeat.*

The end of a year comes, and everyone goes.

Coat-hangers are everywhere with Christian names on them in a place where only surnames are used. The horsehair mattresses are rolled back on the iron beds. On the dormitory floors lie empty brilliantine bottles, ice cream spoons, fragments of balsa aeroplanes, peppermint cartons, and screwed-up mothers'-letters like bleached hearts. With symbolically silent bells, on a hanger without a name, the red and yellow costume of the jester in the school play dangles empty as though no one has ever sweated in it, postured in it, forgetting lines of words.

Duke's College dormitory—any dormitory; any dormitory—the world one sleeps in, and departs from, leaving a little litter, a place for others to clean up, a mattress for others to sleep on, and to rise from to depart.

In 1942, the year of the fall of Singapore and the Japanese bombing of Darwin, I resign from Duke's College, and move to Prince Alfred College. My reasons are uncomplicated: more money and less work in a more highly organized school, a much larger, older, and greater school, a Headmasters' Conference, *Whitaker's Almanac* school. That it is a Methodist school is, in my explorer's mood, of interest. I do not have in me the infusoria that causes the ferment of turncoatism, nor time for the game of moving myself from the Church of England square into another square marked Roman Catholic or Buddhist or free-thinker or atheist, nor do I wish to know what makes Roman Catholics, Buddhists, free-thinkers or atheists tick. I am, however, interested in hearing what can be heard of the ticking without a strained ear, and in sniffing out what is different in the anatomy of a Methodist school without going to the bother of becoming a Methodist.

I resign from Duke's also because there is no more reading in such a small book, and it is not a book to re-read without weariness and, perhaps, distress. The two years have been full ones. Apart from successfully shouldering the senior pupils—whose fathers are paying the money which provides me with a horse-hair mattress, middies of West End beer, and Argyle socks—through the portals of examinations into the hurly-burly beyond, into dad's business, back to the land, into the army, the navy or the air force, I have been busy about my own purposes. These are multi-coloured. There is dancing at the Palais de Danse, or at the two unlicensed night-clubs, The Blue Grotto and The Four Hundred Club, to which one takes one's own bottles of whisky or gin. An attempt to join the army is frustrated; I am not patched up well enough to be shot at by Germans or Japanese, so I find myself compèring marquee performances at Red Cross garden parties and, in the summer holidays, stitching wheat bags or working on the flax-fields.

Here, bent like Millet's gleaner, I bundle up the scutched and retted flax-stalks. They are spread in wandering silky stripes over the undulations of field-mouse-haunted paddocks, and I erase miles of these stripes, tying them in sheaves with acrid-smelling green hay-bands, and leaning the sheaves into stooks for tiger-snakes to hide in.

At the most private of my purposes I have been, on and off, engaged throughout the two years. When the composite consciousness of the boarding-house has wavered down and down like a lead-line, and has reached its limit, dragging uneasily in the mud of the sea-bed of sleep, I sit writing in the Masters' Common Room. By pulling down the blue enamel lightshade lined with white—it is one that is balanced over a ceiling pulley by a large porcelain egg weighted with lead-shot—I make myself a circle of radiance on the ink-stained table, and shut out the surroundings, the bookcase of ragged textbooks, the empty red ink bottles, the broken pencil-sharpening machine screwed on to the mantelpiece, the split cricket-balls in the waste-paper basket, the canes lying behind the dead potplant on the window-ledge, the megaphone in the grate, and the gowns hanging behind the door.

All these gowns, except mine, resemble old umbrellas or Tom o' Bedlam's tatters. Admittedly mine is newer than anyone's except the Junior Master's, but he has already encouraged the rag-fair effect popular among schoolmasters so that my gown, dry-cleaned to the blackness of a melodrama roué's cloak, hangs there as though ready for Mr Rochester and high drama. This Byronic touch is my affectation as the-beggars-are-coming-to-town affectation is theirs.

When, finally, I correct the galley proofs of the stories which I am having printed, the completion of the labour, *that* terminal reached, prompts me to consider making Duke's College a neck-and-neck terminal. I leave it with no more than the etoliated and fleeting sadness felt as consciously doing something for the last time.

The Headmaster and I shake hands with, on my part, sincerely dishonest firmness for, although I have got much information and joy from experiences in his school, my instinctive mistrust of him seems to have been proved. The school he presented to me in the first place was the prospectus school. I was prepared for the real one. We duel once only. He says he does not owe a month's salary I know he owes. I tackle. His face red, his eyes racing about like cockroaches, he says, "*Please*, Porter, lower your voice. Let us talk this over like gentlemen." Gentlemen! What an invitation to collusion! Lower? I raise. I pillage a large vocabulary, and enjoy some anger, a dish I do not often touch. The cheque appears. Neither of us apologizes to either. The quicksand of routine and to-morrows engulf the set-to.

Really, nothing new has been learned. He knows who he is. He is his own microscope. I know that every part of the sea is salt. I know too that truth is cubic, unmovably heavy, a mono-lith with so slippery a surface that no distinctions can be scrawled on it in the bad handwriting of those who write on walls. A year after the duel, therefore, while still obeying in-stinct with compliance and detachment, what to do but shake hands with a fraudulent candour?

Good-bye black rose, Cassandra rose, unpruned one dropping your burnt-paper petals and black hints on the doorstep.

I am driven to Prince Alfred College in a Royal-Family-black hire-car, petrol-nurtured. No charcoal-burning rucksack on *its* lacquered back. The car is provided by one of my pupils who has a hero-worshipping crush on me or is being a "bland, mysterious Oriental" affecting a crush for his own "inscrut-able" reasons.

On the day of my departure Wee Soon Wat is the nineteen-year-old Chinese son of a millionaire Singapore merchant, and precious to the father as Number One Son of Number One Wife. During the early war years many such valuable *objets d'art* are shipped over, and stored in the warehouses of Austra-lian private schools. They have come as evacuees from English schools or direct from schools or tutors in their own countries, Bali, Thailand, Burma, Cambodia, countries with Turkish-bath climates, reeking of frangipani and excrement and the wood-smoke of the tiny cooking-fires of poverty.

Wee, brazen with wealth, impervious to hint, reeks of *Soir de Paris* brilliantine and talcum powder. He and I arrive at Duke's College on the same day. His luggage of half a dozen suitcases of immaculate vulgarity, and four cabin trunks with brass-gold locks the size of alarm-clocks, makes my luggage look like a Brontë governess's carpetbag. Gold is Wee's keynote—gold-rimmed spectacles and sun-glasses, gold fountain-pen and Eversharp, gold wristwatch on band of gold, gold-stoppered crystal bottles for tooth-powder, mouth-wash, and laxative pills of Malayan manufacture, gold-backed military hairbrushes, gold stud-cases, studs, tiepins, cuff-links, cigarette-case, nail-scissors, and a number of gold-filled teeth.

At first, the seventeen-year-old Wee is the darling of school and boarding-house. He is super-exotic with his curious sandals and dragon-embroidered dressing-gowns; has an amusing accent —half-Public-School-pommy, half-fake-Yankee; has the Chinese love of displaying wealth; is handsome, and a good cricketer and swimmer. Inside two months he is reviled as the Oriental Bastard, and his special-permission jerry, hitherto respected as another addition to his charms, begins not to be under his bed at night. If it is, it contains rolled-up dead snakes, or chemicals which react noisily to urine. The masters watch with interest the god with his "weak bladder" lose worshippers one by one because it is seen to be a smug god, spoiled and arrogant, a too pi telltale, and a bore. When the Headmaster, bypassing worthier boys skilled, after years of Duke's, in its deadly and delicate laws, makes Wee a House Prefect the god is torn down for ever from the pedestal. He buys with gifts of cigarettes, model trains and chocolate frogs a handful of lip-service worshippers, younger boys hungrier than they are perceptive, or more cynical than they are dedicated to adhering strictly to mob movements. These yes-men call him Oriental Bastard only behind his back.

Wee becomes a tiresome disciple I am always having to beat off, becomes one largely because I give him some after-school English lessons. I give them reluctantly, because extra time to gambol outside in the world of balls and parties and upper-crust suppers and beaches and saloon bars is infinitely preferable to extra money. In a larger school with many English masters, some of them more than willing to mulct a wealthy father who will pay for his son's pampering, I should have turned down flat Wee's offer and the Headmaster's support of it. At Duke's, however, I am the sole and nearest thing to a pipeline between an anxious Chinese stripling and Shakespeare's obsession in *Macbeth* with time, night, and blood. I stick out enacting pipeline for a term. To save my face with myself I refuse money. To save his face Wee tempts me with gifts, *nouveau riche* gifts which I make him send back to whichever emporium they came from. The nadir is reached when Wee, having seen me idly hitting a golfball with a wood-hafted stick called a cleek on the parklands opposite the school, turns up with a vast receptacle of crimson leather, a golfbag of the sort used by Miami estate-agents in co-respondent shoes. The crimson is embellished with pockets and strappings and edgings of white leather, many chromium-plated buckles and studs, and from the well of the monster protrudes a blinding faggot of chromium-plated sticks. He is so depressed at my this-is-the-last-bloody-straw-Wee rejection of the labour-making device that I suggest a bottle of Scotch whisky and a fifty-tin of cigarettes will be an ample Collins for predigesting *Macbeth* for him. He cottons on to this. Whisky and cigarettes are presented. Wee is not Wee for nothing. Whisky and cigarettes continue to be presented. They follow me to Prince Alfred College. The manna ceases to fall only when Wee joins the Australian Army and, in spite of a knowledge of *Macbeth* and the possession of gold-backed military hairbrushes, is killed somewhere.

I am never, consequently, able to have the experience of accepting his invitation to stay at his father's mansion after the war.

When I am in Singapore years later no memory of Wee Soon Wat stirs while I am steering myself through the more citified and tourist-overrun parts, nor in Raffle's or the Cathay, not even among the glittering gimcrackery of the Chinatown market stalls but, at a Kafka hour without a number, in a stifling and stinking rookery.

I am lost but not disquieted: there is spare time for me to be lost in.

It is late enough for the brothels to be reduced to no more than a crack of pumpkin-yellow light and a yellow smell of durians; sleep has struck down the beggars lying like corpses in the storm drains. Only the pariah dogs, beaked and hollow, walk the weeds with me.

Why think of the youth inset with gold?

I see him in the chocolate-and-gold school blazer inclining his brilliantined head to sniff at the glass of supper milk, an action peculiarly alive and mind-steered and animal-human with its suggestions of pre-experience and possible aftermath. Why did he always sniff at milk as though it were a Borgia stirrup-cup? Why, when he was alive and sniffing, didn't I ask him why, instead of leaving it until a moment of resurrection when his simplicity is made a silly mystery in a tropical slum?

Why won't the dead die?

I switch the lantern-slide.

That is Wee, his old-ivory body in a skin of saltwater beads and streamings, standing in the morning sunlight at the Henley Baths. He is the newly arrived Chinese boy who has just won a long-distance swimming race, and turned fascination to idolatry. His worshippers, hoarse from barracking, surround him with the fervour of those surrounding the next man to be crucified for their pleasure. Nearby, withdrawn under their sunshades, more than luminous in the luminous shade of their sunshades, stand his elder sisters, the Misses Wee, undulant as Kwan Yins in their cheong-sams.

A pariah dog circles me, far-off, but it circles me and the ghost of Wee. Are they beggars on the bed of the storm drain, or corpses of beggars? Wee, this is the Singapore you invited me to. Where are you? You used to ask me to use the unfitting Christian name you had picked out for yourself. "Say to me Ronald," you would say. Okay! *Ronald*, where are you with the Royal-Family-black hire-car that takes me to Prince Alfred College?

As the hire-car moves up the driveway of Prince's, and draws up under the masculine branches of the Moreton Bay fig-trees opposite the school porch, the schoolmaster sitting by the ostentatiously gracious Wee is not merely the schoolmaster he thinks he is. He thinks of himself as a good disciplinarian who has learned the ropes in a large port-and-sea-side school during the worst of the Depression years, as a facts-Mr-Gradgrind teacher with a reputation for examination successes, as an

167

anodized schoolmaster who will not let ells be taken, never gives an inch, and whom no boy can faze. He is to find out that this sellable self does not travel alone, but is accompanied by a glamorously disreputable twin, an unsellable being brewed of myth and mirage.

Admittedly I dance the Conga and the Hokey-Pokey in night-clubs, get merry from drinking under-the-table whisky, arrive home just before the milk-man, have my name in the Social Jottings page often enough to make me seem to be a Cary Grant playboy squandering unearned increment, and appear at inter-collegiate sporting contests in the company of charming women, but, so far as my pupils are concerned, I should be no more than a happy hymn-singer at morning prayers, a vigilant corrector of manners at table, an energetic teacher, and a just caner.

This is far from so.

My *alter ego's* name—mine!—has already beat me to Prince's on the interlocking system of gossip which connects schools in a city of Adelaide's size. This *alter ego*, capable of gestures absolutely contrary to my just-so-far-and-no-further nature, steps from the hire-car with me, the swashbuckler who has legendarily sailed into prayers in his tails with lipstick on his dress-shirt and cocktail-shaker in hand, has taught in an Ivor Novello dressing-gown, is a womanizer, and a two-bottles-of-Scotch-a-day man. The giftie the gods have given me is to see myself as others see me—straight from *Decline and Fall*.

If I find it possible to understand how this dasher has come into being, it is impossible to understand how, years after, hard-headed and amiable hearties of middle-aged men can tell me—and sincerely believe it—that they were sitting in prayers on the mornings I made the tails-and-cocktail-shaker entrances, were present the day I punched a taxi-driver, and knew I had had a Chinese manservant.

Now, after early denials not believed, I equally submit myself to the depersonalizing and repersonalizing of me that Old Boys go through when I am trapped with them. Let them have their legends. I know the facts. I have, for instance, rarely seen a cocktail-shaker, and have never held one. If one permits others to objectify *toujours gai*-ness as a cocktail-shaker, it is one's

168

own fault if one shudders, if a goose walks over one's grave at the thought of all the dropsical evidence stacking up and stacking up while one has been circumspectly drinking lapsang-souchong in Twining's, coconut-milk in Nandi, or orange-juice for breakfast.

Any schoolmaster who takes full advantage of the portability of his qualifications to rove from school to school comes in touch with hundreds of schoolboys, most of whom are colourlessly average, extras in a crowd scene, unidentifiable faces in a group photograph. Turn one's back, and they have grown into those unplaceable men advancing on one with the robust cry of "Sir! I'd have known you anywhere."

I know, now, the grisly drill to be gone through, the handpumpings, the exchange of unshared memories of the Old School, the revelations of man-in-the-street careers long ago foretold by forty-seven per cent for a paraphrase of "Childe Roland" and the depersonalizing-and-repersonalizing of Headmaster and masters and myself so that there is the impression of being in a Pirandello play, of having been badly impersonated years ago. Not knowing what to say to these mediocre men invoking their mediocre boyhoods forces one into faking a killing bonhomie, for there is an unwritten law that schoolmasters be interested in the adult hibernating in the yahoo whose acne flamed like a spray of Cartier rubies all the time *A Passage to India* was being cooked into examination-passing gobbets.

During the years I spend there teaching Senior English and French, and Middle School Art and Economic History, Prince Alfred College is in charge of J. F. Ward. He is the only Head, apart from my first one, P. J. Green, I have been able wholeheartedly to respect, able to call sir without regretting the politeness of conforming to custom. Other Heads I later work under haven't the ichor in their veins which transforms a mere man or a brilliant man into a flawless Headmaster. I avoid, as much as possible, calling any of them sir. All the ingredients of this ichor I do not know but am aware that the receipt includes absolute clarity of mind, diplomacy, fearlessness, instinct without blinkers, and a species of clairvoyance that does away with the need for suspicion, snoopery, accusation, or even enquiry.

A good Headmaster knows the names of every boy and the

169

exact proportion of sin and virtue in every boy, knows which maid is up-the-duff, which member of the school board has to be directed away from an eccentric idealism or a romantic materialism, which window is broken, and which groundsman is malingering. J. F. Ward's kingdom has many subjects and, at first, I am so impressed by his handling of each and every one of them that, for a while, I have the suspicion that my admiration for him is relative, that he is not great, merely better than the Headmaster I have left in the house with the unweeded garden, the desperate rose, the rusted chip-heater in the bathroom, the triangular skeleton of a corner wardrobe in my bedroom, the rain-gutters blocked with tennis balls, and the Common Room with the linoleum so worn that the ridges of the floorboards are defined. My early self-suspicion passes. I perceive that J. F. Ward is a great Headmaster.

The main school buildings of Prince Alfred College, the original structure, set in playing-fields and elderly trees, is E-shaped, towered and turreted, lofty college-Jacobean with arcaded verandas, and a basement warren of kitchen, pantries, sculleries, dining-hall, store-rooms, infirmary, sewing-room, laundries, changing-rooms, and the apartments of Matron, the tuckshop woman, and the housekeeper. The whole structure is so disposed that, in a wavering light, and when the seagulls are rising and falling over the playing-fields as though they have been put in a disarray by a vast ladle stirring the air, it seems a square-rigger furrowing the present with its freight of futures.

The servants of these futures, from octogenarian Board member to the latest wartime maid with a Veronica Lake coiffure and Fu Manchu fingernails, make a large crew which the Headmaster captains with imperturbable genius, despite the fact that the school is filleted of backstops. Younger masters are at the Front. So are those senior boys who should have been being rowing or tennis heroes, school- or house-prefects. Youngsters not yet jelled are being pseudo-seniors. Stopgap masters with a taste for wardrobe drinking, pubescent boys, or the maids, come in one door and go out the next. The well-trained maids who are now in the army, navy, and air force have been replaced many times by mock-maids, country sluts from the hinterland after an easy job in the city so that they are available to the American soldiers whose talkie accents and prison haircuts—which everyone is soon calling crew-cuts—are being heard and seen everywhere in Adelaide.

The inconveniences caused by the passing endless belt of unsatisfactory basement and teaching staff try-outs are made more inconvenient by a large increase of boarders, boys whose fathers are away at the war, and whose mothers are munition-factory workers or otherwise war-efforting. Above all, the sandbagged lower regions of the school have to be in perpetual readiness as a casualty station. Elsewhere in the school grounds and buildings the customs of the time are adhered to—slit trenches, shovels, buckets of sand, windows criss-crossed with strips of white paper, extra fire-extinguishers, blackout blinds, and, on stair-landings and in corridors and dormitories, light bulbs painted blue and enclosed in shades like narrow black megaphones which, for some undiscoverable reason, are ringed at the bottom edge with punched holes. There are fake air raids. The sirens go, and the boys crouch under desks. At least, that is all I recall. Gas-masks? I forget. The only personal amulet against dropped bombs I remember as having a vogue is a cork on which are tied by string two pellets of cotton-wool; the cork to be gripped between the teeth, the pellets to be plugged in the earholes. Prone in a gutter is, I think, the recommended position while wearing the device. Air raid shelters? There are massive concrete drainpipes with wooden benches inside disposed here and there throughout the city.

During the brown-out and the beer shortage the wireless plays many yearning English tunes of the "When the Lights Go on Again" pattern, and saucier ones like "I'm Gonna Get Lit-up When the Lights Go on in London", but "Run, Rabbit, Run" is the song the school takes up and becomes addicted to for weeks. Indeed, this song and the knitting of balaclavas, along with paying to smash Japanese crockery at fund-raising fairs, are the only wartime enthusiasms I recall the boys having.

The balaclava-knitting enthusiasm is inspired less by an anguish over the freezing ears of warrior fathers and uncles and brothers overseas than by the shrewdness of the Comforts' Fund organization in their choice of an agent, a young woman in uniform who has all the aplomb of a musical comedy star. From the dais in School Hall she makes it seductively beyond doubt that to knit balaclavas or scarves for the brave ones fighting in dangerous zones is not only a duty. It is manly. She makes *manly* sound like *male* or *Clark Gable*. The King is not ashamed to knit. She clinches the matter by promising to hold several classes in knitting for those boys manly enough to want to learn the art, the War Effort manly art. Since she has a tip-tilted nose, very blond curls bubbling out from under her cap, and legs like Betty Grable, the classes are large despite the fact that the Head points out that those—er—manly enough to take up the task will not be permitted to let waning of interest be an excuse for unfinished business. Soon, it no longer strikes me as incredible to hear myself, when on prep-duty, being importuned by the grumble-and-squeak voice of a fifteen-year-old high-jump champion, "Sir, may I get on with my knitting, please? I've finished my work." Nor does the sight of boys stabbing away like Madame Defarge at swabs of knitting as they lean over the first floor veranda-rail looking into the lucent purple labyrinths of the jacaranda outside the ground-floor infirmary. Nor do I do anything but wait as though it were conventional schoolboy behaviour, my hand patient and unsurprised on the dormitory light-switch, while a six-foot, thirteen-stone, eighteen-year-old football captain sits bolt upright in bed chattering, "Sorry, sir, sorry. Half-a-mo', sir, if thou wouldst. Just this row to finish . . . I'm hurrying, sir . . . really . . . hell! Dropped a stitch . . . sorry, sir, sorry."

Prince Alfred College is too deeply rooted and thick-set a growth to lose more than a leaf or two in the diminished winds that reach it from the war. The clock ticks, the timetable is carried out, the bell rings, the tuckshop opens, the library closes, the vaulting-horses are left to graze on the tan-bark of the gymnasium floor, the trapezes give a last quiver, and relax until next time.

Nothing can halt the calendar.

All that has happened before and before, happens again and again. Showers every morning, church every Sunday morning, boredom and billiards and Chinese checkers every Sunday afternoon, high tea every Sunday evening. Easter, end-of-term theatrical performances, annual sports meeting, annual boat race, annual tennis tournament, annual prize-giving. The wandering segment of the staff wanders to the appointed place at the appointed hour on the appointed day—school barber, cricket coach, tennis coach, music master, singing master, gymnasium trainer, rowing coach. The cook boils four hundred eggs. The school carpenter mends the billiard table. The sewing mistress patches sheets. The housekeeper opens the store cupboard, and the odd-job man gets out two four-gallon tins of apricot-and-pineapple jam. The infirmary Sister gives the sick boy his barley water. The groundsman, and the groundsman's nag with an old school boater on its head, roll the grass at the practice nets. Matron and the tuckshop woman, off duty, sup on crayfish sandwiches and ale, and listen to a rebroadcast of a Winston Churchill speech.

Matron is English, from Bath, the tuckshop woman is Scots. World-wanderers both, hard workers and perk-collectors, they too have the flashing eye of the adventuress. As establishment adventuresses, professional and respected, they have tongues of contempt and arsenic for the maids, amateur adventuresses with the sexual morals of rabbits.

I? I teach again as I taught before. Skelton or T. S. Eliot, Tennyson or Gerard Manley Hopkins, *Hamlet* or *Pygmalion*, Rémy de Gourmont or Alphonse Daudet, this year's crop of adolescents or that year's, the forced-feeding of fact and the jabs with the hypodermic of objectivity are the same. Exams are passed. I take my cheques from the bursar with no twinge of conscience. The Old Boys, the *nouveau riche*, the wheat farmers, the social climbers, the ambitious storekeeper, the clergyman on cut rates, the airman bombing Berlin, the head waiter well-heeled from tips, the orange-growers and minor squatters and country-town businessmen, the dead-centre middle class, the fathers of my pupils, all get their money's worth.

I produce *Lady Precious Stream* with the School Captain in the title role, and *Peter Pan* with a Dutch consul's son palpitating in mid-air on the carpenter's contraption of wires and pulleys. *Lady Precious Stream* is very good. *Peter Pan* comes apart at the seams. The proceeds go to the Red Cross.

By the end of 1945 with, apparently, blue-birds over the

173

white cliffs of Dover, and Jimmy asleep in his own little room again, I leave Prince's for the next caravanserai, in my luggage the dazzling reference I seem to have earned. Coming from J. F. Ward, chairman of the Australian branch of the Headmasters' Conference Schools, it is an open-sesame document.

Outside routine, and four o'clock, and the ten-foot fence of cast-iron spears that rings in the school, I carry on much as I always have. The settings differ, the people differ, the beer has a different flavour and the hotels a more solid elegance. I am older and more innocent. New beliefs are superimposed on me like layers of paint, but the layers do not run together or mix, and earlier layers are not effaced. As within me, so outside me. I continue to live a mosaic life.

I've no illusions about the quality of my intelligence. I have only enough to be anti-intellectual, anti-academic, and much more than wary of Culture and its fringe activities such as Adult Education, Summer Schools, Discussion Groups, and Critical Seminars. It is odd, therefore, looking back, to observe myself in a kind of ragged maypole dance with Adelaide intellectuals, culture-cranks, and academics. As though paddling at the edge of the strange lake at the Café Petrushka hasn't been enough paddling in silly water to last me until death knocks me off!

I find, by searching the shelves of memory, that this introduction to the cultural life of a provincial city is the work of a Prince's master. Call him A. A. is directing an Australian play called *Daybreak* for the Adelaide University's Theatre Guild in their homely little theatre, The Hut. Knowing that, as an all-too-cocksure yokel youth, I have acted for Gregan McMahon, a famous Australian director-producer, A. begins to twist my arm. Years before, I have found out that no amount of theatrical training could produce a Hal Porter to out-Irving Irving. Nevertheless, the arm-twisting works. Behold me then, my cloak on the noble swirl, playing a do-gooder young Oxford man with a Be-Kind-to-Convicts kink who makes more trouble for the already troubled Barretts-of-Wimpole-Street household the play is about.

Once idly involved I remain idly involved, undedicated and un-intense, a year or so after A.'s services to Prince's have been terminated, and he has somehow—without the priority voucher at that time required—crossed the border of South Australia to become, first, a waiter in a Chinese restaurant and, later, a reputable bigwig in the Australian Broadcasting Commission. A. is himself an intellectual, author of one novel and some esoterically cerebral poems, a student of the Royal Academy of Dramatic Art, addicted to verbal fantasy and the intellectual's tipple—claret. He is a vastly entertaining boon-companion of the eccentric kind. As a schoolmaster incapable of keeping swine quiet enough to hear the pearls drop, he is hopeless, and his dismissal foreseeable.

High above the workaday noises of Prince's—pigeons among the chimneys, gulls on the playing-fields, lawn-mowers, cutlery rattling in the dining-room, the gym-teacher's barkings, the housekeeper being imperious with the greengrocer—rises the din of Fourth Formers apparently holding the Rites of Spring and, soaring well above that, A.'s Shakespearian-soliloquy denunciations of the heedless revellers, "You blocks! You stones! You worse than senseless things! You drippings from the gibbets! Cretins! Dregs!" His rantings at the Fourth Form are a strictly pentametric patchwork of A. and Shakespeare. I have to send after him A.'s Shakespeare folios in suitcases of dirty singlets, toeless socks, and claret-mottled flannels, to be picked up at an over-the-border railway station because, rather than live out his term's notice, he leaves unceremoniously and instantly on receiving it. How he crosses the wartime borders I cannot imagine.

I appear at intervals at The Hut in such diverse cultural offerings as *Medea*, *The Petrified Forest*, and *They Came to a City*.

Once landed on even the outermost guy-lines of the sticky web of culture-addiction it takes a little while to disentangle one's feet without absolute uncouthness. Entangled, I look around a little at what offers in Adelaide, backing slyly away by centimetres behind what seems to be an interested advance. As a youth I have been unable to give allegiance to the Melbourne cognoscenti, the Bread and Cheese Club, Louis Lavater, R. H. Croll, Furnley Maurice, and J. S. Macdonald. A few years later I find it even less possible to liaise with the International

Brigade fans and the let's-all-pretend-we're-agonized-proles writers clustered around the Café Petrushka, and the New Theatre with its productions of Clifford Odets's and Sean O'Casey's plays, and of group-written dramas about entombed coalminers and canaries. I am equally unable to understand either the aims or the products of Adelaide's three literary-cultural septs whose three high priests, each powerful enough to their satellites, I have ships-that-pass encounters with.

Max Harris, an Adelaide University undergraduate, slender and handsome as Flecker's Hassan or a Syrian sweetmeats-vendor, is editor of *Angry Penguins*, a lush magazine by war-time standards, and *avant-garde*. My limited education, and the fact that I've not yet caught up with all the great *arrière-garde* writers and painters who might have given me pointers, leave me flummoxed. Harris does use one of my already published short stories in *Angry Penguins*—no cheque!—and, apart from its cheapness, I don't understand why. No one could be less *avant-garde* than I.

I blunder through this group quickly, and just as quickly through the Jindyworobak group of poets. Indeed, several meetings with Rex Ingamells, the Jindyworobak high priest, are so upsetting to my old-fashioned notion of the nature of poets that it is difficult to believe the evidence of my senses. It is not his appearance, nor his public behaviour. I no longer expect poets to look like Rupert Brooke facially, be like Byron morally, or to be romantic gadabouts like Robert Louis Stevenson. However, drinking porter-gaffs with Ingamells and his rolled umbrella in the Red Lion, I find I am not drinking merely with a pleasant high-school teacher but with a quiet fanatic intent on making aborigines fashionable, and on screening poetry submitted to him, not as a check on its poetic content but on its content of Australian images and words—Australian meaning, mostly cobberistic or aboriginal. Since each editor is entitled to kill his fleas in his own way there is nothing to say into my drink except, "What an *aw*fully interesting idea—like a cookery competition with everyone using the same recipe." What startles me is the information that he spends from his own high-school earnings to assist the publication of other poets' works. When he tells me this I know that I have been drinking with a unique man. Altruism so lofty transforms him before my eyes into someone as untouchable as Jesus. It is only disciples or opportunity-takers who can touch lips to the hems of such shining robes. I am too selfish to be a disciple, too much a fatalistic opportunity-disdainer to get my cut from the largess of noble zealots.

I don't know, anyway, if poems or aborigines are worth it.

Harris and Ingamells are casual acquaintances of mine. The third high priest, Charles Jury, is a close one. I meet him on the night he returns to Adelaide after many years overseas, and a long Norman Douglas kind of life in Greece or on a Greek island. He is dapper and world-stained, affects shyness, and his shape intends being plumper. He has returned to be, I think, a professor in some section of the Adelaide University subsidized by Jury money.

His acolytes differ noticeably from those in *Angry Penguins* and Jindyworobak circles where the bunch is a mixed one. Jury's offsiders—at least those of them I meet—are not all as wealthy, academically geared, and as socially eligible as Jury, but each has at least one of the qualifications. Just about this time it is becoming clear to me that the caste system works as efficiently and with as unsparing a delicacy in the literary world as it does in the underworld, the bed-sitter world, the working-class suburb, the church, the army barracks, and the slum. Perhaps it does too in the prison and the lunatic asylum. I do not hop on his cultural roundabout or infest his conversaziones, and must take for granted that his published works have the value they are said to have. My knowledge of Greek stops at *gnothi seauton*, and the sort of quoter's Greek found in the Foreign Phrases section in old-time dictionaries, the *Everything passes, nothing remains* sort that has the resonance of a jam-tin in translation. Greek-less, I am unable to confirm how Simon Pure the Greekery of his elegies and lyrics and verse-dramas. His Lord Leighton and boys-upon-a-frieze-of-marble-drawn approaches to his compositions stir me as little as the careful passions of his blank verse. As writer and high priest he is not my cup of tea.

As grog-crony? Another kettle of fish altogether.

Satire is an anti-toxin against the disease of taking the world seriously, and he is satirical, a sly mocker with the air of a once-beautiful but now broken-down faun. He and I, sometimes accompanied by his swanky sister Elizabeth, and a sturdy, well-heeled spinster called Lucy Lockett, enjoy many claret-coloured after-hours symposiums at the Botanic Hotel while outside the searchlights probe the chinchilla clouds with tender precision. Of all these nights of laughter and chatter, scarcely a syllable remains. I have even forgotten the long intricate risqué stories of which he was a masterly raconteur, and which I filch from him, and dine out on when I later go through a now inexplicable period of dining out on dirty yarns. In deciding one day—click!—to give up this borrowed skill I use my mental windscreen-wiper so efficiently that not only does it erase the yarns and the ability to tell them but all the best of Charles Jury's Whistlerian remarks.

Adelaide, a squarish city, is surrounded on all sides by wide parklands. Prince Alfred College is on the outside rim of the eastern parkland, and overlooks it. From my tower room, there is a view over the playing-fields and school trees, and across the tops of the parkland trees to the late-Victorian skyline of the city—spires and clock-towers, domes and mansard roofs, stucco krateres and insurance-building groups of statuary, chimneys and flagpoles and wireless aerials. Four o'clock and, unless I am on the prep duty which turns up every few weeks, the day's work over, I walk through the parkland, following the winding and undulant path between the eucalypts, olives, pines, elms and oaks that brings me out on to East Terrace. On the corner of East Terrace and North Terrace is the Botanic Hotel. From the hotel's first-floor veranda can be seen, opposite, the Botanic Gardens and, west of it, the hospital, the university, museum, art gallery, public library, Government House and, farthest off, Parliament House and the railway station.

The Botanic Hotel is run by the famous Underdown family from Alice Springs, serves well-cooked unsubtle meals, has a good wine-cellar, and an Edwardian saloon bar whose head barman, Paul, has the accent and manner of a stage butler. In the saloon bar I am taken up by a group of happy-go-lucky resident doctors from the hospital. They are a particularly close-knit group, nearly all old boys of the Church of England St

Peter's College, one of Australia's most lavishly endowed and tranquilly snobbish Public Schools. The old-school-tie alliance has been strengthened by their living in each other's pockets at the hospital, and by a mutual enthusiasm for, among other things, interstate air hostesses, drinking, parties, and motor-cycles. Individually, of course, they have other enthusiasms—Beethoven, speed-cars, racehorses, contract bridge, even the new-fangled existentialist writers—but the common-factor ones give the group its quasi-Regency-buck coherence. My acceptance by the pack—a foreigner several years older, and an unwealthy schoolmaster—mystifies me a little to this day; but it solidifies Adelaide for me, provides me with friends outside the package-deal, no-choice kind that go with Culture or Prince Alfred College, and continues the old-gang-of-mine, pumpkin-patch drinking pattern begun in Bairnsdale.

It is with and from these gay young men with their ears to the ground I increase my vocabulary by such new expressions as blitz, prang, euphoria, geiger, Nissen hut, trainee, maquis, technicolor, spiv, I couldn't care less, oomph, Fifth Column, goodbye-now, hair-do, Quisling, reportage, flak, gremlin, and expendable. War is a virile sire.

They also teach me to lose a fear of crossing roads inherited from the accident. It is not a fear of being killed so much as a fear of not being killed but mangled, and thus made dependent on others for the dropped fountain-pen, the emptying of the bladder, the cutting of toenails, the goblet of water. They teach me by intentionally taking me as a pillion-rider on their hell-for-leather drives through the night. Why I should regain confidence in crossing roads because I have been passenger on death-courting open-throttle jaunts with half-tipsy motor-cyclists is an operation of psychological chemistry beyond my ability to analyse, although it is curious that I still have a flicker of traffic fear in staid cities such as Turin and Zürich, and none at all in the heart of Paris or Milan.

For the rest, my friendship with them allows me to add something to my knowledge of hospitals. I have seen my mother die in a private one, have seen what goes on behind the scenes at the Framlingham sisters' private one, and have played the part of insufferable patient in a public Roman Catholic hospital.

What happens in the residential quarters of a large public hospital surprises me, then. The surprise is less than it would have been if I had not got inklings, as resident master at Duke's and Prince's, of the fermentation that takes place in the atmosphere when a group of males live together, the gradual accumulation of many particles of unreleased primitive feeling and sensory irritation. In a school boarding-house a spontaneous combustion of these emotions results in little more than the dormitory raid, the pillow-fight, or the midnight feast. In an officers' mess, inhabited by men who have had an intimacy with death, the periodical ceremonies during which the atavastic boil is lanced toy with death—four years after I leave Adelaide, and am member of an officers' mess in Japan, I witness blood-chilling games with bayonets, for example, in which mutilation and death at the bar counter are missed by millimetres.

Worldly men, accustomed to lies, do not try to understand the spoken words but try to catch the meaning behind them. Civilized young men, herded together, accustomed to the formulae of social exchange, try to investigate the inner ape, the animal recklessness and primal madness that are under hatches by day. Each, egging himself on, eggs on the other. The pillow-fight takes wilder forms.

In the wartime nineteen-forties my medical friends, the more reckless of them, relieve their confined spirits by periodical eruptions of some showiness. The resident doctor's bathroom is large. By plugging the door with towels, and leaving all the taps running full pelt, it is possible to make the room into a swimming pool. It is less possible for the swimmers to be patient enough to wait for the pool to disappear down the plug-holes. When the door is unplugged and opened the water sweeps along the corridor and down the stairway, fortunately both of concrete. It is along these same third-floor corridors that motorbikes, brought up in the lift, are ridden.

Boys and breaking bounds, resident doctors and motor-bikes on the third floor, are the same, the game of defiance without danger, of relief without blood-letting, of throwing a bun to the leg-roped primitive man. Even the mixed parties occasionally given in this all-male zone, in which each man knows exactly how good or bad with a scalpel his next-room neighbour is, have something of the air of Ladies' Night at the Corroboree.

For the Guy Fawkes party in 1945 I arrive late. The men who were doubtless smooth and perfect little gentlemen three hours before, and will be so again, are at the stage of giving the community male his run—dropping beer-bottles competitively down the lift-well, throwing lighted fireworks through transom-windows into rooms of squealing good-time girls, riding motor-bikes in the corridor, setting off huge rockets from the balcony to soar over the city. I suppose men have to prove something to men beyond what they prove to themselves by being good at their jobs, or by being husbands. A man cannot without danger be a silly fool as a doctor (or architect or plumber's mate or dog-catcher), or as a husband. He can have the relief and pleasure of being a silly fool with other men who are having the relief and pleasure of being a silly fool with him.

Japan is defeated and occupied. One by one my hospital friends go there as army doctors. By the end of 1945 I am without a pack to travel with. Foreseeing this, before the end of 1945, I have applied for a position as Senior English Master at Hutchins School in Hobart, Tasmania. This is not solely because my friends have gone, taking with them their whims-and-whams, their clan jokes and wisecracks, their neuroses and their zest for frivolity, leaving to a new batch of resident doctors their rooms decorated with Petty girls and wine-labels, rooms where I listened to Beethoven records or "I'm Dancing with Tears in My Eyes", or talked and laughed the night away. There is also the itch to move on.

The writer, having picked up all the copy he can in Adelaide, prods me. Emotionally, I am more deeply entangled with the place than I think. Self-renunciation is, nevertheless, required. Fortunately self-renunciation is not a wholesale suppression of desires and passions, it is more a willingness to be reduced to those elements which allow one to obey instinct with detachment, and without a quibble. Having, as ever, made a snip-snap decision to move on, I find that detachment is rather a weight-lifting solo that prolongs itself, for the Hobart job does not begin until February 1946. It is less difficult to leave a well-run school and a familiar and friendly staff than it is to leave J. F.

181

Ward, for whom my deep admiration is grained with a deep affection.

This affection begins early. At first it is little more than gratitude for his understanding of my divorce, which is in the air at the time I answer his advertisement for a new master. At the interview I answer his questions with absolute truth. Coloured truths have become as boring to me as white lies, and I am at the stage of trying to remember always to eschew them. I do not always remember because I used to be a free-wheeling teller of lies not only when it seemed necessary but also, for no reason at all, when it amused me to exercise myself in lie-sculpture. My treatment of Mrs Tretheway on Strzelecki Ridge revealed to me that lies to others are lies to oneself. To attack her for reading my letters was a lie because I didn't care if she read them. Cruelty to her was a cruelty to the better part of myself.

Apart from this pernickety attention to integrity, *so* self-satisfying, I am, as I sit facing J. F. Ward at the interview, most interested in finding out how he acts—and how a Methodist organization acts—if I don't keep my mouth shut. This I can do because Olivia has promised a noiseless divorce. I can answer his, "Married, Porter?" by a postdated lie of "No, sir," but, outside my Truthful Willie intentions and my curiosity about reactions, above all, I know he is too valuable and too wise a man to lie to. Ultimately, one only tells lies to people one can't respect or like.

J. F. Ward's nickname with staff and schoolboys is Boxer. His son John's nickname for him is Rex. I learn this because John, an intelligent and harum-scarum senior who shares a dormitory-study called the Dog Box with another senior, is a talkative youth, and the Dog Box is next to my tower room.

Rex, whatever the son intends, is a fitting nickname for the Head who is in appearance and manner kingly. Over six feet tall, ramrod straight, deliberate of movement and gesture, dressed without either foppishness or dandruff-on-the-collar mustiness, he has white hair clipped like a neat boy's, and a face unmarked by the spoor of minor disturbances, a controlled rather than a bland face. The *noli me tangere* aura of this impressive whole is added to by his gold-rimmed spectacles;

the lenses seem always to reflect a great light, and lend him the all-seeing and luminous gaze of Zeus.

"Married, Porter?"

Here goes.

Olivia is divorcing me for desertion. My fault, I say, for not imploring her to join me. Yet, since she has made no move to join me, I have consented to the divorce only if I haven't a cent to pay, and if it is a quiet one.

"Like a quiet thrashing?" says the Headmaster, and the corner of his mouth winces.

Next, hitting the nail on the head: "Why shouldn't the divorce be quiet?"

Here goes again.

This time the Head's office, with everything exactly in its right place, at the right angle, everything dustless and polished, is filled with people exuding a stronger scent of Laife than Olivia or I, deadpan and checkmate, exudes. I explain that Olivia's actress sister has just admitted, unhesitatingly, and with all the silver trumpets blowing, to being the mistress of a Sydney biscuit-tycoon playboy in the brilliantly illuminated action for divorce brought by the tycoon's wife. This would be neither here nor there, despite the newspaper reports, if it were not that, still emitting rays of glamorous scandal, she is advancing on Adelaide to act in a season of marcasite-studded plays— *Reunion in Vienna, The Man Who Came to Dinner*, that sort of thing.

"And you think," says the Headmaster, "that your coming divorce may therefore be not as quiet . . ." The corner of his mouth winces again. ". . . as quiet a thrashing as you'd hoped?"

Thrashing! I sense that he regards the divorce as no more than sharp punishment for foolish behaviour, for the stupidity of marrying in haste.

"It's just, sir, that I shouldn't like reflected notoriety to affect my chances here."

"It won't. A last question, Porter. What are your views on corporal punishment?"

I tell him. When I have finished, "Come with me," he says.

He guide-tours me through the boarding-house, downstairs first. Then, by the stairway outside the almost subterranean dining-room hung with Julian Ashton paintings, we climb up and up through the dormitory wings until we reach the tower room. I sense that the job is mine, but not until he says, "This used to be my eldest son Russel's room. I think you'll find it a very pleasant one", do I know for sure.

It is naïve of me to be grateful for his unperturbed acceptance of the coming divorce, but I cannot not be grateful. What I have not needed to tell him on that first day is that there should never have been a divorce for I should never have married. Love, mere common-or-garden love, is no excuse. Not for me.

I don't know when I begin to sense an uneasiness that husbandship, however deep my love for Olivia, is wrong, a lie, a danger. I do remember clearly exactly when the uneasiness, the mercury far down in the bulb, suddenly runs to the top of the tube, marking off a temperature against which is printed Danger.

I am in the Melbourne Public Library. I have been there for hours; page after page of my notebook has been filled with sentences about assassins and their victims. The little green-shaded desk-lamp, the fountain-pen ink on the writer's corn of the middle finger, the great domed roof of glass turned down over me like a bowl, all have become hateful—I see they are hateful when, the last sentence for that evening written, my attention turns from the hours of labour back to myself.

Why am I here? Why *really*?

I don't want to be here taking notes on these sorts of dead people. The writer doesn't want to write half-hour plays to advertise a tinned soup he wouldn't buy even if he were poorer than he is. Why are the writer and I sitting like a fly under the upended glass bowl? Because the husband says so. What makes a husband? A wife. At that moment, in that place, that evening in August 1939, the mercury leaves the bulb, and goes up like a lift to mark an unsuitable temperature, one that I cannot live in. I want to be a wild dog. To hell with twin kennels, the bitch, the chain, the puppies to be de-wormed and paraded.

Not knowing myself as well, then, as I do a few months later, it seems to me that when the mercury goes down, and with it my apparently momentary treachery to Olivia, the going-up has been just one of those things, fatigue, over-concentration, a slipped mental disc. Let's pretend nothing happened. The wild dog, notebook in trench-coat pocket, inky finger concealed in glove, hurries out of the library to meet Olivia. The mercury is never allowed wittingly to rise again. Even when the decision is made, while in St Vincent's, to give up the idea of writing for money, it is not made as a gesture against earning cash to keep a wife, merely against writing for money. To this day I rarely write for money. I take money for what I have written. To me the difference remains important. I shall never be a best-selling author with my own study and desk but can write what I want to.

If the mercury is never allowed to rise again, it rises of its own accord, slowly, slowly, slowly. Useless to pretend that, by willing myself not to allow the mercury, the thought of wild-dog freedom, to rise, it will not rise. It has started to rise when, distressed at leaving Olivia exhausted after months of playing the ministering angel without dropping a stitch, I watch her standing with her three sisters on Spencer Street station, watch until they are out of sight, and find that the distress is not lessened. However, lichen on a rock, there appear the first tiny colourings of relief. I get into pyjamas, dressing-gown, and slippers, share the bottle of Scotch my wife has given me with two air force men, bask bounderishly in the fact that they have seen the bobby-dazzler women farewelling me, clean my teeth, climb into the Mohammed's coffin, and sleep blind as the train bears me towards the sunrise on the hills over the border.

Meantime the mercury rises, and the lichen spreads.

All very well for me to write love letters in the same cramped Common Room at Duke's, and on the same inky table under the blue enamel shade where I write the short stories.

The love letters seem true, as my love seems true.

What is true is what is not in the love letters.

We exchange facts about people and events outside ourselves. We exchange what we think is love, and what we continue to call love, in bouquets of words. At first, like the bouquets of words picked to pieces in divorce courts and murder trials, these are of blossoms torn wildly from the plant, full-blown and bud, dewdrops and bees and leaves with caterpillar-holes punched in them—at first.

The day comes when the bouquets have dwindled small, sprucer, almost as scentless and artificial as the posies held by ringleted and long-dead women standing stock-still before a canvas landscape to stare at a shape hunched beneath a photographer's black cloak, a shape that sees beauty upside-down, and removes colour and dimension from it, and reduces it to the size of a playing-card. I am no longer sending artless sheaves of flowers to a Venus with entrails who drinks riesling and has fifty pairs of shoes, but tastefully small wreaths, perfectly circular, with the *I love you* on the black-edged card as dodgily written as a blackmail note, not a blot, not a misspelling, not an erasure.

It is in what both Olivia and I do not write, in emptinesses volted with, on my side, the discharge from a desire for franchise stronger than my desire for Olivia and, on her side, the emanations from a patience wearing thin, that an invisible code like a disembodied pain electrically traverses the distance between us of miles, days, weeks, months, a year, another year.

We know each other too well not to know that, having got what we want from each other there is nothing more that we want to get from each other.

Pickled in the brine of absence, my need for wild-dog liberty thickens to a cunning stubbornness to have it, without making a move, even if I already seem to have it; Olivia's need for a man to look after her when she plays the role of being a woman, and a man to accept her overpowering gifts of loyalty, sweetness, serenity and ingenuity when she is being a human being, thickens to ruthlessness.

Love is love, let's get divorced: thus Olivia.

The news of her decision is given me by the lawyer father of one of my doctor friends. I say, "Let the woman do what she wants to do." Whatever I think might happen does not. Nobody official and anonymous sends me a pasteboard ticket-of-leave or a gilty diploma to tell me that she and I are legally sundered and that I can now bay the over-bayed moon and bite the bitten sheep. I first know we are divorced when I hear from the housekeeper at Princes that Olivia has married a South Australian wheat or sheep farmer.

Ah well, I have written to her that South Australia is an enchanting place, although I mean the most southerly parts, and Adelaide itself with its gulf-side suburbs, its Henleys and Brightons and Glenelgs reproducing along the rim of more-than-Mediterranean beaches, and under East-of-Suez sunsets, the engaging amenities of early-twentieth-century seaside resorts—the jetties with aquariums on, the tea-rooms, the weighing-machines and chocolate-machines, the sea-front boarding-houses, the tamarisks, the merry-go-round all looking-glasses and barley-sugar columns of brass, the cast-iron drinking-fountains with their dolphins and scallop shells, and the *chinoiserie* bandstands. For me this cross between the Côte d'Azur and Southend (not that I have seen either in the nineteen-forties) *is* enchanting. Urban, suburban, the wine-growing valleys, the mansions and stone villages in the hills near Adelaide, these I know.

Inland and outback is the South Australia I know nothing about except from what is experienced during a never-again holiday on a sheep property where, restricted by the infinity of a white sky, and encircled by the limitlessness beyond a white horizon, I am glad for the walls and ceiling, the ante-rooms and galleries of night to be run up quickly after sunset, for this hideous form of wealth to be hidden.

Day has no ceiling, no walls. One inhabits an eternity populated by sheep and foxes where black geysers of crows explode out of the floors of dust, and anatomies of windmills shiver in the heat. What appals me most about much of inland Australia is its lack of consequence to all except its victims. Even victims, however, have tethers to come to the end of.

If one has put one's stakes on, say, the flesh, and has gambled long and, inevitably, has finally lost, there is nothing in the landscape to free anyone, except the semi-crazed, from humanity and oneself. It is a country without consolations, and without a message.

Adelaide for me, rather than this. Rather than this publicity on a dusty shelf, the privacy of the city. Not the city for all that is there in the way of culture, philosophy, what is in vogue aesthetically—that is a barren and inorganic reality, a bucket of bones—but for the reality of late summer and early autumn when Adelaide, more than any place on earth, and as simply as pouring tea from a pot, pours from a lavish cornucopia into gardens and parks and markets and arcade stalls a cascade of carnations and grapes and melons, guavas and Michaelmas daisies and tomatoes, zinnias and belladonna lilies and tuberoses, lavender and quinces and cumquats and pomegranates, roses and roses and roses. This natural opulence is somehow middle class, like a Mrs Beeton dinner-party table, like the perfectly pitched vulgarity and comfort of the houses with their cellars, thick stone walls and deep porches, like the gloves and hats of the women, the self-sufficient statues in the squares, and the wedding-cake façades of the public buildings.

Looking back, I find that, as much as my life there is a mosaic one, it is a middle-class and upper-middle-class mosaic. This is purely a matter of circumstance, and the limitation gives me more chance to observe the fine distinctions of caste behaviour and class neuroses, not apparent to non-Australians, which exist in Adelaide, differ somewhat from those in Melbourne and, I am to discover, differ perceptibly from those in Sydney, Brisbane, and Hobart, less perceptibly from those in Perth. Such shades of social conduct are best seen in the middle or upper middle class. It is only when there is a solid and developed design of material safety that refinements in manners and morals appear, even in a democracy as free and easy as Australia's.

I think that last sentence is not my own but J. F. Ward's. If I return before midnight to the boarding-house from wherever I've been, the Head invites me into his study for a talk.

At ten every night, the few unlocked doors of the boarding-house are locked. Each resident master has a key to the front door, behind which lies the entrance hall. To the left is the bursar's office, ground floor to the tower I live at the top of. To the right is the Headmaster's study, door open, desk-lamp on, and J. F. Ward more nights than not at work, upright as a Buddha, his hands illuminated like something in a reliquary, and holding the steel-nibbed pen with which he writes. His handwriting is fine, flowing, unmistakably legible as, I've since found out, is the handwriting of the authors and scholars with the most unsullied intelligences. I mistrust illegible writers. Almost always they turn out to be poseurs, fools, people so vain that they are careless of the sensibilities of others.

As Miss Abramson, the journalist Jewess, used to at 28 Collins six or seven years before, he calls out when I am closing the front door, "That you, Porter?"

"Yes, sir."

I move towards his door, and see the lenses of his spectacles gleaming.

"Are you too tired or tipsy to have a talk?"

This is P. J. Green and Friday afternoon at State School 1409 over again, with the difference that the conversation is two-sided. One of the reasons these late-night talks are so delightful to me is that the Head, this straight-backed Methodist Olympian, cool and controlled, reveals that he is "boyishly" interested in many of the things I am also "boyishly" interested in. The difference in state accents and words is one of those things. I am, at this time, reviewing books for the literary section of the *Adelaide Advertiser*. The review copy of Sidney J. Baker's first book on Australian slang and accent, which I lend to the Head, sets us both bloodhounding. He has the advantage of being older and a South Australian. My advantage is a newer ear. I can never convince him that the South Australian pronunciation of words like little, cattle, giggle and bottle sounds like littoo, cattoo, giggoo and bottoo to me, although he agrees that his state says the Golf Trip and St Vincent's Golf, Golf being Gulf elsewhere, and golf being goff with the upper middle class. We do not, however, enjoy only these finicky interests, nor do we talk shop. He has a passion for Lewis Carroll, Edward Lear, Hilaire Belloc's *Cautionary Tales*, and Anstey's *Turnabout*.

In recalling this man, so important in my sit-down-you're-rocking-the-boat life, I prefer to see him as I saw him on one of those midnights. All the doors are locked, all the lights save his are out, the lower part of the school is sandbagged, the searchlights search outside, everything says "Haven!" and "Gone to earth!" On the floors above and below, his kingdom of sleepers is filed away. He sits erect, his hands and the book in the cone of radiance from the desk-lamp, and reads the account of Alice, monstrous and trapped in the tiny house, kicking Bill the Lizard out of the chimney.

I prefer to recall him so.

My last memory of him, in the same study, in the same swivel-chair, the mid-morning daylight of January 1946 pouring through the high bay-windows, is of a man who has just heard that John is dead, the son who called him Rex, and used to live in the Dog Box next to the tower room.

Men whose tenderer emotions have been subsidized by Christianity, and are exaggerated by sentimentality, incline, generally, to feel sympathy for another man, even an enemy or a bore, seen at the moment when fate has lifted him on to the O-Absalom-my-son square of the chessboard. When both sorrowing David and dead Absalom are the sympathizer's friends the sympathy is uselessly doubled, as mine is on that morning of brilliant weather twenty years ago. My conventionally automatic shock is intensified because I both selfishly and unselfishly want to take away a last-time-ever memory of the Headmaster as I've always known him, a man who, in an age of political, social, artistic, and religious languor and decadence, has convinced me more than anyone that there is more value in character than possessions, in the spirit than in the material.

Often, the sons of figureheads such as headmasters and bishops affect a rebel warp. John does. Not only is he an animal in danger from the community because he is the Head's child, he is a brilliant student. This increases his danger. He is also intelligent enough to play the runagate with much skill, breaking only those school rules that will make his defiance swashbucklingly attractive, and not embarrass the Headmaster into any action more out of the ordinary than a good caning. John's flung-down gauntlets, and the Head's just punishments, are of public value to both in the waspish, treacherous, impressible, and sensitized tropic of the boarding-house.

The last time I see John he is semi-tipsy, and in a spanking new sailor's get-up. During the war years this is not unusual: the last time I see many of my ex-pupils they too, having been transformed into national men by a soldier's, sailor's, or airman's outfit, are rehearsing to be the tough-guy men they think the uniform should enclose, and are trying out alcohol as a first step. A pattern becomes familiar.

One day, there is eighteen-year-old Smith Major saying "Yes, sir" and "No, sir" and having trouble with *King Lear*. The next day, it seems, there is Smith Major in raw tan boots and fresh thick khaki appearing at my elbow in the saloon bar of the Botanic Hotel—"Thought I'd find you here, Hal!"—bold from nervousness, and with an invitation to dine with him at the South Australian Hotel, the posh centre of Adelaide revelry by night. Why my school nickname is always my Christian name is beyond me.

These dinners are usually catastrophically conspicuous even in a building cluttered with American servicemen and their peroxided and overdressed floozies. Behold Smith Major, self-possessed as a cat-burglar, ordering with a lavishness I must accept, and tossing down drinks with an I'm-a-man recklessness it would be uncouth of me to try to subdue. When he gets near tears at the orchestra's playing "There'll Always be an England", it is time for me to simulate a need for his company to the lavatory so that he can relieve his desperate unhappy-happy condition by being sick in the proper place rather than, as one early-on Smith does before I am trained in the danger signs, into his hat. Although the deed is done neatly and with *savoir-faire*, the problem of carrying a hat brimmed with secondhand grog the length of the South Australian Hotel dining-room is not one to be faced with relish a second time.

My first and last drinks with John Ward are drunk in the tower bedroom. I have been on duty. Prep is over, the last door is locked, the last good-nights said, the last dormitory light is out, it is eleven o'clock, and I am in bed reading *Tommy and Grizel* again, and wondering why one of the other English masters thinks Barrie namby-pamby and Hemingway ruthless, and why I think the exact opposite. There is suddenly the sort of hullabaloo on the landing outside my door which suggests—Oh God!—that there is a pyjama'd deputation with the exhilarating news that a sprinter senior is in a Gordian knot of cramp, or a moaning junior about to have a burst appendix. There is a loud knock.

"Enter."

It is John, dressed as a sailor, and clutching a bottle of Vat 69 Whisky.

"Ward!" I say. "Out! Immediately! This is a respectable boarding-house."

"Fret not, sir," he says, closing the door. "Fret not, I'm not here to sully your virtue. Rex sent me. Where are the glasses?"

"In the cupboard. You can fill the jug with water in the bathroom. Why did the Head send you here?"

"I suppose because it's nearer home, and he and *la mère* can go to byesies with a clear conscience knowing that I'm *having* my last night-out, but only on the next floor, and not in a brawl with Yanks in a back lane. Our Rex is a wise old owl."

Yes.

Yes, a wise old owl.

He lays his hand on my shoulder after prayers next morning.

"You look pale, Porter." The corner of his mouth—it winces.

"Yes, sir."

"Nothing serious, I hope."

"Nothing serious, sir."

"John looks well." He says this as one informing the air.

"Yes, sir." I'll bet he doesn't this morning, I think.

No more is said, but it lets me know that John is telling the truth when he says, "Rex sent me." A wise old owl, willing to learn more wisdom from his youngest child.

After the 1945 school year ends, and my job at Prince's as a schoolmaster, J. F. Ward suggests that, until I go to Tasmania, I may stay on in my tower room. This is money-saving, and wonderfully convenient. It gives me time to get rid of the possessions I have surrounded myself with during the five years in South Australia. Once again I drift around giving away books and bric-à-brac I need never have bought, and the pictures I then think mean something. I hack away this time more snail-shell than ever before. Whatever it is that warns me that a conglomeration of bower-bird nonsense is not to be mine for many years, warns me right; whatever it is that tells me my ambling from place to place is going to speed up to a canter, a gallop, is right.

On the last morning at Prince's, the day is so dazzling and still that the inn of night ahead and the hound of wind at one's heels are not to be thought of.

It stands yet, like a vast diamond in which I cannot see the flaw I have seen.

The taxi-cab has appeared, silver and glittering, under the canopy of the Moreton Bay fig, and stands where Wee Soon Wat's hire-car stood three years earlier. The driver puts in my luggage while I return to say good-bye to the Head. I know he is in his study and that, fitted and stacked high above him and behind him and below him, are rooms and studies and cubicles and dormitories, stairways and stair-wells and corridors, all empty except of empty things, wardrobes with nothing in, lockers of air, skeletons of beds, fireplaces without fire, baths without water, a kingdom of closed doors and blind windows, a kingdom without echoes.

At the Head's open door, "I've come to say good-bye, sir."

As so often his eyes are hidden behind the coins of light on his spectacle lenses, as always he is sitting upright, as never before he is not working. A pastel-coloured slip of paper sits under his hand on the white blotter. His hand stirs as though the paper is alive. He clears his throat.

"This tells me John is dead."

Truth is not matter to be minced.

Since I do not know what to say, my throat improvises a brief noise of its own for which I think the dictionary has no single word.

"In Yokohama. An accident."

I still don't know what to say.

I say, "I don't know what to say, sir." My voice indicates that my eyes are about to fill with tears.

The Head puts a stop to that.

"Porter, please. I've waited here to tell you about John because I know you were fond of each other. I've waited to say good-bye. I've not had time to give in to my own sorrow."

In this rebuke, this plea for his own first rights as a father, these truths uttered with effort, I see that the rock is rock still but is to split, that the cry of David for Absalom is to come yet will not come until I leave the kingdom of empty rooms utterly empty. We shake hands. We give each other back to each other.

"Good-bye, Porter."

"Good-bye, sir."

Though we write letters several times a year until he dies, J. F. Ward and I never see each other again.

Four years later I put a bunch of leaves and flowers on John's grave in the war cemetery at Yokohama, a dormitory cemetery, each bed the same size, shipshape, no bed uglier or prettier than the other. The offering looks like something in the wrong place, something that would have made me say, years before, "Ward, if those cricket boots are not off your bed by the time I look in again you'll be writing out twenty-seven words with fourteen letters in each."

The aeroplane out of South Australia, violently deforming animal truth, violently illustrating that time and space are illusions, takes me over a border unmarked on the air, over the hills hidden below the clouds, over the hills and far far away. Far away, and farther away than miles and hours.

In Melbourne, earthed again, I find that, before the aeroplane to Hobart takes off, hours by an earthbound clock must be spent, on an earth and in a city I have become a stranger to. I hide myself, so that the past I have arranged in my mind will not have a chance to change its shape, by sitting through Laurence Olivier's *Henry V*.

Thus, unbumped-into in street or bar or café, those enclosed in the flask of other years and other places can remain enclosed, unaltered, their colours and garments and shibboleths still 1937, 1938, 1939, their every insect gesticulation known, their midget voices piping old clauses and squeaking old songs, their tiny pre-war images repeating endlessly actions they have years ago forgotten—Miss Beveridge, Schultzie, Leon Hogan, Esther in her waitress's black dress, Audrey winking behind her eye-veil sprinkled with midnight-blue sequins, Minka sidling between the green curtains of the Café Petrushka kitchen with the six-penny tumbler of tea, the slice of lemon, and the two cubes of sugar, on the fluted glass saucer. Since no man bathes ever twice in the same river, in the waters that move on replacing themselves, let me not pretend the waters are the same, let me not

194

seek to meet on a windy street corner the three Misses Gregory
with their rosewood-dyed hair, Olivia's three sisters like models
from *Harper's Bazaar*, the three runtish Arthurs from the carpenters' benches in the back room of Arcadia Display Specialistes, three languid drifters from the Street of Leaning Trees
allusively nibbling bruised apricots, or three street-women on
their way to the Broadway Café, one of whom will say, "Who
wrote this? Tell me who wrote this:

> *The cherry trees bend over, and are shedding,*
> *On the old road where all that passed are dead,*
> *Their petals, strewing the grass as for a wedding*
> *This early May morn when there is none to wed."*

Let me meet no phantom from one past in this gap between
another past and the future, between South Australia and Tasmania.

I first see South Australia, just after sunrise, as a landscape
pagan, bronze and violet, Polynesian.

I first see Tasmania, just after sunset, as a landscape desperate,
assailed, and sinister.

The aeroplane, jolting and dropping into chasms of nothing
above the hell-broth of storm-clouds over Bass Strait and Tasmania, is not able to land at the Hobart aerodrome until a long
time after it should. We must wait in the attics of air, wheeling
farther south to where, at last, through slots in the streaming
veils of mist, there is Tasmania, the gothic littoral of a thousand
marine paintings, precipices of bitter grey basalt, insolent tusks
of rock, iron-coloured waves smashing forward an enormity of
water to run like skeins of smoke up the fissured scarps. Nothing is missing except the tormented windjammer, jagged masts,
shreds of sail, careening to its doom. These ramparts at the edge
of civilization, ceaselessly murdering water to spume and
vapour, are not of the twentieth century.

Nor, as I first see it, on a night of gale and downpour, is
Hobart.

It takes me a long time to find accommodation. I try to tell
myself it is mere fatigue and the icy rain that make me feel I
am an Ishmael in the London of Dickens, the narrow steep
streets, the drains gulping and retching, the cobbled mews, the

names of the hatchet-faced hotels I am turned down at—The Man on the Wheel, The Ocean Child, Sir William Don, The Ship, the thin and acrid beer, tepid from wooden barrel on the counter of a waterfront tavern where the taxi-driver and I drink while asking advice.

Where, you pock-marked barman, where in the rain, is a bed?

Anywhere will do—a Night Refuge, Fagin's den, underneath the Arches.

We are directed to a boarding-house which has pretensions. It calls itself the Astor Private Hotel. The reception desk is in a hall haunted by the smell of galoshes, and cumbered with Benares-tray-topped tables, a cast-iron umbrella-stand, alabaster pedestals topped by equestrian statuettes of bronze, and throne-like Chinese chairs of ebony inlaid with mother-of-pearl peonies. Antlered stag-heads protrude from the panelled walls.

There is one room vacant for one night only, a penthouse room on the flat roof, a shuddering unlined box, probably once a caretaker's. The wind scourges it. The rain falls, falls and falls.

Where is the dazzling morning over the border, the diamond with the flaw of pain in it?

Before I sleep I fight an instinct warning me that I am on an aggrieved island, that the water gobbling in the roof-gutters, and pouring off the asphalted roof can never wash away some taint of plague sensed everywhere. There has been a hell here to which Hell is a crèche. I tell myself again that I am the victim of fatigue, irritating weather, and a mish-mash of impressions—the end-of-the-world precipices; a city momentarily like a setting for Jack the Ripper; grisly convict tales of cannibalism, sodomy and the triangle; the Australian legend that Tasmania is an island of incest and haunted architectural follies; and the sailors' stories heard years ago in Madame's Williamstown Wine Depôt that Hobart is one of the most immoral ports in the world.

After ten hours' sleep I wake up to a sunny day, and though, faint but persistent, a nerve of instinct still throbs warningly, it now has nothing but itself to sustain it. For the rest: sailor lies are sailor lies; Hell is only a house of cards; where is the Jack the Ripper rain? how *can* cities "absorb into their very stones the emanations of a squalid and shameful past"? and so on. Listen! A thrush sings; and all the leaves are laundered; all the pillar-boxes filled with love letters, receipts for paid bills, poems.

Hutchins School, although small, slap-bang on a main street, with a century-old pub across the road, buses John-Bulling by, and a brothel or two in the next street, is Hobart's Eton, is one hundred years old in 1946, and self-consciously—in miniature—sticks to the architectural conventions of ogival windows, ivy-covered tower, arched colonnade, attic dormitories, and fives court.

It follows the routine of the Church of England private school: scholarship and sport, dormitories and day boys, compline and the cane. The staff has the same constituents—masters who have outstayed several headmasters, a Matron who knows the world, frisky maids, an ex-schoolmaster bursar, a homosexual master, visiting teachers of this or that, and a housekeeper who much resembles in appearance the Italianized Virgin Mary. It is an older and larger microcosm than Duke's College, a much smaller and slightly older one than Prince Alfred College. The boarding-house dining-room is also traditional: midday dinners, regular dishings-up of sausages, Irish stew, rissoles, shepherd's pie, and curried something. Tasmanians are kangaroo-eaters, and minced kangaroo on toast is a meal new to me. It crops up weekly on the menu. So much for the school itself except to say that the library contains such treasures as the Gould bird books from the Lady Franklin library, and a Breeches Bible. The library is built over some old swimming baths which, through a trapdoor in the floor, has been filled with thrown-out books.

At Hutchins I am in the unusual position of having been appointed Senior English Master without being interviewed by the Head. Doubtless J. F. Ward has been my advocate. The new Headmaster and I have not met, have not sized each other up. He is not only new to me, he is new to Hutchins, and new to headmastership. His background is nebulous to me but I seem to recall that he is a bishop's son married to a woman connected with an Australian political family, and that he has

197

served his schoolmaster apprenticeship in at least one English school (Wellington?) as well as in Australian ones. Since our brief relationship of two terms is to end in such disaster that my name appears in the red type of the stop-press column and in London dailies, it seems pertinent to select from my ragout of abilities and convictions, weaknesses and whims, such of them as get me to Hutchins, and such as get me very quickly out of it.

Ultimately, I blame myself for not listening, on the gurgling roof of the Astor Private Hotel, to the morse code of my instinct which I do believe, if listened to fully and with the atavistic ear, can be decoded. One doesn't listen, of course, because fate is making those other noises. Singing "I Want to be Happy", one skips towards the man-trap.

There is no doubt that I get the Hutchins job partly because of my long experience. In 1946 I have been teaching for sixteen of the nineteen years since I began in 1927. As well, the references from the headmasters of Williamstown, Duke's, and Prince's credit me with schoolmasterly qualities then in vogue —I note myself as being "an excellent disciplinarian", "a highly stimulating teacher", "a loyal and likeable colleague", "hardworking and enthusiastic", and of "sound moral character".

Thus I enter Hutchins.

Thus, so far as I can see, I go from Hutchins with the word loyal the only one in doubt.

The Headmaster and the Hutchins School Board, as will be shown, have—or assume it advantageous to have—other ideas.

Added to the stock schoolmaster qualifications is the extramural qualification which makes headmasters, as though presenting the keys of the city, off-load on me the overseeing of the school magazine and the library—a literary reputation. This bud has opened just enough for me to have become "one of Australia's rising young writers who could develop (blah-blah-blah)", and to be invited to contribute to anthologies and periodicals. The invitations are accepted only when I've something already done, something off my own bat. This assures me that the contribution is as muse-inspired good as I can make it, and not as editor-plotted bad as something off a bat handed to me, the bat that, as recently as twenty years ago, has attached to it the label: *An Australian Topic Only. Between 2,500 and 4,000 Words.*

Fervently nationalistic, I do not object to *Australian*. Fervently nationalistic, I object to *Australian* meaning what the editors of that time intend it to mean—an outback yarn peopled by cardboard characters whose *again, says* and *all right* are *agen, sez* and *alright*.

A schoolmaster qualification I haven't is a university education. In 1946 it is a qualification less looked for by astute headmasters, and much less the rage, than it is to be later. There are many schoolmasters, then, who have not been to a university. They are soon to become a dying race.

It is not, however, my homely enough abilities which bring disaster. Convictions are the trouble. At thirty-five, my convictions, most of them no more set than when I am twenty, appear to be more set because the expression and defence of them, when I am cornered, have the illusion of added strength from my added years. These convictions may appear eccentricities to others. Having adhered to them for so many years I tend to regard them as convenient sagacities. Barren negatives, they are hardly virtues, and I do not regard them so. Eccentricities or sagacities, my convictions have placed me in the position, at the age of thirty-five, of still never having seen a horse race, greyhound race, speed-car race, bicycle race or Test match. I've not seen a boxing or wrestling contest, have never gambled, owned a motor-car, bought on credit, paid for lust, or taken a lottery ticket. Old convictions, all of them. Among recent ones is the belief, spawned nine years before in the Café Petrushka, that leftists are not quite sane in a special way. A bee in the bonnet, an honest-to-God personal bee, often makes an otherwise trite human being a livelier and more palatable one. A borrowed bee in the bonnet, a destructive one that anaesthetizes humanness when it settles, makes a trite human being into a mental robot, bottle-fed on propaganda.

My antipathy towards any move seeming to me leftist is responsible for a splashy gesture that lands me bang in the middle of a scandal.

Not that I think the Head is a leftist. Precentors, bishops, the Governor, and various Holy Joes, are always popping in and out of the school; he is married into a family notorious for its political conservatism; and, during Sunday services at St David's Cathedral, while he does not cross himself with Anglo-Catholic frequency and fervour during the Apostle's Creed, as does the homosexual master, he is pretty austere and pietistic about it all. At first meeting I dislike him but do not mistrust him. Dislike is a bagatelle. Headmasters are not there to be liked by either staff or boys. Respect's the thing. Whether it is immature and absurd to take a dislike to a whole man just because his mouth is horizontal as an inquisitor's, no-lipped, locked, is a question I can't answer because so many authors and so many Christians have made so much of facial signposts to character that one sees an almost complete being build-up—like a dinosaur skeleton from a toe-joint—around such snippets as "mean little beady eyes", "a frank open countenance", "sensual greasy lips", "a weak and vacillating chin".

Dislike or not, he takes me to his house next door to the school, pours out gin, and shows me his beetle collection. Since I am wary of tight lips, not a gin-enjoyer, and disposed towards an animistic belief that an inch of beetle has half an inch of soul, the Head's politeness does not temper the dislike although the mouth tells me about incidents on a cycling tour of Europe, the gin is downed, and one of the beetles is pure Dürer.

An elder school by Australian reckoning, Hutchins is as overgrown by an ivy of traditions as its tower is overgrown by traditional ivy. At night, from the tower leads, one can see, in the street behind, the twelve-paned windows of the Regency cottages and the light shining through their red brothel curtains. In front, across the road, where the more reckless seniors sometimes sneak for a drink at night, one can see what appear to be ticket-of-leave men in ragged overcoats wavering into the Duke of Wellington. Above all of this, an aurora australis reproduces the icy weather in colour with slowly shuttling fringes of green and silver.

The Head, fresh to both Hutchins and headmastership, and doubtless keen to cut a dash, sets about reorganizing the school. He is not the diplomatic softly-softly-catchee-monkey sort of man, rather the harshly textured new-broom sort with *Clean Sweep*! his slogan, and is young enough to tread where angels fear, no matter the time-honoured corns to be trodden on. He treads on some immediately, removing in the first fortnight or so any doubts the watching and waiting staff and pupils have about his nature. Whatever his long-range plan is, the first moves in it are hackle-raising. Inflexible decisions are made, back-to-the-wall stands are taken, dramatic punishments are given. The tone and temper of the school are set, so early in the year, at *Uncertain—Storm Coming*. In the Common Room, the black-gowned staff, in Daumier groups, say, "Tut-tut " and shake heads, hoping that the fretful and already sour winds of the inner weather will drop, and that the air will warm up.

I couldn't care less if the Head ordered Maori designs to be tattooed on every boy's face. He's the boss. I think that some of his moves are too strong, too early, but feel that none of my business, as it certainly isn't. I cannot foresee that, come winter and sleet, come snow falling like white leaves on Mount Wellington, come June, I shall be feeling that what authority is up to *is* my business which, still, it certainly isn't. In February, March, April, and May, however, I sail from class to class contentedly hammering facts into heads and, the school day over, sail out to examine the new world.

In Adelaide I am fascinated by what is not in Melbourne—roast pigeons for sale; crimson radishes as big as quinces which one peels like a peach before eating; pies and green peas—floaters—to be bought at three in the morning from canvas street-stalls; tea-tree fences; sailcloth waterbags hanging on railway stations:; the architectural oddity of upper-floor verandas extending only halfway forward over the fully forward lower veranda; the cows ONLY notices in parklands, and the GENTS FOR SALE notices in fish-bait shops—I do not know maggots are called gentles. I pick up the local expressions *parklands* for *park*; *Wyandotte* for *plonkie*; *handle, schooner, middy* and *butcher* as names for beer-vessels; and notice that rich pastries, cakes, and buns seen nowhere else, many of German heritage, are displayed in pastrycooks', that a drink of German origin, hock-and-lemon, is a favourite in summer, and that the reception desk of a hotel is more often than not on the first rather than the ground floor.

In Hobart and Tasmania, the collecting of local idiosyn-
crasies of vocabulary and custom, hitherto an intriguing sport,
suddenly seems the most trivial of things to do. I note that
tissue is used for *cigarette-paper, cordial* for *soft drink*, and
that cider is drunk much, and such unusual mixtures as beer-
and-raspberry, and schnapps-and-sherry. Then I stop. There is
bigger game. For the first time in my life I am consciously and
intimately in touch with a form of evil, not evil so powerful as
to satirize itself and be not really harmful, but evil moving as
naturally as blood through veins, an impulse drugging enough
to blot guilt from the mind. I keep on recalling, with irritation,
for I want to find out for myself, the sailors' opinion of Hobart.
To this end I visit the world-notorious Blue House in Sala-
manca Place but am still too ingenuous to find its proprietress
any more than a friendly harpy, and her waterfront pub any
more than a brawling thieves' kitchen, noisy and dangerous but
hardly—surely?—wicked enough to merit the sailors' "one of
the most immoral ports in the world". Perhaps Ma Dwyer, with
whom I become matey, protects me—the fearless matriarchs
of such rough-house dives do protect, as protecting a pet fool,
wide-eyed blunderers-in—from what my eyes are too wide
open to see. What *did* the sailors know? What? *What?*

If I am irritated at not being able to forget the sailors' pronouncements, I am more irritated at not being able to forget
the "shameful past" theory.

I am quite willing to blame what I do stumble across and into
on to myself, to an accidental run of eye-opening revelations,
to fate. It is not good enough. Beyond the London-in-1840
atmosphere of Hobart, and the ordinary people living ordinary
lives, there hovers in another dimension a kind of miasma from
the putrescent remains of old bad dreams, old lonelinesses and
lunacies, old and calculated sins against the Holy Ghost. Sinners
no longer sin by the card because whiffs from this miasma,
drifting across like some outrageous sal volatile, seem to stimu-
late infamous emotions so that tip-cat people act and interact
as though the walls between right and wrong are air.

Whether I still believe this is doubtful.

In 1946, surrounded by what appears to be an abundance
and persistence of evidence, in a Hobart where neurotic Jewish

refugees (known as reffos) are putting off their sackcloth and ashes, but not their guilt, and beginning to flash the culture they smuggled out of mad-dog Europe with their jewels, where returned bachelor servicemen are drinking out their war neuroses on deferred pay, it is less doubtful. Let us say I almost believe. The sort of evidence inclining me to belief involves men and women—and not only men and women but that incalculable relationship of husbands and wives—whose lives follow a pattern of sordid and uninhibited relationships plotted, apparently, by Iris Murdoch. I become an onlooker to relationships I am compelled to learn every detail of as, with a glamourizing frankness that has nothing whatever to do with the less glamourous truth, I hear man and wife spill the beans, while the wireless plays "Mood Indigo" and "Sentimental Journey", and I keep on tearing into their sherry as a puritan-concealing ploy. To define to myself why two highly educated, nearly charming, far too articulate Monsters of Depravity should seem harmful, and Audrey, the street-woman who winked at me when she was a pretty schoolgirl, should not, I have to remember the callously gay and guiltless faces as beans are Oxford Groupishly spilt, the cerebral excitation (the whiff of the miasma?), and the patent pride in being emancipated, special, free from bourgeois repressions.

These sorts of men and women—and I meet enough of them —in retrospect make my blood run cold. As selfish as the leading characters of a tragedy already aware of their destiny they claw their way, stepping on the mouths of minor fallen characters, towards shameful conclusions. In 1946, although the accidents of life sometimes make avoidance difficult, I arrange that my apprehensions do not get too near my consciousness, by mixing with such couples as little as possible. Because Hobart is a miniature city, everyone is socially underfoot, and ubiquitous enough not to be easily bypassed without something extreme in the way of action.

The most pleasant way to avoid those belonging to a social-intellectual clique afflicted by what seems to me, then, a local malaise, is to find a group of people as unintellectual as I with whom to fool away those hours left over from being a busy-bee schoolmaster, a gardener, a solitary writer, a secret

203

lover, or a nosey-parker exploring back-streets slippery with grits of sleet scraped from a firmament of ice by the upended ploughshare of the mountain.

The group I fall in with, a pub-crawling group with its headquarters in the Back Bar of Hadley's Hotel, is composed largely of ex-servicemen who, having escaped for a few years from Tasmania, have the more expanded and less analysing and amoral natures I prefer friends to have. They possess a double appeal because they are the first returned men I have intimately known and because, whatever else the war has done to them, it has erased the insularity noticeably affecting less fortunate stay-at-homes, and has made them skilled in the refinements of give-and-take comradeship. These men are among the few human beings I sincerely regret leaving when I leave Hobart; their warm absurdity and casual sensitivity and gift of self-mockery are among the few things I remember about the place with un-alloyed contentment.

For the rest I dance, dine out, go to parties, do a little amateur theatrical work, and observe that the caste system in Tasmania is an uneasy one. Perhaps this is so because there are so many pages of Newgate ancestors deliberately cut or torn from the early records of convict arrivals, so much inbreeding, so much distorted English gentility, so many dotty aunts and alcoholic cousins and crumbling Palladian mansions contained in so small, cold, and craggy an island. It is not a place to whis-per in. Nerves vibrate at the level of the skin. I notice, for the first time in my life, that people seem to cling to life less from belief and certainty than from habit, as a rat clings to his nest in the muck. Perhaps I should have noticed this before, else-where. Do I only notice because I am older? Or because I am in Hobart?

I drift in the direction of scandal by easy stages, my path lined by disquieting things which are the more disquieting be-cause no one else seems to find them so.

Take St David's Park. It is a pioneer cemetery. Except for several elaborate examples of the monumental mason's work the gravestones of the colonists have been uprooted, and the area made into a municipal version of a garden with lawns, con-trollable trees, bandstand, drinking-fountains and lavatories

arranged over the dead. Faced with what I regard as desecration, I am at the same time faced with what Hobart regards as
a civic nicety, the conversion of a human rubbish-tip into a
tasteless little park.

In 1946, not having seen this sort of thing before (and only
rarely since), I am thrown off the centre on which I have been
put by centuries and thousands of square miles of unmolested
"sacred burial grounds". Why is Hobart the only place that
thinks otherwise? And, more sinister, why?

I am asked to do a painting for sale by auction on behalf of
some charity. The evening is to be *very* bohemian, suggests the
gilt-edged (and expensive) invitation card, and very social, with
knights and their Ladies to rub shoulders with while we drink
the grog (donated), eat the saveloys and tomato sauce (a
plebeian food just being taken up as original and smart), and bid
for the works of art. The Governor provides a drawing of a
sailing-ship done in pencil when he was a midshipman. It is
painstakingly bad. The Governor's Lady provides a sheet of
paper covered with Indian ink. This is called *London in a
Black-out*. Considering their artistic merit, these vice-regal contributions are sold at prices relatively equal to the price of a
Vermeer. It is the Premier's drawing which discomposes me.
There is obtainable in the kind of shop selling *The Decameron*,
nudist magazines, and fur-rimmed *pots-de-chambre*, a postcard
of a little boy peeing on the snow. He has already marked "A
Merry Xmas" on the white surface. Below, a caption states:
"And a Happy New Year if I've got enough left". The
Premier has done a large copy of the postcard—it must have
taken hours—and his lack of control over pencil and paint-
brush and proportion has resulted in the phallic exaggeration
seen in the graffiti of public lavatories. Once again, as in so
many Hobart places other than St David's Park, I find myself
wondering—why haven't I bumped into this *just* out of plumb,
just askew sort of thing elsewhere? Why does everyone else
think it not at all extraordinary? Do all Premiers behave so?

Why should I think that to bump into the homosexual master's pet, a lout in pyjamas, leaving the master's room at two
in the morning is unusual? Or that the din of a quarrel between
the barmaid from the Imperial Hotel and another resident

master, coming from his bedroom at the same hour of the morning, is exceptional? Why, in Hobart, do I trip over soiled tangles of linen so often? Is it because, and only because, everything is so close to everything else that little can be hidden, or that islands are less civilized than continents, unashamed of the dirty facts?

Why should the Headmaster and the other headmasters and headmistresses of Hobart's private schools decide not to have the King's Birthday holiday?

The announcement is made some weeks before the King's Birthday. The Common Room staff, about sixteen of us, expresses dismay. The expression varies in intensity to match the degree of cynicism or susceptibility of each member, but the dismay is a corporate one. The dust from the Headmaster's earlier spring-cleanings has been settling. This on-again house-cleaning, bewildering to us, would stir up enough irritating new dust if the holiday to be swept off the calendar were an ordinary one. A traditional Tasmanian school holiday involving a gesture to royalty is not an ornament to be swept out, and thrown on the rubbish-heap, without causing uproar. The uproar begins outside the school. Letters appear from angry Old Boys in the Hobart newspaper. For the teaching staff a touchy problem of public behaviour comes into being. From the others in the Common Room I learn that we are each sharing the same experience of trying not to appear fools without opinions, while at the same time not being disloyal to the school, the school being the Headmaster whom everyone suspects, rightly or wrongly, as the nigger in the woodpile. For years I have scarcely talked of my job outside school, and have avoided or dropped as companions those schoolteachers given to talking shop after the show is over. Now I find myself being either obliquely or bluntly grilled about Hutchins. My dearest back-bar friends are easy enough to fob off. The truth does them. Since they are friends I can be disloyal, vituperative, and condemnatory without feeling guilty, even though some of them are Old Boys themselves. The problem is the one of walking the high-wire of *délicatesse* for the buttonholers, for incensed Old Boys who are no more than acquaintances, for up-in-arms mothers and fathers met at parties, for courtly old men, slightly

206

a-tremble, with pearl tiepins in their silver-grey ties, characters from the Forsyte saga: "Bit stiff, y'know, Porter. Puts Government House in a rotten spot. What's this new fellow like? I hear he's bit of a bolshevik."

I have always, as much as possible, concealed puritanism, conservatism, and fresh-water ideas behind frivolity, and the Paul Pry writer behind both. Each time I have to play the part of the well-behaved schoolmaster unwilling to be disloyal to the Headmaster, my conservative self, already restive, becomes more so and threatens to leap from cover.

Finally, the staff invites the Headmaster to the Common Room, and attempts to indicate diplomatically its fears that the decision to cut out this particular holiday is unwise. The Headmaster listens, his face set, and says nothing. The surface of his cup of tea, untouched, becomes covered with a greyish scum. When its points have been made, the staff finishes at silence. For the first time the Headmaster speaks; the tone of his voice is the wind through the keyhole: "I am, after listening to this disloyalty, more than ever convinced that there must not be a King's Birthday holiday." He rises. "I expect loyalty from every member of the staff." He leaves the Common Room.

For me the word loyalty does it. My placidity ruffled, I take myself for a walk along the sunset waterfront, mentally trying to fight down the conservative who feels some action is needed. The sun dies as any enemy dies, vomiting blood, baleful with hatred. The conservative wins. A week before the King's Birthday I write a letter to the Hobart newspaper, wryly conscious that convictions in this form are a misuse of language, and that in presenting a case for conservative behaviour I am being unconservative, that I'd be less of a fool if I'd written a sonnet instead. The letter is not published immediately.

The King's Birthday dawns, a Monday.

The staff has decided it is more than likely that no boys will turn up because so many loud-mouthed fathers, in clubs and pubs, have said they will not send their sons to school. When I come downstairs the Common Room greets me like a rebel hero. The letter is in the paper. Oh dear, oh dear, oh dear dear dear. Through the Common Room window I see crowds of boys under the elms. If any are defiantly absent it is few. So I, silly man, am the only mutineer, the solitary stone-thrower, the dupe of my own convictions.

The bell rings.

At Hutchins the formalities of entering the school hall for prayers differ from those I take part in, pre-Hutchins and post-Hutchins, anywhere else. On each side of the double doors stands a boy holding a tray of hymn-books. The school moves to its chairs in order, junior boys first, middle school, senior school, house prefects, school prefects, and, finally, to the chairs at the back of the hall, the masters in their gowns, so that the view from the dais is of a stairway of faces rising row by row from the young and unmarked to the increasingly older and increasingly marked. This the master who plays the piano sees, and this the Headmaster sees. He waits outside the double doors until the school is standing, each in his place, all quiet. Then, in cap and gown, he advances down the central passageway, mounts the dais, and gives the number of the hymn to be sung.

The Headmaster gives the number, at Hutchins School, Monday, King's Birthday, 1946. The pianist plays, as usual, a line or two of the hymn. Next he plays the opening note, and begins the accompaniment.

There is nothing to accompany.

He stops.

There is silence.

It is a silence louder than sound. It is a silence of many wills, manufactured in secret, a home-made bomb, and it has been thrown with satanic skill.

A flash of inner elation—I'm not the only mutineer!—is instantly dowsed at the sight of the Headmaster's face. This is the one time, before or since, I witness the novelistic cliché of a face turned ashen. From nowhere a brutal punch falls on that centre of feelings one conveniently calls the heart. However strongly I have felt about him before, and however much I think of him with contempt later, at that moment I am shaken with pity. How hard human beings are. How abominable are these hundreds of boys, row upon row of bowed heads, row upon row of absolutely still figures, stiff with defiance. Before them, from the gibbet, in neat suit, clean shirt, subdued tie, in discreet socks and polished black shoes, spectacles on nose, watch on wrist, mortar-board on head, gown hanging just so, red-backed hymn-book in hand, dangles the nudest man I hope ever to see, stripped to the nerves, to the hollow at the centre of all men, empty-handed, and unutterably alone, dangling from the gibbet, dancing on the air.

He dances badly.

For the next twenty minutes . . . hour? . . . eternity? . . . he tries to make the school sing. Since he will not cease to try, each time his will is silently disregarded the will of the mob thickens, battening on the display of adult impotence, and forced to watch shameful dancings on the air when all that has been expected is a clean-cut execution. The staff must watch too.

Separated from the dais, and the embarrassing and unskilled man on it, aware that an attempt at support would be rebuffed, the masters remain standing at the back of the hall waiting for a sign from—from where? At last, the Second Master, a tall, respected, and rugged man who has taught at the school for decades, makes his decision, and moves to the doors. We others follow. As we walk to the Common Room the rabble bursts from the hall behind us. By the time the masters have collected their wits there has been a display of the kind of wild animal behaviour we can deal with. It is mainly the puppy madness of the younger animals. The more Machiavellian seniors are appeased. They stand in groups, faces grave with the purring gravity of cats full of flesh, and scarcely notice the smaller boys writing on the walls that the Head is a communist, and unhooking the school bell, and capering around squealing, "Down with the Head!" about a man they have forgotten.

"Down with the Head!" has the same note as "Isn't this fun!"

A master finds a hand-bell. It is rung commandingly to say all schoo̶l̶ ̶masters are not yet dismantled. Within minutes the classes are in their rooms. My first class is Matriculation English. As I enter the room there is a roar from the youths. It soars into a sustained shout. The letter! I have forgotten it. I realize that, before prayers, the Headmaster has not seen the newspaper left by the postman in his study, because he has come, as every morning, straight from his house to the hall.

I stand stock still until the shout topples. I do then the ice-voiced disciplinary trick, the cheap and easy one that never fails: "I see you can read. Very well. Accept the fact that I've made a gesture in the vulgar press, and that you've made a vulgar gesture in the school hall. Now, open your *Macbeth* where we left off on Friday."

And, while I teach into their unflawed silence, I wait for what must happen when the Headmaster sees the newspaper.

Not long to wait. The door opens abruptly. The Sixth Form silence drops to a deeper level, and jams. All eyes turn as on one switch.

The Headmaster.

Still with his pitiful cliché face—haggard, drained of colour—he stands there.

His eyes!

The rest of his body says nothing while the eyes, in one sword-flash glance, inform me that he has read the newspaper letter, and is out for blood.

The door closes.

I suppose, really, it is a look of "unadulterated hatred". It is certainly another of those first experiences one is always having, and is accompanied by yet another. For the first time I feel hard or, rather, feel the birth of hardness, the wafer of ice stiffen on the surface of some inner pool.

The bell rings. I go to my next class, conscious that the school, like an engine that has just been overhauled, cleaned to its innermost, oiled, recharged, is running smoothly. The Headmaster throws a spanner. Halfway through the lesson a Fourth Former comes with a message. At mid-morning recess the Head wants all senior boys to gather in the school hall.

Sipping at their cups of tea the masters watch, through the bay window of the Common Room, the seniors enter the hall. The Headmaster is within, alone. The rest of the boys are gathering outside, idle sticky-noses. The staff, waiting and watching, wonders if the Headmaster, the perfidy of males surely all too clear to him, has been egged into making this mysterious and dangerous new move by his wife. A wife, like Lady Macbeth, is loyal and, to the Headmaster on that June morning, must seem the only loyal one in his nightmare.

Years later, from men who are senior boys at the time of the Hutchins School Rebellion, I hear versions of what went on in the hall. Knowing the reminiscences are sure to be, especially with such subject-matter, cock-and-bull, I do not fully believe that the attacks on the Headmaster when he attempts to justify his holiday ban are as brilliantly blistering, such models of oratorical invective, as they appear in legend. I have, indeed, no clear picture of what happens inside the building at all. The only real information I have is that a man who has handed power to a group of schoolboys an hour earlier and, bent on justifying himself, cannot wait until this weapon falls from their silly fists, has chosen to closet himself with the same boys, the weapon still freshly delightful to their hands, in the very hall of their triumph, the echoes of their silence and his pleas of "Sing! I order you to sing!" still infesting the rafters.

It is a brief closeting.

The Common Room watchers have scarcely eaten their ginger nuts before the doors of the hall are torn open like the gates of the Bastille, the seniors explode angrily into view, and the rebellion is on.

What was a family tiff is now a public scandal.

Within fifteen minutes the school is empty of boys, and the seniors have chivvied the last juniors out of the school grounds. For a while they are to be seen running around on the road as aimlessly as newly decapitated ducklings until the newspaper photographers and reporters who have been summoned by a more malicious senior arrive to organize, photograph, and muck-rake.

That an outside-the-school world considers I have planned the rebellion step by step is a privilege of ignorance, and concerns me not a whit. If I become, as I do, déclassé with one set of fools, I also become the standard-bearer on the ramparts with another set of fools. That I am one of a dozen guests sipping sherry and nibbling oyster patties with the Governor and his Lady on the evening of the revolt is a pretty freak of circumstance and is, I hear later, considered to indicate that the noisy splashes are on the surface of very deep water indeed.

Not concerned about the outside responses, I am—and deeply at first—concerned that the Headmaster should be pretending to imagine I have been plotting with the boys like a Guy Fawkes. He knows that the letter has done no more than record the staff's disapproval of the decision of private school headmistresses and headmasters to do away with the holiday. He knows that I reserve a certain power of initiative for the classes, and teach them with my will intact, and have no further truck with them beyond an act of hail-fellow-well-met to offset the down-Fido! class-room discipline.

He is pretending because he is up to something.

The wafer of ice doubles and redoubles itself, and hardens.

This is not a matured headmaster like P. J. Green of Williamstown, or J. F. Ward of Prince's, with whom one's quirks, conceits, and weaknesses are as safe as one's integrities and strengths. This is an ambitious young male with whom one's integrity and strength are less safe than one's weaknesses. A weakness he can openly and fearlessly attack. An integrity has to be sniped at from the undergrowth. For the next couple of months I become, mentally, a moccasined Deerslayer with ears pricked for the crack of the broken twig, the whisper in the leaves. It is an exhilarating and back-to-childhood game in which the tactics used against me are as revolting as the defence tactics I must use. Direct confrontation is useless. The Head's eyes at the Sixth Form doorway have said, "I'll get you!"

How?

Knowing that events in this sort of warfare never shape themselves to expectation, I clear my mind of side-tracking expectations, leave it open to expect any sort of malarky, and let the ice harden to iron.

I ask no questions about newspaper reports that the Hutchins School Board is "considering what action is to be taken against" me and, to this day, have no idea what goes on backstage. On-stage, the Headmaster's first move is the lovers' tiff one of not speaking.

After a fortnight of this, I try confrontation in his study. He will not look at me.

"I shall," I say, "be quite content to resign. New positions will be being advertised soon. If you're unhappy at having disloyalty around like Banquo's ghost, I'll gladly vanish."

"The Board," he says, "expects you to stay on."

"The Board only knows about my work and attitude from you. Does that mean you expect me to stay on?"

For God's sake tell the truth.

"The Board makes decisions in these matters."

"Only on the advice of the Headmaster."

I am talking to ectoplasm.

"I am very busy, Porter."

He has not looked at me once.

We are all very busy that second term in 1946. As well as the ordinary school work, there is the undistinguished revelry that goes on during the celebration of a school's centenary, the showing-off, speechifying, and spit-and-polish brouhaha. My contributions are a re-cataloguing of the library, the designing of a new stage and fittings for the school hall, and a production of *Lady Precious Stream*. I know that the June rebellion is now as remote as Agincourt, and as uninteresting as the murder before last to everyone except the Headmaster and, through him, the Board. Although there are no rustles in the undergrowth it would be reckless not to be aware that the sniper lies there holding his breath, so I remain aware. In the term holidays I travel about Tasmania sketching the decaying sandstone mansions with their porticoes and lime avenues and broken sundials and oak groves, the empty inns, the abandoned shot-towers and kilns and pigeon-lofts and barns, the well-kept convict prisons, and well-populated church graveyards. I return to the boarding-house to find a letter from the Board giving me a term's notice.

At last! Out of the undergrowth at last!

I know exactly what is to be done. It is Sunday. I pack my cases. The clock of my whole being ticks faster, and more loudly. On Monday, at mid-morning recess, I go to the Head. This time he is looking at me. Our wills intersect. Hard eyes face hard eyes.

"You remember I offered to resign?"

"Yes."

How, I wonder, does he kill his beetles?

Why does he kill them?

"You know that the good positions I could have applied for have now been snapped up?"

He does not answer.

"This notice has been deliberately delayed to inconvenience me."

His eyes flicker, but he has an answer: "There will be good positions available again at the end of third term."

"During which time I sing on street corners?"

"I don't understand."

"Yes you do."

"You will be teaching here until the end of third term."

"The Board expects that?"

"Yes. The Board expects that."

"Then I should like to talk their expectations over with them. Now."

Having said this, I expect delay. I am in luck. The Headmaster's first telephone call to his strongest supporter on the Board, a university professor, achieves results. Within ten minutes the professor arrives. His approach—he is a fattish man—is the smiling, hand-outstretched one, "Well, well, well! This is our clever producer. I was very impressed, Porter, with your production of *Lady Precious Stream*. It was . . ."

"I know. Very good."

I have to outplay two men, and must not let up. If I can outplay only by cheapness their cheapness, that is what must happen. There is one card in their hand whose value is hidden from me.

"Professor, the Headmaster tells me that you expect me to stay until the end of the term."

"That is so."

"The Board is quite happy for me to stay?"

The pause is a pause. Then, "For the sake of the boys."

"You want me to stay for the sake of the boys?"

"Yes."

I play the card I have been waiting to play.

"Why have you dismissed me?"

The professor's face breaks, and immediately mends itself. "Porter, you will receive a first-class reference, and—"

"Why have you dismissed me?" This is the card I am after.

I am astounded at the answer. From the moment when the Head appears in the Sixth Form doorway I know that, by hook or by crook, he'll have me out. He must have searched hard and long for a reason. Ten years later an Old Boy journalist tells me that the Head has cross-examined him on whether I have given him whisky to drink and cigarettes to smoke! I wish I had known that in 1946. What other barrels he scrapes the bottom of in search of reasons I don't know.

Why have they dismissed me?

"Because you haven't a university degree."

"You employed me without one. You turned down university applicants."

"We have had a change of policy. We feel that a master without a degree is not properly qualified to teach senior boys."

"But you expect me to go on teaching, unqualified, for another three months? Teaching senior boys who are paying for qualified teachers?"

There is always the moment when the first quiver of the top shows that it is no longer spinning fast enough to remain vertical. The professor and the Headmaster show the first quiver. They speak together, uttering the only near-truth they have, "For the sake of the boys."

"And if I say the boys can go and jump in the lake?"

"At least let us discuss this like gentlemen."

O God, not that!

I say it, "O God, not that! If I say—"

The professor, "Get out! You can get out of this school!"

The Headmaster, "Be out of here in half-an-hour. . . ."

The professor, "Get out! Get out! Get out!"

They are shrieking, vermilion-faced, shrieking like parrots on fire.

Since I have been ice-bound calm, it is easy to remain so a little longer, "I shall want a cheque made out for the rest of my salary until the thirty-first of December."

I go to the Common Room, and telephone a taxi-cab. I bring my luggage downstairs.

I leave Hutchins School.

A lawyer friend picks up the cheque later. I can either return to Australia or stay on in Tasmania seeing what else comes towards me bearing misshapen gifts. I stay the few months longer and, ultimately, do very little more than prove that

Hobart and I are antipathetic. Explicable? No. Valuable experience? Without the shadow of a doubt.

If nothing else, I should never have been able to write a word of my Wainewright novel, a work I consider among my best, if I had not lived in Hobart for a little time, and done what he must have done—listened to the sour-smelling Rivulet lapping under the Palladio, walked the yards and corridors of the Hobart Gaol, toiled up the crook-back streets, seen the cross of snow that yearly curdles in the crevices of Mount Wellington on the stony roots of which the little stone city is riveted, and skipped my hand along the area railings of cottages with their windowsills holystoned as though worn by footsteps, and their doorsteps hollowed by generations of feet as though worn by holystoning.

Apart from regret at leaving my back-bar intimates whose reckless gaiety and attitude of to-hell-with-psychology-Picasso-and-apocalyptic-poetry I agree with, and a handful of charming friends, it is relief and refreshment to take off from Tasmania. I notice, in retrospect, what I do not really notice there and then, that these friends are nearly all non-Tasmanians, or Tasmanians de-insularized by having lived on the Mainland (the Tasmanian term for Australia) or elsewhere. I am still, after all these years, not quite certain what it is in my nature that has so often made me run foul of people and institutions in Tasmania. The latest of a tiresome progression of duels, on and off throughout the years, is as recently as 1965 when I am self-cornered—by the same breed of conviction that self-cornered me in 1946—into bringing a Hobart newspaper to court for suggesting that one of my books is written to attract the attention of censors. There is always—why?—a twist in my Tasmanian experiences. In this latest one it is that I am one of the few Australian writers who approves of Australian censorship.

Regret at leaving Hobart friends, all of whom I am pretty sure to see again, is less distressing than regret at leaving my garden at Hutchins which I know I shall never see again. To leave the gardens I have at Duke's and Prince's does not cause deep distress because I have seen some seasons through, birth to death, and an act of fulfilment has been committed. At Hutchins the garden is a few months old, is just beginning to break the crust of winter, and the narrow buds of daffodils and narcissi I last remember must always be remembered so, unopened, furled, nosing the still Antarctic air for the taste of spring. Spring, in cold countries, is a more exquisitely poignant illustration of resurrection than it is in warm countries, and it seems to me of a piece with all else that is happening to be thwarted of seeing, in my borrowed plot of land, the opening and unfurling, the full-faced defiance of frost and dark, I have looked forward to. It is, but I cannot guess this, the last garden I am to have for years.

When I write to J. F. Ward, outlining my part in the Hutchins scandal as objectively as a bias permits, he invites me to return to Prince's. That river has, however, been swum in. Having begun to see Australia, I am keen to see more. I keep my eye peeled for a vacancy in a reputable school near Sydney which is, by reputation, Australia's most dashing and flamboyant city and, by fact, its largest, oldest, and most strikingly situated.

Until what I think is the right school comes along I remain in Hobart, and do little of value to anyone, and get some mould on my tranquillity. I do form an amateur theatrical group called the Hobart Theatre Guild, and direct a production of *Hamlet*. This is notable for at least one thing—the use, almost certainly for the first time in Australia, of fluorescent lighting on a silk cyclorama. To me, now, the labour on *Hamlet* indicates the extent to which I have become harder, the extent to which my confidence has remained unmutilated. I don't mean self-confidence: I suffer the illusion that I've no illusions about my limitations, and cannot therefore extend myself enough to disappoint myself. I mean that my confidence for cause-fighting, despite the Hutchins storm in a slop-basin, is unmutilated. The desecration of St David's graveyard has so startled me emotionally and "historically" that the possible bulldozing of more "historical gems"—and Tasmania is a casket crammed with them—finds me joining the ranks of other warriors on behalf of the Theatre Royal, Australia's oldest theatre, in danger during the nineteen-forties of being knocked down to make way for something progressive. A car park? *Hamlet* is the contribution and, no doubt, it plays a small part in the wood-man-spare-that-tree move.

I am thirty-six when I leave Hobart in 1947, and, although there is an almost immediate thawing of the hardness picked up there, enough remains to be of value. I should prefer to be as I was, no slivers of ice in the system, when I first came to Hobart where too much was learned too quickly. It is, how-ever, ultimately better that I acquired this useful quality of hardness abruptly because, all too aware of its existence, I can control it, and let it grow no farther along my veins. Had it entered by creeping degrees I'd have been less conscious of its effect on my love of human beings who are too precious and dangerous wholly to hate, animals decoyed by love, and living in agonies of imagination.

Nevertheless, it is as well that I have not thawed right back to the isn't-everything-fun view of life when I arrive at Knox Grammar School, a reputable Presbyterian school in a middle-class Sydney suburb. Within the first week it is obvious that I have landed myself in another trouble spot. The writing on the wall of this school is in neon of a different colour but, to my now acuter senses in this field, it spells the same word—Rebel-lion in the House. This time—the callousness at work—I decide to keep out of the ring, watch the nearest exit, stay a term doing whatever the Headmaster says must be done, and move on.

Coming from the long-underwear-in-winter, tepid beer, ten o'clock closing of pubs, and sleet in the street, of Hobart, to the steamy sub-tropical atmosphere of Knox I am, as ever, en-thralled by commonplace things which seem to me as exotic as if I were in another country.

In a sense, I am.

Frangipani grows like a slum weed. Its scent, hitherto appear-ing to me to suggest expensive débutantes, becomes Woolworth and stifling. Unrecognizable birds with astringent voices dash in and out of the school camphor-laurels; a hedge of red hibiscus lines the path to the dining hall; *Strelitzia regina* stands in Aztec groups on the brown lawns. Canteloupes and ice cream appear often on school menus. There is a large swimming pool, and fretful palms moving their fronds like spiders on stalks. The boys and the less hardy of the masters change into shorts when they arrive at school. Trays of water empurpled by Condy's Crystals stand outside the shower rooms as anti-tinea foot-baths. The dormitories contain double-decker bunks of metal. My bed is overhung by a canopy of mosquito gauze that smells like an old singlet. Among the few non-whites at the school are two huge boys from Nauru, chiefs' sons, who look as though they have been stove-polished, write meaningless sentences in exquisite copperplate, and giggle behind their hands with the teeth-hiding gesture of Japanese girls.

I am well away from Knox Grammar School when *its* rebellion occurs, and have no clear idea what it is about.

I do know that the Headmaster finishes up as a person of importance—the curator?—in the Hobart Art Gallery and Museum. The Art Gallery I recall as being a gesture to culture rather than a treasure-house of masterpieces—Tasmania is not a wealthy state. Of the museum the most memorable exhibits are its convict manacles and nineteenth-century costumes, a piece of furniture that is a combination footstool and spittoon, and a pair of Queen Victoria's black silk stockings with her monogram at the top.

Two only of the Headmaster's foibles affect me directly and might, had I not fled from Knox in time, have stirred me again to rash action.

As Senior English Master I am prepared to accept, as at any school, other fill-in subjects and family extras. Before Knox I have done a variety of these chores—umpired cricket matches, taught Middle School Latin, run school magazines, produced *The Monkey's Paw*, accompanied groups of brilliantined boys to end-of-term dances at girls' schools, fired blank bullets from starting-pistols at sports meetings, and sat with justly mocking schoolboys through elocuted performances of *Twelfth Night* and *Julius Caesar* by culture-constipated amateurs. At Knox Grammar I am told to take Sixth Form Divinity, by custom the Headmaster's subject. I take it without a protest, although to teach the subject requires a technique I do not possess, and an evangelical blandness for which native cunning is no substitute. I do what study is possible at night in the Sydney Library. Protest none—even on the grounds that I am Church of Eng-

219

land, and the school and the boys Presbyterian. Protest takes a harder and slyer form—I get in touch with a schoolmaster agency to find out what might be coming up at the end of first term. I do this even before facing the first Sixth Form Divinity lesson disguised as a commercial traveller for Christ.

The Headmaster's other foible is easier to knuckle under to. Schoolmasters at Knox are forbidden to smoke in front of the boys. Although a heavy smoker, I find that the fiat irks me only at certain times.

At four, the last class of the day dismissed, there is a walk of several hundred yards to the boarding-house. It is taboo to smoke during the walk: one is visible as a giraffe to boys. It is equally taboo to smoke anywhere in the boarding-house except in the prim and polished master's sitting-room or in one's bed-room-study. Since I've been used for years mindlessly to lighting up the moment I am outside the class-room, it is interesting to control myself, to pull myself up with the cigarette already out of the packet (tins are becoming a thing of the past), and a grinning Macdonald or Macarthur-Onslow saying, "Go on, sir. I'll keep nit!" It is more interesting to control the mind, as I walk the several hundred yards, from questioning the Head-master's common sense in applying this ban to a number of men several of whom are older than he. Why doesn't he make it easier by specifying that only non-smokers apply for jobs? It would cut down the need for him to s-t-r-o-l-l from behind a tattered banana-palm, waving his forefinger like a French traffic officer at a wanton smoking master, to say, "You know the school rule. Put that out, please."

There is, however, a more irksome hour.

When the hot midday meal is over, and each huge blue enamel teapot drained of its gallon of strong tea, the chairs scraped back, and "For what we have received the Lord make us truly thankful" said, the school straightaway assembles on a playing-field at the back of the school. In all the muggy heat, the cedars sullenly fuming, the bagpipes yowling, the full-bellied school marches round and round and round. On more fervid days, now this boy, now that boy, keels over in a faint.

Meantime, presumably of its own volition, the school dog lies watching and panting in the shade.

Meantime, also in the shade, and decidedly on the Head's ordinance, the staff watches and, not allowed to smoke, its avid smokers gnaw the nicotine on their vandyke-brown knuckles, or retire like corrupt messenger-boys to smoke in the lavatory.

My scant three months at Knox do not give me enough time to find out exactly at which point between adult and child the Headmaster draws his moral line—I presume the line is his, not Presbyterianism's and John Knox's—for this is the only school I teach at where the boys are allowed to have home-made wireless sets and pin-up girls of the Lana Turner sort in their dormitories.

To prevent myself from developing unnecessary feelings of revolt I drop smoking altogether until I am out of sight and hearing of the school. The free-and-easy drinking of the past also becomes a thing of the past: Knox is built in a "dry" area, a shire that does not permit pubs. The nearest, a vast modern atrocity, called, I think, the Greengate, is miles away by bus. I visit it a couple of times with some of the masters but decide that this is too much fag merely for booze; teetotalism is easier by far. I wait with relaxed patience, teetotal and non-smoking, to give the Head notice, and to move on to Ballarat College, to my native state of Victoria where I've not lived for eight years, to a provincial city both wealthy and romantic, to a school I have checked and re-checked as much as possible. There have been too many footprints on my serenity since I left Princes. Anyway, after experiencing two good headmasters, and three headmasters who go back into their boxes, I am hoping for a third good one.

Having long ago, step by step, made oneself as efficient and gracious as one's limitations allow in the give-and-take of daily existence, no longer crying aloud for miracles as when younger, no longer putting faith in beautiful absurdities such as eternal love and endless peace and sin-free days, attempting always to grub out the root of cut-and-come-again cynicism, to remain optimistic of people, it is vexing—and not salutary at all—to find oneself where it is impossible not to walk into the cobwebs streaming from another and boss mind, cobwebs that stick to one's own and servant mind, clogging sympathy, smudging a lucidity hard come by and driving a maturing man to cry out, like a child tired of hide-and-seek, "I give up! I'm coming out! I'm not going to play this absurd game any more!"

Because I leave Knox Grammar in a fashion expressing "I'm not going to play this absurd game any more!" the departure is a relief undiluted by regret of any sort at all. Having earned my money there by enacting the competent automaton, keeping my blinkers on, my eyes on my feet, and my mouth shut, it is very much more than likely that no one remembers I was ever there. Admitting that one term is a brief stay, admitting quirks of circumstance, it yet seems to the point that I have never been recognized and bailed up by a Knox Old Boy but am always bumping into Old Boys from every other place I ever taught in, and not only in likely places such as the Melbourne Post Office, or the marble halls of Australia House, or on a back road outside a fly-blown one-horse bush town, or a Greek liner ballasted to the plimsoll with Australian tourists, but in some far less likely places, doing not usual things—picking lily-of-the-valley in Fontainbleau Forest, taking a rubbing of Heloïse-and-Abelard's tombstone in Père Lachaise Cemetery, eating in a Greek restaurant in Edinburgh, drinking Samos wine near Byron's signature carved on the marble of the temple at Sounion. What is more and most to the point is that, even on my many trips to Sydney, not once have I been accosted by a Knox Old Boy. It leads me to a conclusion that, in suppressing myself at Knox, in playing the role of a meek one, I render myself invisible. One is not, it seems, really visible unless one reveals most of oneself, unless one makes oneself visible.

Thus rested and refreshed, with strengths and weaknesses untapped by several months of disuse, I arrive at Ballarat College full of beans, and only a little leery. There is no need for wariness of any sort. I am instantly attracted by the Headmaster, the staff, the Matron, the Cook (a slender blond giantess whose country cooking is of the sort I've not encountered for years), the ambling provinciality of the school with its hard core of efficiency, and the city of Ballarat itself. The cobwebs on my vision detach themselves—pouf!—they are gone. Almost my first move is a letter to J. F. Ward to tell him I no longer feel I am on the wrong side of the looking-glass, that my convictions can be stowed away, and I can put on my Touchstone costume again.

When I leave Ballarat College about eighteen months afterwards it is with more regret than I realize until later. I leave because I have been offered a job so unlike anything yet attempted by me that I am as excited as though starting a first job. It still—faintly—intrigues me why it is offered, because the offer implies that I certainly appear to be to others someone else than I appear to be to myself. It is too fascinating an offer to turn down even though I am very happy at the college, where nothing out of the ordinary occurs except an invitation —the first ever—to join a schoolmasters' union. This is the one and only time a conviction has to be aired in Ballarat. "No!" is, however, all the airing necessary.

Since I am so doubly happy, after Hutchins and Knox, it is only fair that the happiness should be tempered. Pain serves its purpose here. My hip injury, after nine mute years, begins to speak loudly of itself again. At first, until I learn the art of speaking more loudly than pain, of cannibalistically eating it, and digesting it, it seems to hamstring rather than merely temper happiness. It takes a while to find that, in the long run, pain does not destroy happiness, contentment or serenity. Pain, indeed, has its glamour, and its intrusion on the senses merely makes the outward expression of happiness a little more difficult because this requires action, and, just as thought is the denial of comprehension, and desire the denial of wisdom, so is action the denial of repose. Repose—inner repose, that is, central happiness, the repose of the soul or whatever the mystery is— seems, for me, the flour in the bread of contentment.

To have to perform repose-destroying actions to keep repose undestroyed is a conflict not without failures but is a conflict I must win, can only win alone, by myself, because pain is incommunicable. To someone else, however sympathetic, however imaginative, my pain is as ungraspable as reality, as ungraspable as the salt in salt water.

Except for this contest within my own body, I am, when I leave Ballarat, much the same piece of topiary work that arrived, a bush that has been clipped, shaped, twisted, and fed with some deliberation. For years the shape has altered little and, no matter how many times it is transplanted in the next twenty years, remains unaltered except for the stealthy leaf-picking and sap-decelerating work of those years. The main branches are set.

Those set branches! Those habits, the same then as now!

I am infinitely outmoded.

All very smart to have come to obvious conclusions that modern men are masked animals, that speech is often the camouflage of ignorance, that many of the upper class are only the lower class in disguise, and that the surest way to defeat others attempting to reform one is to be heedless of one's own fate. All very well to fall in and out of lust, to open and shut doors, to tell the truth, to feel one's hair thinning, to look around and listen around and find that an unfelt wind has blown many things out of range. All very sorrow-making to discover that sorrow is man-made, selfish, and mortal. All very boring to know that civilization is gangrened with boredom because it can never stick to one set of ideals. All very boring to know that boredom is immortal. However—however, one has to clean one's teeth.

I clean them now, just as I clean them then. Euthymol Tooth Paste. Kent bristle brush. Right teeth, turn brush, centre teeth, left teeth. Scrub tongue. Gargle. Spit. Every morning. Every night. Drunk, sober, in landlady's bathroom, P. and O. cabin, King's Cross, Beirut, Ballarat, Bloomsbury, three miles above the Pacific Ocean, basement at the seedy end of Knightsbridge.

There are dozens of these habits, and a thousand muscles perform what is decided on decades ago.

The cold shower every morning—Wright's Coal Tar Soap.

The Ingram's Shaving Cream applied in three dabs. Left, chin, right. The Kent badger-hair shaving-brush. Right, chin, left. The safety-razor given free with a tube of shaving-cream in 1928. Left, chin, right.

Left sock. Right sock.

Right shoe. Left shoe.

Nails of left hand trimmed with scissors. Nails of right hand filed.

Tie, wide, woollen and Windsor-knotted. Hand-made brogues by Geo. W. Bunbury of London. Two meals a day.

Eight hours' sleep. "Dear boy, this!" and "Dear boy, that!" Whisky and water. No ice. No watch. No rings. Read *A Tale of Two Cities* again—the twentieth time? This is the little silver box with the things that are in it thirty years ago still in it today—the same dress studs, cuff-links, silver toothpick, magnifying-glass, leather buttons that "might come in handy", the 250-year calendar never used, the teeny-weeny gold safety-pins, the white pebble with the black stripe through it.

Why not put on the right sock first, buy a narrow silk tie, stop reading *A Tale of Two Cities*, and saying "Dear boy!", and using Euthymol and Ingram's? Why not put rings on my fingers, ice in my whisky, a hat on my head, and throw out the pebble, and the leather buttons that will never come in handy, and all the habits?

It is too late now, as it is too late then. Anyway what is the point in this sort of delousing—were I to change everything, from shaving-cream to religion, throw out everything from pebble to conviction, were I to do everything that is done in Rome I should still not be a Roman.

It is too late, much too late, to start for any destinations not of the heart—oh, much too late.

In Ballarat I first become aware what a number of private habits I have picked up, and how many schoolmaster ones. I have a vision of myself handing myself on from school to school like a plate of sandwiches, always the same sandwiches. There I am saying the same things about *Macbeth* and Tennyson and the position of French adjectives. There I am producing *The Mikado*, correcting the same mistakes in answers to the same examination questions, announcing through a loudspeaker at the sports meeting the same words: "Next event, the Under Fourteen Four-Forty. Will the boys taking part go immediately—immediately—to Mr Godbehear at the south end of the track." "Afternoon tea is now being served in the School Hall." "A black and yellow silk scarf has been found in the drive."

Outside school hours I appear in Ballarat Amateur Dramatic Society productions, and where once—was it in 1890 or only last night?—I was a juvenile lead, now I am the mature man with hair silvered at the temples in plays by Priestley, Bridie,

225

or Novello. I direct *Lady Precious Stream*, a chore, a habit I can perform with my back turned.

Drink? A great deal. I am in a sprawled-out provincial city with a ranting and roaring gold-digging past; and the emanations from that past (so it seems to me) have the gold-happy, devil-may-care, I'm-my-own-man, diggings flavour, as the clenched-up stony city of Hobart had emanations from a convict past (so it seemed to me) with the flavour of eternal exile and elaborate corruption.

Although a city crowded with Italianate public buildings all stucco caryatides and Corinthian pillars and parapets topped by urns; with colleges and churches, spires and pinnacles and domes; edged by public parks with conservatories and European glades and 1884 statues of Flora, Pomona, and Hebe; with avenues and trams and markets and theatres and cinemas, Ballarat retains much of a country atmosphere. An inch outside the suburbs, already rusticated by orchards and fowl-yards and shock-headed gardens, are the dairy farms and sheep properties with their miles of fencing, their windbreaks and shearing-sheds and milking-yards, their paddocks blazing green for the milder seasons, bleached and tousled for summer, with a ground-mist of fog-grass, and smelling in late afternoon like haystacks.

The masters at Ballarat College are all good drinking men in the Australian country tradition and, haunting the nearest pub to the school with them, I am soon in the whirlpool of Ballarat hard-drinking life. As an unattached male with a handy tool-kit of social tricks, a set of tails, the savoir-faire of a cad, a collection of dirty yarns filched from Charles Jury in Adelaide, and untenanted time on my hands, I find the scene littered with invitations to parties, balls, bucks' nights, pub-crawls throughout the district, Sunday morning revival sessions on Pims to freshen up after Saturday night parties, and Sunday afternoon parties to tail off the Sunday morning ones.

Among the liveliest and wittiest of the high-flying crew I become a member of is a Roman Catholic family of Irish descent whose financial interests are many—the land, the Ballarat Brewery, and a huge hotel at St Kilda, a seaside suburb of Melbourne, a mile or so from where I am born at Albert Park, two blocks away from the sea, in 1911.

226

I stated earlier that I do not know why these people, wealthy, vivacious, intelligent, hard-drinking but hard-headed, should have offered a penniless playboy with a gammy leg and a repertoire of risqué stories the job they do offer—as assistant-manager in the George Hotel, St Kilda—but it is offered, and accepted. The year is now 1949. I have been working since 1927, nineteen of those years as a schoolmaster, and have not an inkling how the intricate machinery of a hotel, famous since the eighteen-seventies, works, but the scrap of paper has blown across the trail, and is recklessly to be followed.

I resign from Ballarat College.

·It is not until Ballarat is an hour away from being a thing of the past that I remember that Father and Mother had their honeymoon in Ballarat, at Craig's Hotel, next door to which Adam Lindsay Gordon once owned stables, and in which, during his trip to Australia in the nineteen-twenties, the Prince of Wales stayed. I am glad the recollection of the honeymoon has not come earlier to suggest a tear or two, not of brine but of sentimental syrup.

It is better that I was unaccompanied by the ghosts of a man and a woman, years younger than I, love's animals dressed in their new honeymoon clothes and their new privity and their new happiness, as, wasting the life they gave me, I pry and stroll where they must have pried and strolled thirty-nine years before—among the monkey-puzzle trees and wych-elms in the gardens, along the rim of the lake under a 1910 harvest moon, past the marble lions into the miniature Crystal Palace where the marble man and wife, she dangling the marble infant like a larger amulet, he controlling the marble cloak that billows and curls above and behind them as they gracefully flee the cataclysm of Pompeii on perfect marble feet.

By the time I reach the George Hotel, St Kilda, in early 1949, I am tall enough in years if nothing else to see my own piddling landscape of space and time turned face upward for inspection, and can see, *just* see, the crinkle-crankle of my own footprints leading up to me. Minute footprints across a minute terrain that was once so illimitable and pure but has shrunk to the size of a child's glove, grubby and worn into holes. It is a terrain that can, as the glove can, be washed and darned and dyed and turned inside out, but the pin-prick footsteps always, always show. Looking down and back at them, I cannot decide (and who or what else can decide?) whether wilfulness has brought me the better or the worse way to where and what I am. Assistant-manager of a hotel! God!

What the angels have to go through! Unable to escape heaven! Unable to avoid looking down! Unable, century after century after century, not to not see that nothing in man lets up, nothing progresses. There am I, the words of the poets washing over my mind, edging it towards truth; there am I, the lies of the scientists and politicians edging my mind towards disillusion; there am I, my own poet and scientist and politician, finishing up like the doggerel in a schoolgirl's autograph album:

> *Look before you leap;*
> *Men are always cheap.*

Or striding up the entrance steps of the George Hotel, through the revolving glass doors heavy as the portals of a family vault, across the draughts-board of black marble and white marble, with all the assurance—all the doggerel assurance —in the world:

> *Love all; trust a few;*
> *Always paddle your own canoe.*

I have never wanted to live, a monastery-pond carp growing weightier and older, safe below the surface that only reflects suns and moons but has none of its own, that reflects the keeper, the god with the single-mind-sized head who throws me scraps from his dreary table. I do not, however, properly realize, until I qualmlessly accept the George Hotel job, how much stronger the vagabond artery has grown, how the years have enriched and are beginning to agitate the blood in it. There is absolutely no impulse to be a tattered-and-torn wind-on-the-heath-brother gipsy with a belly full of windfalls, hedge-berries and brook-water; nor to be an unshaven back-o'-beyond swaggie in a willy-willy of flies, humping a bluey with a bottle of Red Ned in it; but despite a need for certain amenities, I am turning out to be a sort of gipsy or swaggie, one without his own roof over his head, unprotected from the small winds by even a trailing

228

whippet of a missus to have her dirty palm crossed with silver, a puritan con man starting to look like a cashiered colonel, and living by his wits. This latest roof not my own is a lofty one and, on the corner nearest the sea, it nozzles into the sky a pepper-pot tower with a dome of copper scales that salty rains, and fogs smelling of kelp, have licked green.

The hotel beneath the roof and the tower is itself a thesaurus of seventy years' chopping and changing of fashions; its inhabitants cover a number of gamuts.

All in all, to me, the difference between a school boarding-house and the George is not great; the complexities of management are, on a larger scale, the same.

The Headmaster?

Mr Wimpole, whose Ballarat part-owner sister has offered me the job, is the majority-owner of the hotel, and lives there with his wife, but, although I see him every day it is always from far off. Otherwise I meet Mr and Mrs Wimpole twice only. The first time is for sherry, titbits of smoked salmon, cheese, and anchovies on toast, and—I have no doubts—the once-over. Mutual, the once-over.

I remember them as late-sixtyish, frail-looking, fleshless. As people married for decades often do, they seem to have interchanged qualities. He is small, rather like the Duke of Windsor; she somehow matches that impression, feminized. They may be taller and more robust than memory suggests, for their suite, fitted like royal chambers in the Pyramids gloomily into the core of the vast hotel is also vast, and would make a short lad of Gog. One reaches the suite by corridors in the corners of which ceiling-high looking-glasses reflect one's advance as the approach of someone seen before, someone not recognizable in the obscurity of magenta wallpaper and chocolate-painted pillars until one is nose to nose with oneself. The booty of the Wimpoles' overseas trips jammed into the suite is not homely booty—brass-work from India, Dresden figurines, looking-glasses with rococo frills of Muranese decoration, billiard-table-sized nineteenth-century Italian canvases painted in many tones of Bovril, chiaroscuro dramas caught at a point of climax where the upturned eye glitters with a highlight like a wet diamond. Among all this, and gate-leg tables and majolica platters and china cabinets and curtains of burgundy velvet and rosewood chairs, by a stand of potted ferns, a canary in a gilded cage tinily talks to itself as though not in its right mind.

It cannot be said that Mr and Mrs Wimpole have retreated, as well they wisely might, from the post-war world becoming overgrown with the commoner weeds of progress at their very doorstep, but that they have remained in their own world, a world that could be the one before the sinking of the *Titanic*. They dine in pre-*Titanic* solitude, Edwardianly, sacrosanct as royalty, at a table at the head of the dining-room. Sharing the era with them, waiting as it might be for the iceberg to run its fingernail along the fabric of the unsinkable, and let in the coldness and coarseness of the future, are the permanent guests, mainly elderly women, many of whom have lived at the George for decades—Anglo-Indian spinsters, superannuated deaconesses, judges' daughters, clergymen's childless widows, bitches all. Their tables are those along the walls of the dining-room so that intrusive fly-by-nights, the mobile creatures of no consequence, eating at central tables, are fenced in by the elderly, each with her silver napkin-ring, each with a private still-life of little jars and bottles on the damask in front of her—digestive tablets, vitamin pills, Fortnum and Mason chutney, Düsseldorf mustard, Rose's marmalade, Gentlemen's Relish.

The elderly guests, fatigued with indolence, absence their only companion, have concocted—from lips unkissed and songs unsung and letters never received—mean and querulous selves who live only for whining and food. The George, true to the lavish and colonial age it has halted at, is unaffected by the vogue for the food of poverty at that time being introduced into Australia by Displaced Persons, and immigrants from the riff-raff strata of Europe's paupers and peasants, and has a magnificent table, and a service that, although diminished, still has the hierarchic quality of service in the century of Queen Victoria. The old men and women—old *gentlemen* and *ladies*—eat their way with finicky gluttony through every menu, eat from the moment they wake up until they fall asleep. Having, as I grow older, found two square meals a day quite enough, I foolishly think older people, particularly old non-working people, will be content with a doll's meal, a hermit's ascetic snack. I am right off the track. Tea and toast in bed, a breakfast fit for a weight-lifter, morning tea, a heavy luncheon which many of them call tiffin, afternoon tea, an hors-d'oeuvre to cheese dinner, and a large night-cap supper fill their bellies and days.

Food, I see, is the deity of the lonely, the god of many Communions.

I feel far less pity than sympathizers demoralized by tolerance do for the selfish elderly who will not take advantage of inertia, who don't know how to do nothing, who cultivate loneliness and self-pity, and am daily sickened by the queue of old people, whose tables are theirs alone, lined up, a quarter of an hour before the gong sounds, outside the twelve-foot-high double doors of plate-glass sand-blasted with art noveau floralities, a spiteful queue bickering as it stands watching the waitresses within at their last-minute work on table-setting, a queue obsessed and unbalanced, whose world has contracted to the size of a dinner-plate. They are their own gang of disclosures. It is almost possible to see the forked tongue, thin as hair, run in and out between each pair of lips, in and out, in and out.

I see them, the long day's labour of malice, complaint, and gorging over, the final crumbs on their chins, their eyes flat and glazed, creeping from the sitting-rooms to the iron lattice of the lift, past the Satsuma vases and Chinese screens and camphorwood chests and nests of tables, past the life-size negresses and kneeling negro boys of lacquered wood touched with crimson and gold, past the bronze bacchantes mild as milk and tall as amazons upholding marble globes rosily glowing with electric light, past everything, across the chessboard of tiles. The lift ascends with these well-to-do no-hopers.

I think, somehow, to see them in their rooms, in their beds, not lying straight as effigies on old tombs as they circumspectly should be in rehearsal for imminent death-beds, but coiled like adders about the centre-piece of their own heads, asleep with the glazed eyes still open, the forked thread running in and out between lips already parted to emit venom at the steward who brings the first tray of food.

In hotel circles and employment agencies the George Hotel is, I soon discover, known affectionately as Wimpole's Circus, and this small zoo of constipated adders attached to it is the dreariest and most troublesome section. The rest of the Circus is tempestuous, a sea of many winds, its army of employees and coming-and-going guests as lively as the cockroaches behind every *bain marie* in the kitchen. A hundred one-act plays a day keep me agog.

St Kilda, once a fashionable and grandiose seaside suburb, a sort of Aussie Cannes with a better beach, has become tawdry, its one-guinea waves now cheap at a penny. Its mansions along the Esplanade—Belgian Gothic, Greek Revival, Florentine Renaissance, Moorish, even Spanish Mission—have become boarding-houses, or have been subdivided into flats, flatettes, and hives of bed-sitter cells smelling of gas-rings. In 1949, its drain-edges, and front steps, and the stairways descending to the beach zigzag through lawns and palms and gazania-covered rockeries, are still painted with blackout white, and the suburb has become a post-war working-class playground providing all the shoddy and instant pleasures the working-class go in for— a Luna Park, a Palais de Danse, a skating rink, fish-and-chip shops, hamburger shops, ice-cream kiosks, soft-drink stalls, pie-and-tea restaurants, milk bars, penny-in-the-slot machines. In the back streets, blocks away from the sea, are the houses of rag-trade Jews and fish-shop Greeks and fruit-shop Italians. Nearer the sea are several night-clubs haunted by car salesmen, petty criminals, Albanians and their factory-hand pick-ups, confidence men and their molls.

When the wind flings the seagulls about like handbills, and the sea is frothing at the mouth and ejecting corks from fishermen's nets, and rotten oranges from P. and O. liners on to the beach, the spivs and gamblers and Esplanade larrikins and urinal-haunting perverts and burglars and pickpockets make for the bars. The bars include those of the George Hotel.

The George's earlier reputation as one of Melbourne's half a dozen *cordon bleu* hotels still draws guests from the country; its old-fashioned lavishness and service still draw those who prefer these qualities in a hotel. Upstairs, the George is the *Titanic* that missed the iceberg, and has merely got shabby and patched. The patchers are at work all the time. I remember the housekeeper and her bowed-over staff, the sewing-machine ceaseless as creation, the sheets of fine pure linen being turned, the napkins and tablecloths darned, the chintz loose-covers mended, the bath mats re-hemmed. And every day, Scottie, the carpenter and odd-job man, in a leather many-pocketed apron, the wires of a grotesque hearing-aid drooping from ear to ear, hobbles about, dedicated to surgery on the inanimate. His work is so fine that most of it cannot be seen. His love of the hotel and its furnishings, as physical creatures being ill-treated by brute humans, and scarred by cruel carelessnesses, compels him to make the restorations flawlessly invisible—a split chair-leg, a piece nicked from the scagliola top of a console table, a broken cornice—less for a pride in his own craftsmanship than for a sense that he is painlessly healing something that has been hurt. I hear him say, skimming his hand over a wound in wood, "There, there. You're no to worry. I'll be but a wee while, and you'll no feel a twinge. And they'll never know." Sometimes, as when patching the lead floor, polished to silver, in one of the older bathrooms, it is impossible for him to mend and leave no sign. It is then, as much as in the invisible surgery, that the ardour behind his skill shows. The scar becomes a beauty patch, an inlay of lead cut in the shape of a five-pointed star, a Tudor rose, a Maltese cross. His one sorrow is that he can never catch up. For this he blames not the pillaging years, nor even slapdash chambermaids and cleaners, nor the vandal guests ("They would no do it in their own house!") whom he despises, but the fact that he was once in hospital for three months. His pain and inconvenience—nothing. The desertion of the carpets and chairs and statues and picture frames and door-handles—everything. He has lost some time in time, and the maimed suffer; the hotel becomes a hospital without a doctor; the mute patients multiply.

He is a Florence Nightingale unable to overtake a Scutari, not of chipped and scratched and torn human beings, mere fallible flesh and easily replaceable, but of irreplaccable and infallible objects infinitely more precious to him and the world. There is the white finger, unsoiled by nose-picking and lascivious beckoning, to be restored to the statue of Tranquillity that has stood for years under the oil painting of "Dawn at Ronda"; the frame of "Sunset on the Nile" is to be re-gilded; the prints of setters by Thomas Blinks are to have new backing. Scottie can scarcely sit through a staff luncheon of kidneys sauté and turkey salad because, despite the creeper of hearing-aid wires growing from his ears, he can hear nothing except the thin wail of a crippled pedestal, the moan of a Corinthian capital bleeding to death from the injury where a curl of stucco acanthus leaf has been knocked off by a cobweb broom. Patcher-up of a tottering empire of values, he cannot bear, he says, to think of a progressive upstart taking down the framed Buckingham Palace menus hanging in the dining-room. For him, they seem to possess the superstitious assurance of the apes of Gibraltar: when the menus go, his *Titanic* will founder. He knows them, like a prayer against dissolution, by heart, a prayer he will jabber off at the drop of a hint:

Her Majesty's Dinner . . . Monday, 21st June, 1897

Potages	*Tortue*
	Printanière
Poissons	*Filets de Sole à la Normande*
	Aiguillettes de Merlans, Sauce Chéron
Entrées	*Bouchées à l'Impératrice*
	Côtelettes d'Agneau en Belle-Vue
Relevés	*Poulets à la Régence*
Rôti	*Roast Beef*
	Cailles bardées, feuilles de Vigne
Entremêts	*Asperges en Branches*
	Beignets de Semouille, Ananas
	Meringues à la Chantilly, Vanille
	Kiche au Fromage
Side Table	*Hot and Cold Roast Fowls, Tongue, Cold Beef, Salade Romaine*

For me there is, as always, the fascination of observing how eras, kings and queens, history's toughs like Alexander the Great and Hitler, how poets and murderers and national heroes, give themselves away by their food. Scottie cannot hear me saying this for he is saying the same thing, and drawing wonderful conclusions, and reciting Edward the Eighth's menu for the first of June 1904. His university Scots-French is better than my high-school Australian-French. He rattles on (I am looking at the framed menu in the Buckingham Palace chef's pointed handwriting) without a slip.

Madeira 1816	*Tortue Claire*
	Consommé Printanier à la d'Orléans
Johannesberg 1880	*Whitebait à la Diable*
	Suprêmes de Truite à la Valencienne
G. H. Mumm 1892	*Zéphires d'Ortolans à la Lucullus*
Chambertin 1875	*Hanche de Venaison de Sandringham*
	Selle d'Agneau à la Boulangère
Still Sillery 1865	*Cailles Froides à la Russe*
	Poussins Rôtis sur Canapés
	Salade à la Jaucourt
Château Laffitte 1875	*Asperges d'Argenteuil, Sauce Mousseline*
	Pêches à la Reine Alexandra
	Gradins de Pâtisseries
	Cassolettes à la Jockey Club
Royal Tawny Port	*Petites Glaces à la Moscovite*
	Paniers Garnis de Friandises
Château Margaux 1871	*Dessert*

Heigho! The George's menus are also in French; and the Wimpoles, and the permanent upstairs guests, and Scottie and the oldest grey-haired stewards and chambermaids, all live in a Pinero dream that two world wars have not broken.

There is no Americanization in the George, no shilling-in-the-slot wirelesses, no loudspeaker system, no chromium, plastic, ground coffee, tinned peas, frozen food, or tea urns. What modernization has been done can be assessed by the subtractions, the contents of several store-rooms filled with cruets, Venetian glass finger-bowls, bouillon cups, gas shades, coal-scuttles, epergnes, candlesticks, marble clocks, cut glass water carafes, chamber-pots, and washstand sets.

The only recognition of a cruder day is seen in the basement bar, in Ladies' Lounges occupying what were—in the days when Sarah Bernhardt lived in a St Kilda bijou house with her pet tortoises—a smoking-room and a music room. It is to these garish parts of the hotel that the winds scything in over the stubble of the sea drive the fish-and-chips element, and the St Kilda underworld.

That they can be instantly spotted as not to be trusted a centimetre is not good enough for the writer. He wants to get to know them better than their telltale suits and ties and haircuts. There is no time. No-time is a condition not foreseen by someone spoiled after many years of a nine-to-four, five-day-week life with months of holiday. Admittedly the manager's week is a forty-hour one, but the breaks are so arranged that little can be done with them. I seem to be always going back on duty. This cuts out any chance of my enjoying, except rarely, the kind of drinking I enjoy. I stop drinking. Anyway, somewhat on the formula that he who works in a chocolate factory doesn't crave chocolates, I find the idea of alcohol momentarily repulsive, and do not possess the knack of the other assistant-manager who can, along with many of the rest of the staff, do efficient work while half-stewed. Above all, the effect of steady tippling during the day on some of the foreign kitchen staff requires from me a cool mind.

The kitchen and dining-room are under my control and, after a first week of silent observation, I can find nothing more useful to do than try out on these grown men and women the disciplinary tricks of a schoolmaster. Slightly adapted, they work. I find this uncanny until it strikes me that men and women are no more intelligent than when they were children, and often more tractable. That the kitchen is a little Europe of a dozen or so men in whom seethe eight national animosities too esoteric for my comprehension makes the experiment of discipline a fascinating project—the *chef de cuisine* is Russian, the others are Dutch, Maltese, Greek, Latvian, German and, responsible for most of the knife-brandishing, an Italian breakfast cook from Turin and an Italian kitchen-man from Calabria.

No stranger to brawls at the Blue House on the Hobart waterfront nor to flourished knives at Madame's Williamstown

Wine Depôt, I am nevertheless in a different guise in the George Hotel kitchen. There is no seasoned Ma Dwyer or Madame Jorgensen to take action while I am enjoying the fracas as no more than a bystander in another's establishment. A set-to in the George kitchen is a set-to in my own establishment, and I am the stuck-with-it boss-cocky.

I have already settled various minor brawls—sex and damaged vanity the usual causes, and have thereby learned something of the emotional looseness of what I am beginning to think of as my pupils, the truculent arrogance of the Dutchman, the quarrel-making overprotectiveness of the Maltese elder brother Manuel Vella for his pseudo-Casanova young brother Josette, the nobody-loves-me sulkiness of Hans Singer the German kitchen-boy, the yellings, the arm-wavings, the tears about what seems to me nothing at all. I am in touch with a different brand of masculinity, as expressed, to that, as expressed, of Australian friends. The foreign brand seems faked, depthless, centred in sensual skills used only to display those skills. I keep on recalling a half-remembered *Esquire* article by a woman—"Latins are Lousy Lovers"—which seems to point up my feelings. The hot-blooded ones so cold-bloodedly vain about their hot blood complain that the waitresses are rude to them at the serving counters. The waitresses point out that they have merely refused, with increasing sharpness, incessant importunings. It is rejected European masculinity that whines to me like a schoolboy when Australian female directness adds what seems insult to what seems injury.

The first knife-flashing problem I encounter happens one Saturday night about five minutes before the dining-room doors are to be swung open on the guests already lined up like wealthy idiot orphans. The waitresses are at their cedar service tables; the wine-stewards and drink-waitresses at the dining-room bar. I am talking to the hostess who smells of apricot brandy and the clove she is chewing to hide it. From behind the screen, from behind the baize doors to the kitchen, comes a sudden Latin din.

"For Pete's sake!" says the hostess. "What a time to pick! Bloody Dagoes!"

Bloody Dagoes it is. The North of Italy and the South of

Italy are at each other in the kitchen with its white-tiled walls, red-tiled floor, and clerestory windows decorated with transparencies of hares, pheasants, and Muscovy ducks.

The monkeyish Calabrian, certainly as much inflamed by wine as by his unpinned emotions, is raving in his disorderly dialect and, in a semi-squatting stance, is poking a long ham-knife in the direction of the Turinese.

The Turinese, disdainful and pale, less inflamed, hissing, holds a large tin strainer, shaped like a coolie hat and called a Chinaman, at arm's length, a combination of shield and knife-swat. In his other hand he too holds a knife.

The rest of the staff jabber and gesticulate while the ham-knife clangs on the Chinaman. The Russian chef is alone affecting calm. His pussy-cat face pecks at an upraised spoon of gravy as though, under his tall white hat, he is posing for an Oxo poster. His face is positive and negative: good gravy, disgusting Italians.

With no other tricks except schoolmaster ones, I automatically go into an old boy-quelling act, an impersonation of rage that is, this time, enhanced by irritation—Saturday night and every table reserved, and the gong on the point of being pounded.

I let fly with the sergeant-major roar I've not used for years. Noise is the thing. The words don't matter.

"How dare you!" I am louder than I think I can be.

There is silence.

I let it hold. Since I am going to do nothing, and have no real idea what form nothing will take, every second of inaction is useful. What eyes to be the focus of! I advance towards the combatants . . . slowly. I am then astounded to hear myself say:

"You were very very naughty little men. You know the rules of this hotel, and are perfectly aware that Mr Wimpole will not allow murders in the kitchen, particularly on Saturday. If you want to kill each other you *must* do it in your own time. *And* with your own knives. Mario, have you nicked that ham-knife on the Chinaman? It's one of the new ones, you know."

The Calabrian looks blindly at his blade, and then, focusing, squints along its edge.

"She'sa aw kay. Issa naw nick."

238

Issa naw nick at all at all.

The gong sounds.

The brawl's over.

Looking back, I can only think that the foreigners are be-wildered by the nonsensical logic, by an absurdity more absurd than theirs. Perhaps they are glad to be relieved of the problem of stopping their own shindy without loss of face. Men duelling as these two are, rarely intend serious damage. Had a knife in the belly been really intended, a knife in the belly there would have been.

This incident, three weeks after my arrival, seems of little importance. It assumes importance when I discover that I have become overnight a sweetie-pie to the three battered and cyni-cal pantry-maids who witness it, and who have hitherto re-garded me as a nose-in-the-air ring-in. They embellish the incident until they project a gossip's image of me as a dag, and a fearless, superbly tailored Peter Wimsey character. This is curious because what, I think, they are backing by their en-thusiasm is an Aussie victory over Dagoes. My ascent into their harsh and sentimental sixty-year-old working-class hearts is by a descent to practical absurdity. This pocket-edition fame, as jewel-encrusted as a Fabergé egg by the time it reaches the end of a long line of tongues, makes me visible and acceptable as a real good bloke, a he's-all-right character, with the Australian section of the staff—yard-man, furnace-man, waitresses, por-ters, barmen, cleaners, chambermaids, even with the reception-ists, those superior buffers between the world outside the revolving doors and the passionate world behind the baize doors, the world of the waitresses' dormitories, the attic rooms of the odd-job-men, the world of boiler-room, cockroaches, coke-heaps, rats, and rubbish-tins, of the bar-takings being nightly washed in boiling water before they are counted, of the butter being cut into cubes of a certain size. What the foreign-ers think is a mystery, except that the Dutch breakfast cook, a man of forthright delusions, and ambitions far beyond the kitchen, accuses me—because of the "very very naughty little men" remark—of being contemptuous of foreigners.

Both versions give me to think. Both versions are very nearly right, and absolutely wrong.

Perhaps I am contemptuous of the foreigners but not, as the Dutchman implies, because they are foreigners, only because they are tiresome employees and hysterical men carrying on as though, every second day, they are well into the second half of the fourteen Stations of the Cross.

Perhaps I do enact, as the pantry-maids observe, a sort of Algy with many a smooth trick up his smooth sleeve, but it is not to put down Dagoes. It is merely a humorous device to be able to control without friction and passion men unused to frictionless and passionless intercourse, men without humour.

I consider the versions because, at the age of thirty-eight, with a number of other versions of myself rustling about on the track behind me like paper-chase litter, it is apparent that an earlier hope—how long ago that seems!—of becoming crystal-transparent to others might as well be flushed down the drainpipe.

This problem, in one ear of the mind and out the other, is far less engrossing than the problem of an increase of arthritic pain. The increase is due mainly to a more strenuous physical life, a more scrambled arrangement of relaxing periods not yet wisely coped with.

Nothing in the glaringly illuminated region of pain shifts or melts unless one can devote oneself with unbroken concentration to outstaring the brilliance. At two o'clock every day I become free for three-and-a-half hours. I lie on my bed for an hour until I can stare directly into the brilliance without needing to blink. Then, with the stick which I encourage others to consider an affectation like the black Windsor knot, I walk to the beach. Watching the streetless waters centuries-long bored with the streetless firmament they have reflected for centuries, I listen to the pig-headed waves nudging on to the threadbare sand, nudging on to the threadbare sand, nudging on to the threadbare sand, and remind myself of the fact but not the memory that I was born within earshot and sight of these waves, and wheeled in a perambulator, parallel to their parallels, by a woman twenty years in her grave. Staring at this fact, compelling myself to stare fixedly at a chosen fact beyond and behind the wildfire mirage of pain, I find the mirage wavering, cracking apart into wafers that slip one by one away until the

obstruction of disquiet is reconstituted somewhere else in the
outhouses of consciousness.

Usually, when I am alone, with no one to engage my mind's
attention, it bowls about like tumbleweed in a temperate wasteland, catching on nothing, no outcrop of ambitions, no fence
of daydreams, no skeleton of regret or remorse or desire. This,
when pain is of its own accord absent. When, however, I have
fought to be successful in moving the screen of pain away
from the foreground, there is revealed, not the blankness across
which the tumbleweed thoughts bowl to no destination, but an
illuminated map of streets and rooms and doorways, of rainy
lanes and dishevelled beds and windows filled with stars, of
class-rooms and dance-floors and overhanging trees, across
which winds a queue of—oh, God!—Hal Porters. There, in the
van, the perambulator gliding springily along, is the baby I cannot remember being, behind it all the thousands of selves I have
not forgotten being, the thousand variations of toddler, child,
youth, man, the long long caravan arousing no emotion except
the sort aroused by the dull film seen too many times already.

What does arouse emotion are all those others, hundreds
of them, so beautiful, so vile, so good, so cruel—how many?—
who thicken the caravan, walk in their out-of-date clothes beside one of my discarded selves for a brief time, and then move
away. They are those who have taught me what every emotion
between love and hate is, those who, by being themselves, body
and mind, allow me to find out what I myself am, body and
mind. Their fascination lies in the iridescent, oil-on-water
quality of their worth. My love makes none of them lovable,
my hate none of them hateful, my indifference none of them
worthless. What is the effect of their love or hate or indifference on me?

That question, in 1949, with pain making me think of others
to stop myself thinking of myself, becomes less a piece of
abstract fretwork than a situation to get out of, for the effect
of the emotions of those in the George Hotel on me is beginning to show itself.

As much as the writer is spellbound by the persistence of the
hotel in its pre-1914-18 War form into the post-1939-45 War
era, as much as he marvels at the elaborate intrigues and malici-

ous feuds carried on in the corridors repeated to infinity in the looking-glasses, in the high-ceilinged rooms, in cellar and pantry and boiler-room and coke-shed, I am beginning to think he has had enough. Repetition of others' disordered emotions proves something to writers. It proves something else to assistant-managers, the public-relations aspect of whose job makes it impossible to avoid what he'd like to avoid.

I become tired of pouring oil on troubled waters. I have spent enough years acquiring the art of skilled intolerance. This is no time of life to be seeing both sides of a coin. Let the Dagoes stab each other, Saturday night or Wednesday morning, own knives or George Hotel knives. Let the stewards spit in the coffee of nagging widows. Let the dining-room hostess smack the face of the waitress who went to a night-club with the hostess's lover, let her smack the face and dismiss the face's owner. Let there be short-changing, watered-down gin, tickling the peter, betting in the bar, stealing from the storeroom, drunkenness in the kitchen, bitchery about favourite chairs in the guests' sitting-room, luggage-less Mr and Mrs John Smiths in every bedroom, nasty drawings in every lavatory, cockroaches in the consommé.

I do not, of course, let anything of the sort. I do my job with an orderly and repulsive sincerity. This means that, when I am unlucky enough to be trapped into knowledge of what goes on, I try to act as someone (I?) thinks I should.

Oops! there's that lame waiter spitting in the coffee. I wish I'd not but I have seen him. Here I go.

"Just a second, Charlie, dear boy!"

I lift the coffee-pot from his tray, and carry it back to the serving-bench where the percolators are gargling gently.

"Who's this nostrum for?"

"A guest." Charlie's coarse squashed face goes lantern-jawed with resentment at himself for being caught.

"Don't be a dill, boy. Which guest?" I soften the question: "Which bitch?"

"Mrs Beaufort."

"You, of course, may have T.B., Charlie."

"She's welcome to it. She's nothing more than a . . ."

And he's off. His obscenity is lucid, and I get the picture. Because she wants to snaffle the best fire-side armchair in the sitting-room, Mrs Beaufort will not wait to drink her coffee in the dining-room or the adjoining drawing-room where coffee and liqueurs are served. From the remoter sitting-room she has sent him back twice, once for a larger cup, the next time for fresh pots of coffee and milk which, she says, have got cold during his absence.

The expression of passion is always somewhat vulgar, and Charlie is, as he tells of the woman's nightly baiting of him, of her vicious subterfuges, increasingly passionate, increasingly foul-mouthed. I call a halt.

"All right, all *right*, dear boy. I'll deal with the old bag. T.B. in the milk too?"

"Yeah."

"Too generous. But *don't* let me catch you being generous again. Savvy?"

I fill a coffee-pot and a milk-pot.

"I'll take these along to your enchanting friend, and . . ."

He makes a revolting suggestion.

"Don't be coarse. Anyway, they wouldn't fit. How-ev-ah, dear boy, I'll admonish her on your behalf."

The dear-boying, the guying of myself, the use of words like *nostrum* and *admonish*, the chance for him to gabble out his resentment, skim the cream off Charlie's anger. It is now mine. He has been pricked into nasty behaviour by—I've no doubt anywhere—Mrs Beaufort's nasty behaviour. I walk and walk, advancing on her, tempted also to spit in the coffee-pot. Why should underhand behaviour be encouraged with tolerance and extra attention?

"Ah, Mrs Beaufort. All alone! Queen of the hearth! How cosy you look! I wanted to be sure your coffee was hot this time. Shall I pour?"

She knows there is something afoot, and can be sensed to sharpen in defence of her delinquency.

"It's not necessary."

The irises of her immodest old eyes are rimmed by a white line; many years of meannesses have afflicted her face; if life has deceived her it is because she is without guilt or remorse; life's honey has soured on the sourness of her tongue.

243

"Where's that waiter?"

Brewing saliva, Mrs Beaufort.

"Charles? The lame waiter? Charles is very upset about you, Mrs Beaufort. Hadn't I better pour your coffee before it gets cold?"

She begins to pour. That means, "Leave me! Get out!"

"Yes, Charles is *very* upset." I intend to make her bite.

She cannot go on pouring for ever. Nor can she remain silent. She puts down the two pots. She bites.

"I did nothing to upset him. I merely asked for—"

"Good heavens, Mrs Beaufort, I know you wouldn't upset him. I said he's upset *about* you. It's all my fault. I spoke to him sharply for being away from the dining-room for so long. Not away once, but twice, and on the point of taking off for the third time. With the place packed! He didn't want to tell me where he'd been. He's a very nice man. When he told me that you liked to have your coffee here, by yourself, I quite understood. Now, since we simply can't spare Charles at our busiest time, you've set us a problem of organization, but I've thought of a solution. I'll bring your coffee. But we'll get things straight. Charles tells me you're never certain whether you need a large cup or a small cup. I shall bring both. And three sorts of sugar. It was very silly of Charles not to think of being prepared, instead of hobbling backwards and forwards all that distance two or three times. Is there any other thing I've forgotten? Lemon? Cream?"

If I feel pity for this wealthy woman to whom the years have taught little but a skill in indirect and calculated rudeness to servants, it is too faint a pity to stand against my objection to having to tamper with the facts, and carry a corrected message-stick between an old bitch and a disgruntled waiter.

I tire of a number of such recurrent go-between jobs because in diluting the truth with poisonous fictions to make bogus truces between others I am diluting some element of aspiration in myself. I am not, anyway, cut out for this sort of oil-in-the-wheels job.

Fortunately, before I find myself unendurable, before I have reached the point of making a decision to cut yet another painter, the opportunity to go to Japan as a schoolmaster turns up. If there be any moment in my life where it can be said that a corner is turned, that moment is when the Army Education Officer at Victoria Barracks, St Kilda Road, Melbourne, tells me that I am to get the rigmarole of medical examinations, injections, passport, visas, taxation clearance, and so on, over in a fortnight, and go to Japan.

I pick up this well-timed windfall with no surprise. There it is, at my feet, mine by right of letting those feet take unorthodox paths, mine inevitably, the something I have been waiting for without knowing I waited. Japan has haunted me since childhood. Having as recently as 1964 re-read Grandfather Porter's books on Japan which came to me after his 1920 death, I am absolutely unable to understand how a nine-year-old boy got what he did from Bird's *Unbeaten Tracks in Japan*, MacFarlane's *Japan*, Reed's *Japan*, even from Mitford's *Tales of Old Japan*, but he got a great deal. Japan is instantly recognizable, thirty years after first reading these nineteenth-century works. I do not, in October 1949, recall sip by sip the drug I took in those books, but am vividly aware of the lasting effect.

Having broken contact with the relative unreality of the George Hotel, I am prepared to live competently through the busy vacuum of the fortnight, and to tie off neatly the little hanging threads as though I were my own hand-made garment. Fate permits me to go about this without interruption. On the day before I am to fly to Sydney, and thence to Japan, there is one thread not tied. Fate is patient about the tying off of this one too.

I spend the last fortnight with J., a wireless-announcer friend of the days when I am writing the still-born novel in Bairnsdale, and pub-crawling all over the district—Dargo, Lakes Entrance, Sarsfield, Lindenow, Stratford, Ensay, Kalimna, Swan Reach, all those country pubs whose quality is enriched and seasoned by the fact that they serve outside the law. For me illegal drinking is, like stolen fruit, sweetest.

In the morning of my last Melbourne day, I leave J. still bed-bound, promising to telephone her later in the day. I take a taxi-cab to the Collins Street doctor with whom I've an appointment to have my hip X-rayed—it seems wise to take some X-ray plates to Japan as clear evidence, should there be trouble.

I am X-rayed.

Fate, I now see, has let me tie off the last thread, but is already, in the X-ray room, doing some weaving of its own. The doctor's assistant is, though neither of us know it, the sister of the headmaster I am on my way to meet in Japan.

Coincidence? Of course.

She tells me to dress myself, and sit in the waiting-room—she'll bring the plates to me in ten minutes.

In the waiting-room is Olivia.

It is years since I last saw her standing, my wife, on Spencer Street Station, a city's day on its death-bed behind her, her scented lips still felt on mine, scent and warmth on its death-bed.

Olivia.

Coincidence, of course.

What happens is what happened when I first saw her.

A lightning crack runs from heaven to hell down the texture of the high high wall, the thick thick wall, the opaque and multicoloured wall of bodies and minds and time and places and myself, all mortared together to conceal what lies beyond. The crack runs down. Through it strikes the shaft of light, blinding, purifying, dangerous, mortal, the dazzling foe, the radiance I've no word for but love. Love? I cannot define this intrusion of light too brilliant to let me see what lies beyond the ruptured wall, a light in which any idea disintegrates before it can be pounced on. Any word, be it even briefer than love, would be too long.

Since we met, ten years ago, on the threshold of absurdity, it is not unfitting to meet again on the threshold of pain, she with her burden of it, I with mine. How salutary of fate to put her there, to make the reality I am re-entering more real than even reality needs be, to compel me to add renewed renunciation of re-aroused love to my already overweight luggage.

What do we say?

We must have said everything for I remember nothing.

When the unknown sister of the unknown headmaster over the Equator brings me the X-ray plates she tells Olivia that the doctor is now ready to see her. What to do but tell Olivia

246

I'll telephone later in the day. What to do but go through the door into Collins Street and the sunlight.

Am I surprised when I move off the doctor's doorstep slap-bang into Leon Hogan, my first adult man-friend? No. I accept passively that fate is arranging a day of coincidences, is intent on intoxicating me back to the present after allowing me to stupefy myself with six months of facing the past.

I telephone J. telling her what has happened. She says buy party food and grog. I buy them.

On my way back to J., I am in the taxi-cab that stops at the red light next to the taxi-cab containing someone else I've not seen for years, my WRAN sister.

Coincidence, of course.

I feel fate, at this meeting, withdraw from the game. The party, the farewell party, is complete. Fate apparently knows the size of J.'s flat.

The last night in Melbourne, with four of the people I love most—ex-wife, girl-friend, sister, cobber—gives me emotional satisfaction. Deep in the core of this selfish joy is a more abstract satisfaction like that given by a solved equation. All these old relationships, sublimated, make a gathering of fortuitous ghosts clothed in years and flesh, but flesh purified by the strange circumstances of the day into a diversion for the mind, a game as truthful as one can get it. We know too much about each other to hoodwink each other. Lies, semi-lies, demi-semi-lies are not for us. My sense of clarity is recharged. The months of ferrying about in a mist between such people as Charlie and Mrs Beaufort, between the unseen baby in the 1911 perambulator and the man with the walking-stick listening to the waves nudging pig-headedly at the threadbare sands, are over for ever.

If the inhabitants of the culs-de-sac I have been rushing in and out of for years have brought home to me that many people believe in people as foxes believe in geese, that rivalry in vindictiveness is as common and corrupting as rivalry in peace-making, and that too many people are their own priests whom they can blackmail with a censored confession into forgiving themselves, the knowledge is the very knowledge I need to armour-plate me henceforth. That I am able to climb into the

247

aeroplane to Sydney with the armour sitting easily and lightly is my good luck (or the machinations of fate) in spending the last night with those who have the power to scour me down to exactly the size needed to wear such armour with comfort, without rancour, as though I believe it fancy-dress rather than protection.

It is certainly armour I need to wear tranquilly for, in Sydney, I am to be involved for six hours in a rivalry of nations, a diplomatic tiff.

To reach Japan by aeroplane it is necessary to stay overnight in Manila. Earlier in 1949, while I am helping to count silver teapots in a store-room at the George Hotel, or Chianti bottles in the cellar, the Australian government has refused to admit into the country a Filipino called Gamboa who has married an Australian woman. In rebuff the Philippines Government does not want me to set foot in Manila. While it permits army Australians in transit to Occupied Japan to land, I am a different kettle of fish. Employed by the education branch of the army, I remain a civilian, albeit a bureaucratic half-breed called civilian-with-officer-status. As such I have to face the Philippines consul in Sydney to get a visa. In Melbourne the army has said, "They'll give *us* no decision. You've got to be vetted personally. If they turn nasty, we'll send you by ship, but we want you there by plane as soon as possible. Don't put up with too much. They're aggressive sods. The moment they get offensive, tell them to stick their visa, and walk out."

I arrive at the consulate in Elizabeth Bay at ten the next morning, fortunately with plenty of cigarettes and matches, and an empty bladder. It is also fortunate, perhaps, that I've no idea what "offensive" in a situation of this sort means to the army or, indeed, to any other living human being. I can hardly define it to myself. The writer certainly has stronger views than I, but is always willing to let me sweat out a situation on his behalf, long after I have found the situation not only offensive but intolerable. Luckily, most of the time, we work hand-in-glove, and with serenity.

Fate's beautifully timed three-card trick of coincidences the day before has left me as fine as fivepence, calm as a corpse, and unsurprisable. The consular building does not therefore surprise me: a middle-class brick house of the nineteen-twenties halfway down the slope from King's Cross to the bay's edge. Among the Spanish Mission villas, turreted follies, Italianate mansions, and after-Gropius blocks of flats, it seems the milder sort of house a spinster aunt lives in with a cocker-spaniel. It has casement windows with a multitude of panes. Nor am I surprised at the interior.

The interview takes place in a long drawing-room. The spinster-aunt furnishings (Maples-Jacobean, dim brocade, holland blinds with fringed and scalloped edges, Persian carpet made in Belgium) have been added to by some steel filing-cabinets, Gestetner duplicating machines, four tins of Marie biscuits, pedestals sprouting paper carnations of un-carnation colours with tinselled edges, and a large wall-hanging of silky plush depicting Santa Maria della Salute in the midst of a sunset like spilt raspberry vinegar. Nor am I surprised at the consul (or consular representative) who sits, or strolls about, consciously self-possessed, at the bay-window end of the drawing-room, while I stand for six hours at the other end.

He looks like what I have, by years of observation, come to regard as a flashy larrikin. That is, however, merely his adornment: a suit of some flimsy powder-blue material, black-and-white shoes, a tie with a pineapple printed on it, several rings with bulbous stones in them, and a pair of horn-rimmed spectacles he takes off when he writes anything.

Least of all am I surprised at what happens. It is instantly perceivable that insolence is intended. Why not?

There can be no other commonsense explanation of his leaving me to stand the room's length away from him while, in the sort of coloured man's "Oxford" accent which goes (this I decide by the end of the session) so well with black-and-white shoes, he asks the same questions over and over again. Sometimes the batch of questions is asked several times in immediate succession. Sometimes there is a timeless gap of time—five minutes, ten minutes, twenty-two-and-a-quarter minutes, I've no idea how many minutes because I do not wear a watch. Always the same questions in the same affected or educated voice. Name? Birthday? Place of birth? Father's name? Mother's maiden name? Teaching experience? Opinion of the Gamboa situation? Opinion of the White Australia Policy?

By morning tea time he has worked himself so well into his role of languid interrogator with stubborn spy that he is handling his Marie biscuits and cups of tea with all the aplomb of a West End actor pointedly sipping in the pregnant pause, significantly moving the spoon a millimetre on the saucer a split second before he speaks. By afternoon tea time he is, no doubt, more bored than I, and drops these actorish tricks. When he leaves the room, presumably to eat a midday meal, a dreary skinny Filipino woman—his secretary?—now and then asks the same questions, but as though her heart isn't really in it.

Once only, in the first twenty minutes, do I make a request. As the questions begin for the second time, I light a cigarette, When it is nearly finished I ask, "May I have an ashtray, please?"

"It will be better not to smoke," he says. Knox Grammar presents itself to me, and the Headmaster s-t-r-o-l-l-i-n-g out from behind a banana-palm.

"It will be better not to smoke."

He in the crumpled powder-blue is smoking.

What will he do if . . .?

I make the one gesture of . . . defiance? Whatever the gesture is, it is made. I screw out the cigarette carefully on the sole of my shoe, drop the butt on the floor to the right of me, and immediately light a cigarette. Who's the West End actor now? Next butt I drop to the left. By the time the day is over this one-right, one-left game is as much part of the texture of the situation as his questions and my answers.

Father's name? Mother's maiden name? Teaching experience?

"What do you think of the Gamboa situation?"

"I have no personal view."

"Do you think your government is right?"

"Of course."

"Is your government always right?"

"I think it tries to be."

"Do you think the White Australia Policy is right?"

"Yes."

"Why do you think this?"

"Because my government thinks so."

"You agree with your government?"

"Yes. They know things I don't know. I am only a school-master. They are politicians."

Mother's maiden name? Teaching experience?

"What do you think of the Gamboa situation?"

When his afternoon tea is over, and I am still standing where I've stood since ten o'clock, between the two piles of butts, it seems to me that the chances of getting the visa, and catching the aeroplane at Mascot at five-thirty, are remote. An idea appears. I shall say, "Thank you for an interesting day." And walk out. The man is mad. I'm thirsty. I could be hungry. My hip is starting to give me hell. I've smoked sixty cigarettes, and am on my last packet. Surely, by now, offensive means offensive.

That is, however, only my idea. The writer is more tenacious than I. His idea is that, having sweated out the repetitive twaddle, he is entitled to see what happens when it stops, as it must stop. Don't *you* stop it, he advises me, let them stop it.

He's right.

At four o'clock, with an inexplicable crash—frustration? rage? because it's that sort of stamp?—the man slams a visa aslant on my passport. He says I must get three more passport photographs taken. Here is an address. One of his men will drive me there, and to the airport. At a quarter-past four I am outside the house, and about to step into the car when a Yellow Taxi comes up the slope. My feelings are those of one just back from a foreign country. An Australian! An empty taxi-cab! I abandon the Filipino car without a word.

"Listen, mate, here's the problem. Mascot at five-thirty. Passport photographs first—here's the address. While that's happening, can you collect my luggage at Usher's, buy me sixty cigarettes, and pick me up at the photographer's?"

Sydney taxi-drivers are the world's best.

"She'll be apples, mate."

That is Australia speaking, and I know my troubles are over. Apples it is. We get to Mascot with ten minutes to spare.

In this speeded-up film of the last hour I recall one person only with great clarity, the photographer. She seems so slow, so

251

eccentric, that it is only fair to point out that I with my "Hurry, please! Please, hurry!" and doubtless with a glitter in my eye, am quite as eccentric. A description of her from a short story based on the incident gives an idea of why, for the only time in a Keystone Cops interlude, the confidence given by the taxi-driver almost falters:

> He repeated consular urgency to a woman in a fourth-floor three-ply cell—perhaps Elsa Lanchester. A defective torch of archness flickered on and off within her. "*So* understand," she said, at an angle absorbing him, soiled finger along her jaw, as though he were a Spanish oil jar with possibilities.

("Hurry, please! Please, hurry!")

> "Sit," she said, flicking on, indicating a chair of pith lace. She arranged something—bulrushes and 2-shaped swans?— behind him, and pranced into view again. "No, you *silly* girl," she admonished herself, and disappeared to further fiddling—Tintern Abbey?
>
> "Dear-dear-dear-dear-dear, *no*!"

("Please, I'm in an awful hurry!")

> Envy enkindled her to her sinless best. Soon, she began ducking her head under and out from under the camera's witch-cloak, blandishing him into outstaring a felt rat which miraculously appeared in her stained fingers. "Not a dicky-bird," she said, but uncertainly, flicking off to the melancholy of loneliness, of always being left behind.

I give her money to send the photographs, when ready, to the Filipino in powder-blue. The taxi-driver, fortunately for my calm, pulls up with luggage and cigarettes just as I hurtle out of the building. Next minute, it seems, I am in the aeroplane, and able to notice that I am very thirsty, and somewhat tired from the six hours of perpendicularity.

The aeroplane is a wartime Lancaster, battered, and bleakly functional within, but it throbs into movement as convincingly as piano wires encountering the pedal. This is no luxury cruise —smoking is forbidden, the seats are not upholstered, a refrigerator that is not working contains only some corner-shop ham sandwiches and tins of warm pineapple juice. My companions are all khaki-clad: five privates as drunk as lords, several middle-aged women with pukka accents who look like generals and, in the seat behind me, a tipsy Brigadier with the accent of a race-course tout, and a cheap fibre suitcase containing nothing but four bottles of Australian whisky wrapped in wet hand-towels. He is an amiable leprechaun of a man. By the time Darwin is reached we have, by drinking straight from the bottle, used up half his store.

Next day, we reach Manila.

Once through the rubber-stamping at the aerodrome, and on the way to the Manila Hotel in an army staff car with the half-blotto Brigadier, there is no doubt under the sun—an equatorial afternoon sun blurred at the edges like a sucked acid-drop—that the higgledy-piggledy jigsaw picture I have of any country in the Torrid Zone is wrong, not so much in the details (palm-trees, bamboo, rice-paddies, scantily clad people with flat feet, water-buffaloes sousing themselves in warm mud), but in tone, fundamentally. Wherever these ideas of the archipelagos scat-tered like animal droppings in the jelly-like soup of oriental seas come from they are old-fashioned, or there has been misrepresentation or, most likely, since I've not the imag-ination to read between lines, mistranslation on my part. A few years later, I become used to walking through the travel poster, all gorgeousness and mystery, smack into the stench and filth and monstrosities that lie directly behind. In 1949, however, my first leap—the clown through the paper hoop—I am exhila-rated to horror. The horror is no more, no less, than that felt today, but has, at Manila, the unforgettable quality of firstness.

An immediate and violent repugnance against the climate and the light overcomes me, and is, maybe, inherited from cold-country Anglo-Saxon and Teutonic forebears, and fostered by living in the mildest, most southerly parts of Australia.

Manila has no sky. A burden of air charged with vapour from above suffuses with a vapour-charged mephitis from below. The light is steam of light. Heat has no blades to slash and lunge at one. There is nothing to dodge. The sponge descends to smother. One is embedded, overborne. Most abominable, one's mind is entombed.

If, my heredity and upbringing and instincts all being put to the test, I am having humidity-logged quarter-thoughts, the writer is in a visual ecstasy at the first sight of tiptop poverty. On the outskirts of Manila the car, a plated beast bleating viciously and perpetually, is furrowing through a rank crop of what seem human beings. It appears they must be mowed down like weeds for they disappear in a slow swirl at the front of the machine. I look back. There is nothing flattened, no swathe, no crushed and rotten stalks. The unsmiling faces, the seedpods, eddy as thickly behind still as they do in front and on every side; arms upholding shattered baskets of muck that must be food writhe fluidly as sallow tentacles; breasts falter by like bubbles of mud. As we plough this sludge of flesh, the open-fronted bamboo hovels on its banks, like snapshots illustrating the evils of fecundity, like squalid Holy Family cribs at Christmas, offer public privacy with an indifference that, to my pampered Australian eye, seems monstrous—an ancient one-armed thing (man? woman?) fanning a naked baby's pumpkin belly with a tropical leaf; men squatting with glaring eyes around two fighting-cocks, one bloody and ragged; four youths with Latin-lover sideburns impassively, one after the other, stabbing at a dog with pointed sticks; a woman to whose breasts are attached two sucking skin-and-bone children with elderly faces; a crone scrubbing a pied piglet with the fervour of an idiot in a ring of soiled head-scratching girls.

I need only the evidence of my eyes to know this is poverty —the tatters, the bamboo mia-mias, the straw nets of rotten fruit being carried, the mangled domestic vessels, the unravelling reed mats and bamboo curtains. Having seen, it is not necessary to see any more. All the people are made from the same exhausted materials. All hair is black. All eyes are dark. All skin is the same sexless sallow colour—there is nothing of the bristle and gloss of the masculinity I have been used to, nothing of the feminine rotundity and podginess. All faces, old and young, are locked on something that might escape, and the something, although not seen, seems also the same for each. Perhaps the something is nothing. Or a decomposed mind, a blot of mould beneath which lies the maggot of lunacy, the

254

virus of a frenzy to rid themselves of a self-cultivated humiliation.

After some time, and scarcely soon enough, the car turns into a small square in which jeep-sized buses with fringed roofs, red-and-yellow scrollwork, and much merry-go-round brass, are being boarded by Filipinos a shade less squalid in appearance. The buses, hung with them as a rag-market stall is hung with swatches of rubbish, jerk towards a hinterland of sagging greenery and mountains of steam, the bodies swinging like empty garments, boneless, bloodless, with carbon eyes and shut masks.

Our car turns its rump on the hinterland, and moves waterwards, to the edge of a bay of China Sea brine with rusty dredges offshore, and outriggers lying skeletonized on its shoddy beach under some travel-poster palms. In the bay, the Brigadier tells me, are sunk many warships, and an abundance of corpses.

The war being four years over, I have forgotten to remember that there might be a bay enriched by American and Japanese corpses on the left hand and, as we drive along a wide concrete road called Dewey Boulevard, on the right, beyond a frieze of popcorn stands and Coca-Cola stalls and water-buffaloes sloshing in dove-grey mud, all the picturesquely melancholy Grünewald ruins of bombed Chinese joss-houses, embassies, and *churrigueresque* Spanish mansions, under the rifted archways and colonnades of which dark phasmas of people seem to be picking over, so long after the wartime godsend of places to loot, what?

High above all these evidences of man's scientific skill rears an Eiffel Tower topped by *Grant's Whisky*.

The Manila Hotel, a minor skyscraper of concrete cracked like a scorched plate, is prepared for anything, and for me. For reasons best known to the Philippines Consul in Sydney I am greeted with a flourish, and given V.I.P. treatment: a house-sized suite smelling of stale incense; four adolescent attendants —two of them female-shaped, two of them male-shaped—who (why?) project their sexual willingness unmistakably in my direction; and a view from the balcony of the bay of a fiercely lit swimming pool, dry as ash, and stacked with dandelion-yellow rubbish-tins labelled *Trash*; of the *Grant's Whisky* neon and, minor to it and lower, of a number of agitated other neons, Nite Club neons jolting on and off—*Here's How, Jimmy's, Swiss Inn, The Aristocrat, Marfush Gardens.*

After a bath and shower I descend to the foyer. It has the architectural delirium of the nave of a Mexican cathedral and, while I dally to meet the Brigadier, there is much to entertain the writer.

There are the placards—*No Firearms Alowed, When Going the Fiesta Pavilion after 6 p.m. wear you Coot and Tie,* and *Pets Not Alowed.*

A number of dogs connoisseurishly savouring other dogs' behinds infest the foyer, and the arcade leading from it of glass cases and counters displaying alleged Filipino handicrafts— fans, coasters, sandals, embroidered peasant blouses, salad- servers with handles carved in the shape of some slit-eyed, foetus-shaped native deity, and brass nut-crackers in the form of back-to-back nude women with breasts like acorns.

The Brigadier appears, fuming. Not only has he been quar- tered in a ground-floor cell not far from the kitchens, but his lavatory is blocked.

We walk the tessellated and interminable arcade to the bar. It has eye-cutting gaudy mosaic murals but is, happily, almost cool. The bar-counter and a horde of Chinese barmen surround a manufactured central iceberg, a tier of troughs stacked with polyangular chunks of green ice, and plots of crushed ice from which bottles protrude. The Brigadier and I sign chits for our drinks—the army or the Filipinos or someone is paying. Just as well. A small bottle of San Miguel beer costs one peso, about eight shillings in 1949 Australian money. A glass of beer, there- fore, costs about twenty times more in poverty-stricken (as I see it) Manila than in well-off Melbourne. Filipinos, I think, must never use this hotel, an ugly machine merely to mulct tourists. I am wrong. At dinner in the Fiesta Pavilion it is obvi- ous I am rushing through a country inhabited by two races, the disgusting rich and the disgusting poor.

The *No Firearms Alowed* notices seem more whimsical, more mysterious. Who's being warned? Rich man? Poor man?

The Fiesta Pavilion leaves for dead anything I have ever be-

256

fore experienced in the way of hotel size. Crimson pillars like factory chimneys soar to a remote ruddy ceiling. Flights of Chinese waiters and stewards in white sharkskin coats skim the immensity of parquet showily holding trays of food or drinks balanced on fingertips at arm's length above their oiled black polls.

The Brigadier and I, deciding to go the whole hog on some-one else's money, sign chits for Veuve Clicquot. He has ideas of going on to a night-club or gambling saloon someone in Australia has recommended. I am content to watch the rich Filipinos at play: humidity quenches all thought of chasing the spoor of sin. Anyway, it's on tap in my suite, two sorts at least.

Our table, not far from the dance-band seated beneath the concavity of a glowering huge crimson scallop-shell as though seated in Hell's mouth, is accidentally in a perfect viewing spot. I can see the sockless ankles of the musicians, and their split relics of cruelly pointed black shoes (in 1949 I have not seen such points since 1924); the sleaziness of their yellow satin tunics *à la Russe*; and the loops of sweat spreading under their armpits. They play in a morose, muted fashion, and each tune has much the same rhythm, somewhat like the tango. Curiously, their repertoire includes many Irish numbers: "Mother Macree" and "Kathleen Mavourneen" in the tango-ish stop-go time are recallable. Although becoming increasingly anaesthetized by champagne against the heat I know it has not lost weight. The fans sluggishly push their way through it near the ceiling, making heat visible as well as palpable. The dance-band takes no breather, but goes on dejectedly reducing every tune to the same rhythm, the rhythm of a defective heart.

After having seen the poor, I can do no more than call the diners rich. Next to the basket of orchids on almost every table there is a champagne bucket; ostentatious dishes are ostenta-tiously cooked on trolleys beside tables; foods bathed in blue flame are handed; more and more wine is poured; the music never ceases; and yet all is forbiddingly decorous. There is something wrong—I mean that to me there is something wrong. The gaiety is defective, is reined in. It is not that handsprings are expected, or barber-shop quartets, or peals of shrill laughter. At first, a wrongness sensed, I blame my Australianism as much

257

as my own nature, and my ignorance of a tropical world already found distasteful. Then, suddenly, it comes to me that what is wrong (to me) is that these people are half-and-halfers, are playing a dreadful game of being civilized, of being westernized, a charade of dining out in style, of being some version of classy mortals like Carole Lombard and Humphrey Bogart, of spending money however ill-earned or hard-won—and that doesn't matter, for the saint's money is as dirty as the murderer's is clean—only in order to act out their own film. They are their own infatuated audience as they see what they are paying to see and be.

Twenty or more of the women are dressed in *dernier cri* versions of the national dress. Remove the salient feature, the quivering and extended epaulettes the texture and iridescent tint of dragon-fly wings, and the dresses could be those worn by any film star in a cocktail comedy. It now, rightly or wrongly, seems to my champagne mind that the women are living up to their hallucinations about themselves conceitedly, rather than living up to the spending of money offhandedly, joyously, for fun, even if the pesos are blackmarket, war-profiteering, dive-running, grinding-the-faces-of-the-poor, or bodies-and-souls-for-sale rake-offs. Wealth, clean or dirty, has corrupted them no further or enlivened them no more than into attempting an imitation of film stars attempting an imitation of the wealthy. The setting is apt to the borderline of satire: Manila's largest hotel, counterfeit American, with Mississippis of fissures meandering across the terrazzo floors, tide-lines of suicide moths outside, sockless musicians, blocked lavatories, aluminium venetian blinds with snarled cords, lewd nutcrackers, chlorinated water, a swimming pool of yellow rubbish-tins and, in the Fiesta Pavilion, the mongrel dogs from the foyer now and then skidding across the seeming acre of parquet in the great spaces between the dancers, each couple striving to out-exhibition-dance the other couples.

The men, looking like amorous gangsters with their sideburns, parti-coloured shoes, and suits of lavender, honey, pink, and powder-blue (was he ever here, the consular inquisitor of Elizabeth Bay?), behave with the unabating gentlemanliness of lounge-lizards. When they dance, mincing, swooping, tacking,

258

they kick the mongrels out of the way with stylized brutality, and no uncouth intensification of the expression on their faces which is that of approval of their own sophistication.

The Brigadier, fortunately, gets too drunk to go night-clubbing, and wavers away to his cell to sleep. Freed of the obligation to accompany him to further exhibitions of Filipino money being spent, and other placards forbidding firearms, and more boxed-in tropical heat, I walk to the Western Terrace, dimly lit, an open-air terrace of beach-umbrellaed bamboo tables. Half-tipsy and flagging as I am, I notice that the Chinese steward steers me to a table near the balustrade up to which, and not a finger farther, a surge of natives has washed. Through this surf, every second, and like arriving barges, long wide glittering motor-cars float in to the hotel steps—the chauffeurs open the car doors to release more Carole Lombards and Humphrey Bogarts for the Fiesta Pavilion.

Meantime, sipping a Tom Collins a yard away from the balustrade which is where the night really begins, the seething night and surf of heat and eyes and fans and bodies and wheedling voices, I must seem a desirable piece of wreckage, an unaccompanied man, to be sucked out into the foam. The gentle spray of voices floats over the balustrade:

"You dee-siring pretty girl—clean?"

"I guide you to beautiful girl, ver-ee young."

"My neem Mistah Joaquin Pacis. You want pretty boy—black velvet?"

"Look to me. I do all things. Look to me."

Look!

What is there to look at? I pity you without looking, and hate you without looking. You, whoever you are, are no more than a human being. I am one too. There's nothing special or original about you and me. You do all things? Doesn't everyone?

As much as I'd like another Tom Collins without going back to the bar, I haven't the insolence to outsit myself at the edge of this pleading sea, nor the desire to go on rebuffing invitations to wade into its currents of deranged minds and secondhand orifices. I am tired of shaking my head politely at the whispering fans and oiled eyes and shameless voices. How cocksure

259

prostitutes can be! How unsympathetic! I rise, and trail back to the bar.

I leave behind the emptied glass, the vacant bamboo chair, the void I am even when sitting there with a full glass. All the eyes that see and watch me see nothing but a handful of pesos. None who see and watch will remember me, the handful of pesos on the bamboo seat under the groggy umbrella, out of reach beyond the balustrade, on the Western Terrace where firearms are also forbidden. I remember all the faces I didn't see, in the same way as one remembers the seething lake but not each separate wave.

In the bar, the iceberg has lost its ridges and edges; the labels have slipped aslant on the bottles of San Miguel beer; a childish sobbing of green water down an imperfect pipe draining the tiers of thawed ice accompanies me as I drink stark-awake exhaustion towards sleep. Unseen, on the other side of the weeping iceberg, two Americans or one ventriloquist American can be heard great-guying and goddamming, uttering as Americans do platitudes not worth eavesdropping on, talking as American men do from somewhere near their navels, somewhere near their pockets.

I am in a heavenly sleep-walking haze, far beyond feeling heat or permitting thought, when I reach my suite at eleven o'clock.

The four adolescents!

They advance on me, and it is patent that, mollified by alcohol as I am, they are sure I shall make a nuptial choice. Their hands and smiles are upon me. The surf being, as it were, over the balustrade, there is nothing to do but play Canute. I thrust the pesos I have left—who wants pesos!—at them, and:

"Outski! Vamoose! Skedaddle! Home to your mums and dads! Next time, some other year, but not tonight Josephine! Outski!"

They are gone. Their surprise does not leave the suite until minutes later.

Last thing, under the tasselled mosquito-net they have set up over the bed with heaven alone knows what strange hopes, I drowsily read *The Landry Prize List*. I try to remember to ask when I wake what the garment *Pant Skins* (one peso, fifty centavos for laundering them) is. I forget.

I know no more, today, about *Pant Skins* or Manila than I do then. Perhaps, since 1949, all has changed, and the poor, as in Australia, are rich, perhaps firearms and pets are allowed in the Manila Hotel, perhaps the instinctive feeling I have in the Elizabeth Bay drawing-room, in the suburb of hovels, and in the Fiesta Pavilion, that I am in touch with an untrustworthy and corrupt nation tinged with insanity of a sort differing from the Western insanity I am used to, is instinct's error. I've not had time to find out.

After a short period spent in an unknown place one can either keep one's mouth shut on one's impressions or open it to let out what can be no more than generalizations based on what the five senses have experienced in that short time. Today, with memories of nearly two more decades of places and people stacked on top of those of Manila and its people, two more decades of the wicked spites and tireless hatreds of men, it is difficult work to dig down to the true centre of my revulsion, and it would be more difficult to attempt justification of the antipathy to those who have opposite feelings. Instinct, the essence of generalization, proves something only to oneself.

Some famous writer about countries in equatorial latitudes (Henri Fauconnier?) says something like, "Very high temperatures extinguish all human sympathy and relations." I agree. A similar revulsion, sometimes weaker and sometimes stronger than the Manila one, is aroused in me by places such as Panama, Colombo, Djakarta, Bombay, Singapore, and Aden. To say with a shrug of the inhabitants of these places, "The poor swine are victims of the ghastly climate," is, I suppose, as close as I can veer towards sympathy. It is, I'm all too conscious, a suspect sympathy with that undercurrent of greasy toleration one finds in the attitude of those who preach lenience to murderers and rapists and thieves on the grounds that they are "sick". I am still, alas, unable not to feel a quite unfashionable horror at the sight of a crocodile of nine-year-old girls in tinselled saris being shepherded across a gangplank from the Bombay wharf into the Indian crew's quarters of a P. and O. liner, am still unable not to feel that I've no hope ever of understanding or

261

not despising a race that can deliberately mutilate its children so that, scraping their stumps on the filthy road by the Colombo Clock Tower, or mopping and mowing to the tourists coming ashore in launches, they can beg to keep alive the mutilators.

No do-gooder, I do nothing about it. The sword is mightier than the pen. Let them chop off baby Yaseem's feet, and sell little girl Laila to fat old tups. Outwardly, I don't do anything except drop a florin at Yaseem's stumps, thus supporting mutilation, and move on, deadpan. Behind this blankness the writer puts on his wry expression, the So-*this*-is-life! expression. After all, during the Depression, centuries ago, when he thought he was young and un-innocent, he and I read *Mother India* which was bound in covers of what looked like pale grey hessian.

I have taken space briefly to record an example of East-of-Suez techniques of living, and my "sensitive" recoil to it, because it is necessary bluntly to confess that, in Japan, wholeheartedly inconsistent, I never think of recoiling from situations which have something in common with Hindu and Sinhalese ones, and to which the writer ecstatically responds with a This-is-LIFE! expression. Tragedy is misproportion. It is also as relative as the spectacles one wears to look at it.

The snowy ignorance with which I land at Manila, my first foreign city, could have been an advantage. I could have been swept off my feet by its strangeness, titillated by its openslather vices, taken photographs (were I a camera-bearer) of cock-fights, water-buffaloes, buses with a fringe on top, bare breasts, and the Manila Hotel.

Perversely, the curious swag of information about Japan I land at Iwakuni with could have been a disadvantage. I could have been savagely disappointed. Admittedly the swag contains mental notes of hatred scaldingly expressed against the Japanese by returned prisoner-of-war soldiers; mental pictures of well-bred men and women paying to smash Japanese crockery set up Aunt-Sally-wise at social garden parties; and the remembrance of hearing, since boyhood, the word Japanese used to mean gimcrack, jerry-built, trumpery. Indeed, a favoured statement among drinkers excusing themselves to go to the lavatory was, "Must rush! It's my cheap Japanese bladder!"

The swag is, however, also weighted with Grandfather Porter's nineteenth-century books on Japan, with all the hours I spent in a trance before the Melbourne National Gallery's superb collection of Japanese colour prints, with the lacquer and china and ivories in antique-dealers', with the legends and fairy stories and plays I have read, with Lafcadio Hearin propaganda, with the dozens of *haiku* and *senryu* copied in my commonplace books, with the Japanese history I taught as a fill-in subject at Hutchins School, and the pinch of Japanese words taught me by the khaki-clad Japanese sailors met in the early nineteen-thirties when I used to frequent Madame's Wine Depôt, and wander the trembling piers and the waterfront streets of Williamstown.

We descend through the Friday clouds over Iwakuni aerodrome, and glide on to Japan as gliding into the kernel of a cool and pale opal—rain and mist and supple shafts of afternoon sunshine too ravelled to disentangle. Into this mother-of-pearl loveliness strides a hazard from my past. One of the doctors with whom I used to frolic in Adelaide is there to meet me with an invitation to immediate gaiety. I beg off on the grounds that I'll be expected at B Officers' Mess in Kure, a few miles off. He makes it clear that no one will, by the time I reach the Mess, be there at all. He makes it clear that I am in Occupied Japan where, since my job does not start until Monday morning, it will be almost improper to appear before Monday morning in any but a weekend guise. He makes it clear that I'll waste my time being a pious mug. Fond as I am of the tempter, I should prefer to have my first view of what lies outside the aerodrome sober, and without a dangerous old friend at elbow, and am about to say so as diplomatically as I can to this charming leftover from the past when a messenger from the future, a laconic corporal swaddled in a transparent orange-coloured mackintosh, and unfolding an oiled-paper parasol, advances on me from the delicate rain.

"They've rang through," he says, "t' say they can't git a car down for ya. Nor no jeep neither. Ya can go in the train, but."

"You see," says my friend, "you're trapped. Let's paint Iwakuni red. I'll drive you up on Sunday."

The Brigadier, who is seeing Japan for the first time through a pane of whisky, saves me from doing the same.

He barks protectively, "You're coming in the launch with me."

A speckless colonel has met the Brigadier, and has a speckless launch and two speckless privates waiting on the rim of the Inland Sea.

"Ya roight then. Ya home 'n' hosed. Sayonara, mate," says the mackintosh with a smile from which one tooth is absent, and thereupon conveys itself, Queensland, and the parasol out of my life.

Had I gone to Kure by train, car or jeep, I should have passed through Hiroshima, in 1949 a large draughts-board city with the raw and angular air of a frontier town: wide scraped streets, flimsy box-like buildings, rows of saplings still tied to stakes of unseasoned wood and, near the place where the atomic bomb landed, shops and stalls doing a roaring trade with souvenirs and photographs under large placards, in English, of *No More Hiroshimas*, placards sprinkled with doves. These birds, to the Japanese, are the messengers of Hachiman, a war god. The souvenirs are authentic or manufactured gobbets of blast-melted stone or metal; ties decorated with hour-glass-shaped nude women, *No More Hiroshimas*, or Phar Lap's head in profile; Betty Boop clocks with rolling eyes; head-scarves of inferior silk bearing representations of Lana Turner, or the race-horse Bernborough, or Mount Fuji projecting like a sundae from a too pink froth of cherry-blossom; manicure-sets of a dozen instruments embedded in imperial-blue velvet; and plastic statu-ettes of conspicuously pregnant girls labelled *Kilroy Was Here*. I am glad that my first glimpse of Japan, outside the anonymity of the aerodrome, is from the launch cutting through the waters of the Inland Sea.

As the launch moves along on the sea's choppy topmost waters the Colonel statistically indicates the unseeable in the lowest waters: sunken submarines and destroyers, mislaid mines, the largest warship ever built. His death-and-destruction entertainment hooks only on to the farthest edge of conscious-ness. I am disinterestedly conscious too that Hiroshima, the spot marked X, lies a few miles left. It is more than possible that the older cormorants among those hunched like so many Charles Lambs on the spiky spits of islands no bigger than altars, no taller than cypresses, could have been hunched there at the moment the atomic bomb turned Hiroshima into a tourist resort. Most of my consciousness, however, is occupied by the astounding realization that I am seeing, on every hand, what I have already seen in old drawings, seeing outlines long-dead artists and poets saw. What astounds is that, with the mist and rain now withdrawn, and the autumn sun shining like a magnifying-glass, I am not seeing a life-size model of old Japan correct in every detail but, in the middle of the twentieth century, a swallow's flight from where science celebrated itself with a sumptuous bang and bonfire, old Japan enacting the centuries it has been enacting for centuries, giving with a merely daily offhandedness demonstrations and dramatizations of time.

The launch keeps near enough to the shore for me to see the details of a succession of scenes straight from Hokusai's *Mangwa*—miniscule plots and strips of taro and sweet potato terracing the hills; temples and torii sticking their mild old horns out of jaundiced groves of gingko; grey-tiled villages with willow-lined streets where women in blue-and-white yugata shuffle along under paper sunshades; rice-paddies, bamboo copses, pine-trees with their lower branches propped up on crutches, persimmon-trees hung with swags of radish-slices; men in loincloths, up to their knees in water, bending among the poles of the oyster gardens; high-prowed fishing-boats of ancient design beached on the aluminium-coloured shingle; and the countless offshore islands, each just large enough for a rock-fed pine, stunted and distorted, and a stone deity, a fishermen's god, gone blind and bland from centuries of nights and days, wearing epaulettes of lichen and a stomacher of moss.

God knows why I am so feverishly exhilarated by these alive-and-kicking Hiroshige and Hokusai landscapes. Is it because, at the age of thirty-eight, I am beginning to feel that "progress" is becoming the beast to be wary of, the beast getting out of hand, and treading down man for the sake of Man as it lopes, snarling its own name, towards a horizon it imagines? I don't know. I do know that these glimpses of an older and persistent civilization with its long-range values of equilibrium are what comfort me when the launch turns the last cape, and there is Kure, a new and temporary civilization, and my home for the next year and, as such and journey's end, a somewhat refreshing eyesore.

From the edge of the bay the land cants steeply up.

A deadly mural confronts me.

On the higher slopes are bomb-craters, bald scars in the maple woods, mounds and glaciers of houses minced to rubbish. At the water's edge is a geometric entanglement of rusted shapes—girders, derricks, vast skeleton sheds, tanks, boilers, great cogged wheels, superannuated buoys, turbine casings, all of them rust-red. From the launch it can be seen that the seepings from this bombed naval dockyard have stained the earth far below its surface.

Between the bomb-savaged slopes, and the lattices and crosswords of rust, are scattered the grey-white concrete army quarters—hostels, messes, barracks, hospitals, canteens, bootbox buildings with child's-drawing windows and doors, each surrounded by its high wire fence, each with its gate guarded by Australian or Japanese soldiers. Higher than all, on the top of the hill, is the boot-box known as The House That Jack Built, jack being the euphemism for venereal disease. The wire fence here is topped by a ferocious border of barbed wire. At night the arc-lights set at intervals like Byzantine gems in the barbed wire can be seen for miles, a diadem crowning with symbolic brilliance a village where East sleeps with West. I have an imperfect recollection that the imprisoned victims of lust, enjoying the best view of the bay and the islands of the Inland Sea, wear a special uniform—blue?

Seen from the hilltop, to the right of the army area, is the village of Kure.

By 1949 most of the cruder evidences of its bombing have been cleaned up, filled in, levelled out. On a smaller scale it has also the frontier town air of Hiroshima—splintery, treeless, stopgap, with side-streets of bare earth, weedy vacant allotments, out-of-plumb telegraph poles, and the wind-scoured look of a place run up by the poverty-stricken from shards salvaged out of the rubble of holocaust.

My Adelaide tempter friend's prophecy that there would be nobody waiting impatiently to greet me at B Mess late on a Friday afternoon is a correct one. A fat sergeant with golliwog hair and eyes, and other things than new arrivals on his mind, shows me to my room, is sorry my house-girl will not be turning up until Monday, and leaves me. He closes the door. I hear his boots thumping wildly on the coir-matting of the long corridor; I hear him step on to Japan and walk its gravel.

Silence.

I am alone.

Ever since the Army Education Officer in Melbourne dropped the starting handkerchief I have been racing past people and places, the wind hissing by, to overtake myself in this room, to overtake silence and solitariness. The sergeant, closing the door, shuts out the past of seventeen days, the din of engines eating miles, the voices asking questions, all the clerks with printed forms and rubber stamps and illegible signatures; the men with hypodermic needles; the X-ray Sister sister of the headmaster I am yet to meet; J. and Leon Hogan, my sister in her WRAN uniform, Olivia pallid and beautiful with pain; the crazed Filipino at Elizabeth Bay; the gentle butch taxi-driver and the passport photographer with her fingernails blackish-brown from metol-hydro-quinone; the tipsy Brigadier and his fibre suitcase; all those nameless continents of cloud, deserts without roads, alps of foam, hiding all those steamy archipelagos, and all those tepid seas—Arafura, Banda, Molucca, Celebes, Sulu, South China; Manila hiding nothing or everything; the Adelaide doctor cajoling in the opalescent fusion of mist and sunlight; the corporal in the orange mackintosh; the Inland Sea and its gallery of Hokusai landscapes, landscapes never without figures; the final landscape as the winning-tape comes nearer, a coastscape of rubble and rust; the Japanese guard (why?) at the wire gate in the wire fence of B Mess; the fat and flurried sergeant; and—finally—there in the looking-glass of my hideously luxurious room, furnished like the large cell of a show-off monk who has won a lottery, the one I have caught up with. He looks much the same as when I shaved him in Manila, but I know he isn't.

I speak to myself in the looking-glass.

"I think, before you do another thing, you'd better have a sleep."

What I am really saying is: Use this accidental break in the film, this five o'clock silence and slump, this gift of nobody, to wash off in the dark tarn of sleep the lingering stains, the clinging words, the last old colours, the taint of movement, the shreds of torn time.

Lest enticed otherwise, I avoid looking out of the window as I pull down the blind. I close my eyes against the untidiness of the open overnight bag from which I have taken my pyjamas, the shoes and socks lying on the bedside mat, the clothes tossed on the armchair, and plummet instantly far below the surface of the dark waters and, for all I know, could be dead, and heir to the infinity owed me.

When I wake it is night. Deprived of death, one must make do with life. Beyond the enclosed blackness of the room, this night can be sensed electrically quivering, simmering, charged with emanations from hurryings to and fro, criss-crossed with unheard sounds and esoteric vibrations. My mind and body tingle. Night is alive and, resurrected into its fever and blackness, washed naked-clean of the past, I am also resurrected into the future I slept to overtake, and into a bewilderment because there is an immediate perception that the future has overtaken me, or at least drawn level. Something has happened while I was dead. In the room now mine, close at hand, I feel another me, already up and about, a presence in unsteady outline, a muslin figure put into action while I lay like a thing of stone beneath the burgundy-coloured quilt and the grey blankets. Absurd! It is, state the illuminated hands of my travelling-clock, a quarter to eight. I feel for the switch, and turn on the light.

It is not absurd. A future me has begun. My shoes, newly polished, each with a folded sock in its mouth, sit by the lime-green armchair. A fresh shirt, its crush-marks ironed out, hangs, with a pressed tie, on the back of the chair. Where is the overnight bag? Someone has begun to construct me, not in the slapdash manner of boarding-school maids or George Hotel chambermaids, but with the particular, almost holy, care of the angelic sprite of fairy-tales. There is my pressed suit in the wardrobe, the handkerchief set like a love letter on the arm of the chair, my toilet brushes and bottles and tubes, my shaving gear, disposed in an asymmetrically balanced group on the dressing-table, Olivia's photograph standing on the drink-table near an arrangement of pampas in a grey bowl.

All this is, I discover next day, the spectral work of Ikuko-san, my house-girl, whom the distracted golliwog sergeant has bumped into as she is bringing a parcel of her bits and pieces to the quarters in preparation for Monday.

Ikuko-san!

I have loved few people as much, and none in the same way, as I do this squat, bandy Japanese woman who knows more about me, evil and good—if she is still alive—than any living creature. It cannot be that I know all about her for I know nothing but good. To remember her is a distress I prefer to avoid for, in knowing her, I learn the final unpleasant truths about myself, truths lying so far down beneath stacks of carefully posed, hand-tinted, touched-up studio portraits of myself that the presence of these clouded negatives is something forgotten. I am now less liberal to others because I was more illiberal to her, and more stern with my great imperfections because I was stern with her infinitesimal ones. One does not strike angels without burning one's hand.

The night calls me from somewhere in its own distance. Go I must.

As at the Misses Gregory's rooming-house in Mackenzie Street, Melbourne, so in B Mess Officers' Quarters, Kure: a long wide central corridor between two rows of rooms. Is the bathroom in the same place? It is. The shower-room smells of carbolic, the water is hard and heavily chlorinated. I dress in the garments set out by the unknown, the jinnee valet, the phantom handmaid. Because of an impulse to run like a child towards whatever it is that galvanizes the night outside the walls, I force myself to walk the lane of coir-matting with the steady patience of a sensible thirty-eight-year-old man, who knows exactly where Z is. The outer door is thus reached.

Z!

Where are A and B? Where is poor C?

The stars!

The sweep of some immeasurable wing has disarranged them; Z could be anywhere; the alphabet of the zodiac is tousled. A page of the sky has turned over to reveal planets I cannot name although their names have been known since boyhood; the constellations are undone because my eye cannot fix their boundaries for them; the gazetteer cannot be read. Here are nothing but the spillings from broken necklaces; here, more than anywhere, lie the tangles of the umbilicus it has taken me nearly four decades to be able to cut, the chart of paths I am from now on to hurry along, empty-hearted and empty-headed. Here are someone else's stars. The Milky Way has overflowed the levees I knew, to make a marsh of pin-prick twinklings. To me, they are no more than an instant born, they are younger than I. I am too old to know them.

On the height, by the gingko-tree outside the door, I am made dizzy not only by the overhead garlands of stars which my eye cannot nudge into known shapes—the Cross, Orion's Belt, the Mouse, Eridanus, the Peacock—but also by the stars sown in thick dapplings and arcs on the narrow plain below, nearer and bigger stars, the lights of Kure. How sharply and with what zestful ferocity they sparkle! An atmosphere like crystal? No. The patched paper shutters are drawn back in all the flimsy houses; there are no dimming curtains; no light-bulb wears a shade. Each naked pear of glass, dangling on the end of flex, cannot but glitter. It is in the direction of these grounded stars, as unknown to me as those squandering themselves in space, that I descend by the steep cobbled road immediately outside the wire gate where the guard, pecking rice from a bowl with chopsticks, gives me a sharp cockalorum bow, and a smile that reveals teeth edged with a metal resembling platinum.

As though hastening to the Cornish Floral Dance, downhill and downhill, faster and faster I go, double victim of the force of gravity and increasing excitement.

In the unlit room I had felt the buzzing vibrations from some far-off scrimmage of festivity. As I stood near the gingko-tree, bamboozled by a vertigo of stars, I had heard the muddle of twanglings and squeakings and thumpings, and the cryings of flutes, all striving upwards. Now, as I tumble nearer to the electric constellations and trembling lanterns, the mesh of music and sound becomes stronger and less intertwisted, each thread grows separately, almost phosphorescently, visible to the eye in the ear—hands beating on tight little lacquered drums, fingers roaming on bamboo flutes, sandals with soles of paulownia wood clicking like pony hoofs on the slope of cobbles, plectrums of ivory the size and shape of battle-axe blades slashing sour-sweet tunes from samisens, and loudspeaker voices singing from behind slatted visors: "Samisen Boogie", "Apple Song", "I Can't See You in My Eyes Any More", Deanna Durbin and "It's Raining Sunbeams", Doris Day and "In the Café Rendezvous".

Unhampered by the need to decorate raw curiosity with polite small-talk, alone and happy as a child, I am lucky to have this particular first-night baptism in the vortex of the landscape that, from the Brigadier's launch, looked like a doggery. I am to wander, unattached as smoke, the streets and back-streets and alleys of a village festival on behalf of one of Japan's godlets, one of those deities as numerous and carefree as lice.

I am to drift through many such festivals, more townified or more really rustic, later on and elsewhere, as drifting through objectified segments of bygone centuries, with matter and time keeping their former identities, and imposing their certainties.

As well, on this fortuitous first night in Kure, headquarters of the Australian Occupation Forces, I can see where the present soldier-ridden design interlocks with the past.

Every souvenir-stall, tea-house, beer-stand and barber-shop (*Stand Beer* and *Bar Ber* say the signs), every inn, noodle-counter, snooker saloon, indoor-fishing joint, pinball parlour, silk-shop, china-shop, and bookshop is lit-up, lantern-hung, and busy. The little poverty-stricken world is out under the stars; the poverty-insect's ticking is overborne by spruikers, samisens, gongs, and drums; the boy street-tumblers, red-and-black-striped, with cock's feathers on their heads, stand on their hands like caterpillars, spin like catherine wheels.

Babies everywhere, slung in pouches on the backs of mothers: their heads hang like dark fruit, or are in pods of pixie-hoods; necklets of hare-fur dyed apricot, raspberry-fool-pink, heliotrope or jade-green encircle the stalks of their necks. Impassioned children surround the shaved-ice machine, a late-Victorian device halfway between a lathe and a mangle: boys with powdery thumbprints of some disease impressed in their bristly black skulls; little girls, their faces flour-white and their lips painted, in kimono of gigantic yellow and green and orange flowers. Trios of giggling-tipsy men leashed arm-over-shoulder together swagger on muscular bandinesses girt by wilted suspenders from the saké shop to the roast-peanut-seller's stall lit by acetylene flares. A cloaked old man wearing a Sherlock Holmes hat with padded ear-flaps extends his hand to the corsair-haired palm-reader whose lantern sign holds up another hand, sinister, black, gashed and cross-gashed with white. Young men, fresh from the bath-house, strut like samurai, the iron-dark sashes of their grey robes tied in docked stallion-tails on their lean rumps. Young women, in kimono of lavender and violet, navy-blue cold-germ masks tied across nose and mouth, teeter pigeon-toed from stall to stall, their seal-brown eyes expressing verdicts on the value to no one and fools of celluloid kewpies, cigarette-lighters formed like miniature refrigerators, plaster-of-Paris Virgin Marys robed in Reckitt's-blue paint, musical decanters tinkling a stave or two of "Waltzing Matilda", and photographs of Greer Garson and Moira Shearer. The reason for the Greer Garson popularity in 1949 and 1950 Occupation Japan seems a mystery; Moira Shearer's leap to suicide in the film *Red Shoes* assures her popularity. For a while she is so revered as to be admitted to the centuries-old pantheon of creatures folded from paper—the crane, the tortoise, the grasshopper, and the lobster, and I am later on taught by provincial geishas and buck-toothed brothel attendants to twist and mould from the tissue-paper in cigarette packets a tiny model of Moira Shearer in her tutu, and to put the toe-point of the finished model between the painted lips of my teacher so that it is dyed red.

Student youths, slender and earnest in shrunk and washed-out high-school uniforms, peer through horn-rimmed spectacles at the poster of a peroxided Laurence Olivier as Hamlet, and a bewigged Jean Simmons, their eyes orientally slanted, leaning on each other in theatrical anguish among vertical columns of Japanese calligraphy.

A knot of more hooligan youths in Hawaiian shirts are reading, with what inner expression I cannot tell for the outer one makes no comment except none, at a glassed-in notice rimmed by green neon. Several Australian privates, seeming relatively big-boned and bestial and wrinkled, although young "clean-looking lads", are also reading the notice, counting their yen, and noisily debating the yeas and nays of spending them on what the notice offers:

PICTURE, and NUDE CARNIVAL
Tokyo Eccentric Strip Show
organized with
YOUNG VIRGINS ONLY
The Fully Numerous Flowers of Nude Beauties
PINK ROSE IN A SPECIAL ACT
&

with above, Republic present
ANGEL ON THE AMAZON
Could it be up along the Amazon where the
ferocious beasts are roaring?
DEAD BEAUTIFUL WOMAN SHEDDING THE SMELL
OF RIDDLE

Cheek-by-jowl with the stalls where circumspect families are sucking in bowls of buckwheat noodles with polite din, or buying cellophane sachets of seaweed biscuits, are the strip-tease joints and the *cinéma bleu*. Next to a brothel making the thinnest of pretences to be a tea-house staffed by far too many far too pretty waitresses in elegant kimono, is a shop selling shrine furniture, brass lotuses, china Inari foxes with their brushes as erect as squirrel tails, incense-sticks, and porcelain windbells with long rectangular paper tongues on which are written poems or prayers.

It is not easy for me to explain truly to myself, and certainly not at all easy to explain to others, why the evidences seen that night of enthusiastically amateur attention being given to the more lecherous tastes—strip-tease shows, female and male brothels, *cinéma bleu*, pornographic booklets, and obscene figurines—do not seem to suggest decadence, while in Manila the much less seen strikes me as vitiated.

Whether my puritanism is inherent, a matter of temperate humours and a taste for self-discipline, or is based on fastidious

273

and aesthetic rather than moral feelings, is another of the many questions impossible to answer. There is no recollection of the seed being planted; there is a dead-certain knowledge that the plant cannot now be uprooted. Whatever the reason—and maybe it is one not touched on in the preceding sentences—it is true that body-selling and poverty, for instance, which seem so degenerate in Manila, seem in Kure (in spite of the arc-lit comment of the Venereal Diseases Hospital conspicuous as a Hollywood première on the crest of the hill) to possess a quality making them much less than vile, expressions of the life force, expressions of will, rather than of anti-life and hopelessness.

To those who have read thus far an attempt to put down what one follower finds, during a limited paper chase between the years 1929 and 1949, certain shapes must have formed in the mist. The shapes, whatever they are, have coagulated because of or in spite of the writer. A cocksure and smart-alec denial of subtleties that other intelligences can take in is as shape-forming and mist-dispersing as a simple affirmation of situations too obvious to need affirmation. What, to me, seems clear enough is that until I reach Japan in October 1949 I am a shape that lacks some faculty, some key to the door of the maze, some "Open, Sesame!" I appear to be some shape on another plane (offside? lower? nowhere?), or some *other* kind of clot or con-man or mug or idealist.

It is unmistakably true that, until Japan, I have laid hold on little except happiness of a dead-level sort, on trifling distresses, unsplendid victories, and the empty joy that lives in the sad and wonderful truths of others—you there, squatting on a mock-heroic cloud; you there, fat white woman who walks through the field in gloves; you there, pretty girl milking her cow; You there, groaning, "*Eloi, Eloi, lama sabachthani?*" you there, all of you.

However much it is possible honestly to be dishonest, vigorously to denigrate or mock myself, however much it is possible wryly to pat myself on the back or wilfully to put myself on the rack or—most shaming of all—to make emotionally and socially profitable misunderstandings of myself, there is a point where the possible becomes impossible. In the smoke-charged and inferno-hot vastness of din, a cool silence gets to its feet, and stands up straight in the trampled and scorched paddock of mere words, and convictions in words, and love and hate in words, and—then—I know. I know that clumsy years have been spent in seeking to discriminate between the essential and the incidental, and that I have arrived at the time and place where the answer is ready, omnipresent, and mine for the asking, mine for the bare looking.

The paper chase has prolonged itself because a ravenous curiosity of this sort, carted about like a burden not to be put down, is distracted by false trails. Who would expect, anyway, that a whole nation would be needed to show that what I seek without seeking I shall discover without looking, and recognize without instantly knowing what is being recognized?

As always, when writing of a past self, I try to put down what is felt *then* even if *now* has changed the feeling, blackened it, turned it inside out, trodden it underfoot, chucked it over the cliff. The Inland Sea introduction is, let's say, no more than a cunningly reproduced frontispiece of a book to be read. Kure's little festival is, let's say, Grecian urn stuff in the Lafcadio Hearn manner. No Keats or Hearn *then*, no Keats or Hearn today, I have nevertheless tried to keep the description of that first night as naïve as the writer of that night is, which is less naïve than the present writer who can attach what he learns later to what he only senses then.

Since I've already written a not successful novel on Japan, and am commissioned to write another large book about the place, it is necessary sternly to control myself here, and do no more than sum up in a paragraph or two what I find out in 1949 and 1950.

Japanese civilization does discriminate between the essential and the incidental, and has perspective, continuity, and counterpoint. Its landscape is not defiled by its millions but glorified, humanized. In 1949 the mounting petulances of the twentieth century can, in Japan, still be shaken off like crumbs from a cloth. Long before 1949, their hand forced by the monstrous anti-civilization of the West, the Japanese used the gadgets of the West, the machines of war and industry—these enlist from them no profound emotional loyalties. The Japanese are not pauperized, as the West is, by science and the material. Even poverty cannot pauperize those who have spent a thousand years acquiring the art of poverty, an art so profound that even the wealthy, the writers and architects, have acquired economy of spirit as well as of matter. The perfection of the rich man's house and possessions and garden matches that of the poor man's because each employs an age-old simplicity in which nothing is left to chance. In this, the Japanese poor can be as scrupulous as the pure can be unscrupulous.

Atomic-bombed, defeated, humiliated, they escape what could be a suicidal combination of gloom and impotence by continuing to carry on their integrated culture, by living their own lives of Spartan self-education—a pinch of rice for the kitchen god, moon-viewing, tending the ancestral dead, making bamboo cages for crickets, eating bean soup, saving excrement to feed the arrowroot crops, arranging flowers, patching kimono, going about their . . . their vocation of living until they die, *and* getting their rake-off also from the less but particularly from the more barbaric of the Occupationnaires. Not only do they play their parts as picturesquely quaint peasants, fishermen, sieve-pedlars, rice-bran wives, cute children, sweet-potato-vendors, blind masseurs, bonsai-sellers, lantern-makers, and tourist geishas, but they perform as a comic troupe of bar-boys, house-girls, cooks, gardeners, chauffeurs, telephone-operators, typists, clerks, odd-job men, guards and pantry-maids in the British Commonwealth Occupation Force Messes, transit hotels, offices, and the residential suburbs run up by post-war profiteers for the officers and their families. For the sillier or baser needs of Occupationnaires on the loose, or of those Japanese who can afford to pay for them, the defeated engage in the game of buying and selling to the conqueror on an ascending scale which starts at the *après-guerre* girl, the amateur lamp-post prostitute, and finishes at the brothel-magnate, and covers such people as dive-guides, brothel-touts, editors of pornographic books, makers of pornographic pottery, blackmarket-eers, strip-tease women, cabaret-performers, pinball-parlour kings, night-club promoters, and the owners of factories devoted to the manufacture of tourist atrocities for buyers who want them because they think them beautiful or amusing or clever, as well as to the manufacture of fake antiquities, and

276

conveyor-belt rarities, and reproductions of exquisite knick-knacks, to suit the taste of buyers who can be taken in or do not mind being taken in.

Existence for the Occupationnaires at the tag-end of the Occupation has taken on the quality of life on a luxury liner with millions of servants or near-servants, engaging as pretty monkeys, with enchanting manners and customs, and a country which, outside the coarser cities and industrial towns, most of them bombed flat, is a perfect illustration of how superbly men and women can fit fields and woods and groves and temples and villages and inns upon and between the notches and spikes of a land of islands balanced on earthquake and admonished by typhoons, and as lively with deities as with irrepressibly vital humans who have learned to control their emotions without suppressing them.

People on luxury liners are inclined to step outside everyday life with its guarantees and necessities into that almost immoderate region where they become more than themselves. Comparisons are therefore easier because contrasts are stronger. Of the many non-Australians—Americans, New Zealanders, English—encountered in Occupation Japan there is little to say except that, in making a daily balance of human contact with the Japanese, their behaviour is essentially barbaric although affecting to be civilized while the behaviour of Australians is fundamentally civilized although affecting to be up-you-for-the-rent barbaric.

Having learned, very quickly, that I can—for a while anyway—look through myself as through a glass of water because the Japanese ethos has purified me of earlier and gaudier conclusions does not mean, alas, that I can sit in a padded kimono on the tatami mats staring through myself at the snow-coated pine branch and the round round moon. Indeed no. I have to go on being a social camel, ambling along with somewhat the camel's gait, lively yet preoccupied. There is also work to do.

I teach at Nijimura School which caters for the children of Australian officers. There are also some American and English children at the school.

Because the Nijimura teachers are a hand-picked lot among whose qualifications (diverse experience, social flexibility, et

277

cetera) disciplinary power is an important one, the children are kept in order, and taught what has to be taught. As pupils they seem like other children. Outside that there are differences.

They are the first jeans-wearing children we have seen. I feel that sentence intimates more than it states but cannot clearly say why, beyond underlining *first*—the first girl children to wear trousers.

They are also more spoiled and footloose than they appear, almost the forerunners of Affluent Society children. Each officer's house has several servants, so the mothers are, like working mothers, often busy as bees away from home—playing canasta or bingo, selling soap or aspirin or wool or tins of cocoa on the blackmarket, drinking at the Club, taking lessons in Japanese, in pottery, painting, lampshade-making, poker work, lino-cutting, book-binding, and basket-weaving, and scouring the curio kiosks and market stalls for what they are spending their blackmarket money on, some "collection" of minute tea-pots, Satsuma, glass menageries, dolls, chopstick-rests, ivory figurines, rice bowls or carved wooden trays. As well, even the least frivolous of mothers must, as an officer's wife, make appearances at the frequent farewell or welcome parties being held in one or the other Messes, or at the Officers' Club. The children become, by and large, servants' children, and gang children.

Nothing happens except that, in a situation already luxury-cruise unusual, the home—impermanent and foreign at best—becomes less centralized, its pivot out of kilter, family texture looser, and the children themselves adept in the back-alley intricacies of the blackmarket. If a children's blackmarket is not an institution to quibble about, nothing happens.

The school itself—most of the staff and many of the children of which play the blackmarket game (as mysterious to me as *chemin de fer*, and as boring as crosswords)—is for a school of its nature too prodigally equipped. It has, for example, a large theatre, music room, dining-room, and kitchen, and many servants, and is a delightful if absurd building to work in. The one thing I feel unhappy about is its being presented to the Japanese as a "typical" Australian primary school. Because of this

278

"typical" fable there are certain people I do not like to see through my class-room window.

Outside the window there is much to be seen: wine-coloured hills splashed with the gentian stains of forests; house-boys clip-clopping past hand in hand on their six-inch-high wooden-soled *geta*; one of the school gardeners on a bamboo ladder clipping the hair of an immature pine, and puffing a Peace Cigarette—its smell is unmistakable; a yellow butterfly and a black dragon-fly palpitating above a daphne bush as high as a refrigerator; and, nearest, intent as a tattoo-artist, scratching with a bamboo rake on the gravel path the striped current of a flowing stream, another gardener, his hand-towel tied around his head.

Here come the certain people one does not like to see.

A Major who does not know how to pronounce *longitude* and *culinary* is guide-touring into Nijimura School a nervous huddle of people who do know how to pronounce them. They are Japanese dressed in clothes one can only clap tear-jerking adjectives on to—shabby, neat, patched, threadbare. They would be less tear-jerking if I didn't know how wastefully wide to them as the Champs-Élysées the corridor must seem, how boundless and sparsely inhabited the class-rooms, how copious and snow-white the supply of chalk, and brilliantly black the huge blackboards with the bloom still on them, for the visitors are Japanese schoolteachers. The Major, suddenly appearing over-handsome, much too well-fed and obtuse, is heard more than implying that the theatre with its electrically worked curtain and tip-up seats, the kitchen with its *Saturday Evening Post* refrigerators and sinks and electric stoves, the music room with its pianos and music stands and metronomes, are absolutely usual to all Australian state schools.

I wince because, as a voluntary extramural stint, I am one of the teachers who sometimes lecture at night in Japanese schools (which, at that time, are running two or three school sessions daily) and see the worn-out and tumble-down buildings, the meagre scraps of furniture, the makeshift equipment, and am moved and impressed by the high standard of education reached under what would be ruinous conditions to Australians.

About the Occupation itself, with its two-sided aim of

humiliation and democratization, there is no more to be said than *C'est la guerre* or *Who loses wins*, but the wincing comes on when lies of salt are rubbed in wounds that need not be fingered, when the Major who is little more than a nice, vain, no-harm-meant man who reads Paul Gallico and the *Reader's Digest* boosts Nijimura Dependant's School to teachers from the Japanese schools without admitting that the Nijimura one is very far from usual. With repulsive magnanimity I give the visitors boxes of chalk under the have-you-tried-this-brand cloak. After all the Japanese are paying for them. Maudlin sensitivity, of course, from a grown man besotted by a nation of little people who eat raw fish, pickled radish, and dried squid, and whose rice fields are fertilized with human excrement, who have shrines in their department stores, and still believe in the medicinal value of pickled snakes, cremated moles, and desiccated frogs.

This almost maidenly tenderness, from one who cares little about human death but much about human feelings, is always tripping me up.

One evening three of us teachers are speaking at a particularly dilapidated school, a bombed one that has been put together like a house of frayed cards. Two of us, by the brownish light of one bulb, have said our pieces to the students, eighty-odd of them between the ages of fourteen and eighteen, jam-packed before us in a nearly visible fog of scent—camellia hair-oil. The third teacher who, until then, I have regarded as having some nous rises to make her offering to Australian-Japanese relations. For a while she is as efficient and informative and amusing as she usually is. Impossible to guess why she suddenly asks the students to sing "You Are My Sunshine". My blood runs cold with embarrassment, for this is the theme song of Tokyo Rose, Japan's wartime Lord Haw-Haw, and I experience the *déjà vu* switch—Hutchins School Hall, King's Birthday, the Headmaster trying to make the boys sing the morning hymn. The woman has lost her head.

"*Come* along now; come *along* now!" Standing there, fat and forceful, hung with blackmarket cultured pearls, she jollies them, "Come *on*, sing! I know you *all* know this one. I'll start you off."

And she begins, "You are my sunshine, my only sunshine . . ."

And they sing.

If the dark eyes flicker, I do not see them. If there is a subsurface recoil before they sing, I cannot tell if I have registered it. Maybe I am the only one in the room who feels that something unfair has been done, the only one drenched in shame and anger.

I could be doing the Japanese an injustice by blushing on their behalf. Their sense of humour is more sophisticated than mine. Just as it contains none of the sardonicism of the Australian one, so it contains none of the class-consciousness or rights-consciousness or malice of the English one. It has its behind-the-fan quality but it is also very direct. The messenger doves of Hachiman, the War God, standing-in as Doves of Peace on NO MORE HIROSHIMAS posters sum it up. Perhaps the singing of "You Are My Sunshine" for a fat Australian school-teacher of notable insensitivity is funnier to them than I think, and a blush has been wasted. Why, anyway, should one's conscience go tiptoeing and creaking about in back rooms—the Japanese are capable of looking after themselves with breathtaking finesse. Summer 1950, night, an uphill suburb of Kobe, I see them do it.

O-Bon, the Festival of the Dead, the Japanese Feast of All Souls, is being celebrated in a wide square. I have come upon the dancing people after wandering through streets of windbells and stalls, where thick pencils of incense are smouldering on the fish counters, and melons sit in wooden tubs of bubbling water, and shallow tin troughs set on stands down the centre of the street hold large prisms of ice across which passers-by slide their hands to cool them before stroking their cheeks and foreheads. In these prisms are embedded mounds of grapes and roses, or egg-fruit and seashells, their colours perverted and delicate details blurred by the depth of frozen water. Other prisms contain nothing except a white core like earache. It is easy to know there is something afoot: children wear garments burning with tremendous blossoms, many women have on convoluted wigs, there are lanterns of cut white paper with gauzy green fringes. I can hear the music

281

hammering and hacking ahead of me. I arrive at the dance for the dead.

In the centre of the square is a pine-wood platform decorated by red lanterns and white lanterns. Here the musicians, gaudily robed men and women with narrow drums and clacking rods and plangent samisens, play and sing relentlessly while the dancers, several hundred of them, dance round and round and round the hub of music. The wheel of humans has, it seems, been turning for hours, egged on by the blood-streaked voices of the singers, the goad of primitive noise.

Nearest the axis, a teetotum of toddlers, long ago tired, still lift up their arms in floral sleeves, faltering and sleep-dancing through the mist of dust, with tinselled rosy bows on their meagre coiffures. Next, round and round, tirelessly raising and lowering their arms, their fans, their clogs of crimson lacquer, circle the bigger children, the adept boys, the painted girls supple as lizards. Clogs spring out from the dust, and are drawn down; arms gash up into the lantern light; hands clap on the plate-round fans. As I watch the fuming wheel it seems possible to hear, under the tartness of the samisen and the loud stuttering of drums and the clacking of the rods, the friction of body on body, the whirr of hundreds of fans as they slice upwards together against the light. Again and again the whirlpool brings around the same scraps—a sweat-shiny torso, a pair of foot-high clogs, an adolescent in a yellow gaucho shirt, square-rimmed spectacles, lofty wigs, women with the ends of their head-towels clipped between the teeth, a burly man with his yugata-skirt folded up into his sash, a heart-shaped fan shredded by age and eaten by use into holes like an old lotus leaf, the long little fingernails through which the lantern-light shines. Round and round. Round and round. Arms up. Arms down.

As I watch, the dance seems to become imperceptibly faster and yet more tranced, the music imperceptibly more inflamed and yet more numbing, as though these living ones are really dancing with the dead who themselves, when living, danced the same dance to the same music with the living and the dead.

And then—s-w-e-e-p—like one wave, one comber only, cessation and silence.

The music stops.

282

The wheel of muscle and flesh and hair and cloth and colour halts like a merry-go-round.

From one of the streets running into the square a jeep has appeared. It contains two very drunk, loud-mouthed American soldiers and two drunk Japanese girls in Western dress, poor painted things in fake satin with tangled false eyelashes and curled hair and crystal necklaces, looking like a sister-act from a scruffy cabaret. In the silence, the sharp laughter of the women and the ho-ho-ho of the men are almost as visible as a coarse growth. While the jeep jerks across the square this growth decomposes, disintegrates. With an untranslatable gesture one of the sister-act begins to toot the horn, violently and —surely?—mutinously. I can see her eyes flashing with tears or fear.

No one of the stilled dancers, child or man, toddler or woman, and none of the silenced musicians looks at the braying jeep and its occupants. Those who escape from its path step aside as indifferently as from nothing at all, and those who must hear its hullabaloo do not appear to hear it. To me, it seems hours until the yowling hearse reaches the other side of the square, until the horn stops and, behind the tail-light, there appears a second of silence made more explicit by the whistle of a train somewhere downhill, far-off, near the harbour, near Osaka Bay.

The dance begins again.

As though nothing has happened except the comment of nothing, the stringent and ancient music gushes up like a geyser, the bodies wheel round, the hands and fans slice aloft, the feet go on rising above the dust and stabbing down into the dust, round and round.

I realize then how miniature and tinpot the jeep seemed, how like frangible puppets its drunken quartet, how minifying it can be to cross the tracks of the dancing dead and the living dancers, and the music of the past being played in the present.

Yes. I need not have fretted about the fat teacher's insensitivity. The Japanese en masse know what they are about at the centre of reality even if the remoter meadows of their minds are trodden by outrider spirits and haunted by old glories. If their attitude is no more than a comment to themselves there must be, as in suicide, a self-satisfaction.

What, generally, during the Occupation, Australians (Americans, et cetera) learn about Japanese, and Japanese about Australians (Americans, et cetera) is that both are human, a piece of information no one really needs. Learning *about* human beings one learns such things as that some of them might as well be God for all the good the world does them.

This is what Yamaguchi, the aged, skinny odd-job man of B Mess learns about one of the Mess-Presidents who breaks Yamaguchi's jaw because of an error in the dimensions of the hutch he builds for the Mess-President's pet rabbit. The breaking of the old man's jaw is the only directly nasty thing I know about B Mess. The rest is rather like a boarding-school with everyone on his honour to conform to the unwritten rules rather than the written ones.

Being on my honour in a male community is a soda because by this time I am an old hand at living the life of the institution male, and long enough in the tooth to be surprised at nothing. I have, when it comes to mind, one problem only. As a civilian in a Mess of professional soldiers I've not earned the right to certain feelings and sensitivities, and have not the knowledge to understand certain dramatic expressions of emotions, certain vehement loyalties. I am in much the same position as when, nearly twenty years earlier, I am a Junior Teacher at North Williamstown drinking in the Bristol Hotel with older teachers returned from the Great War. Then, I am young enough to be guiltlessly grateful to the tribal elders, the warriors, and am able to forgive myself for being young. Now, in B Mess, drinking and earbashing and singing dirty songs with soldiers of my own age and soldiers younger than I, men from battles and prison camps, I am still the one the witch-doctor hasn't shown the ju-ju to, still the one without the cryptic weal on each cheek. Not only has no initiation blood been drunk, no blood has even been sniffed on the air. I am, therefore, sometimes at a loss when the pillow-fighting side of the male clan takes a dallying-with-danger-and-death form, becomes a glassy-eyed contest of fire-eating. When these outbursts, usually in the early hours of the morning, after deep and deadly drinking in the Mess Bar, do

284

take place the delicacy with which I am as it were protected from participation ("Order us a round of buttered rums, Hal!") is such a ruthless delicacy that it would be improper even to think of wishing to join in. These boil-lancings and turbulent lettings-off of steam happen just enough times, and only with the more raffish officers, and seem to have something of the effect that, in a domestic setting, a wife-beating or a showdown with a mother-in-law would have.

For the rest, the noisier drinking sessions give me an opportunity to add to the collection of wartime dirty songs begun in Hobart in 1946 when my boon-companions are returned servicemen and -women.

New words appear—gen, bod, yakkata, purgee, nong, pesticide, Benelux, and apartheid are among those I recall hearing for the first time.

More, however, than the new-to-me wartime songs—already full-blown—which I foresee the men years later singing at nostalgic warrior gatherings taboo to me, more than the new words which contain the present and the future as the seed does the thorny vine, I am interested in the new feelings being expressed about the Japanese by men in the Mess who have been in Changi prison camp or have fought the Japanese bayonet to bayonet. There comes always the hour when grog traduces men to that last and most insincere of poses, sincerity, and it is then I discover that war is the shortest short-cut to admiration of and affection for an enemy. I listen to men trying to explain to me (to themselves!) why, having turned over the counter marked *Hate* to find *Love* on the other face, they are bewildered that *Forgiveness* is nowhere, even as a sub-title. They cannot, for example, forgive Japanese wartime atrocities. At such moments I am glad that being a civilian gives me no right to remind them that, ten nights ago, four grog-sessions ago, many rum-and-Coca-Colas ago, they told of their own atrocities, and that one reason for not forgiving enemy bestialities is that they cannot forgive their own.

I arrive in Japan when the Occupation is at the-last-rose-of-summer stage. There are still enough wild parties but many of the people who are there at them are not there. They are the men and women who have returned to Australia, the you'd-

have-loved-them people, the legends of whose wit, swashbuck-
lings, beauty and "personality" eke out the diminishing festivi-
ties, fill the blank spaces between the shadowy guests who remain. Someone is always saying, "Oh, but you should've been
here when things were really humming. Wow!" There are still
enough formal dinners and snobby dances at which the officers
are in full fig and I, more than ever aware of civilian singularity,
in tails. There are still masked fancy-dress balls, and amateur
theatrical productions, and organized hikes to temple-and-
panorama-viewing eminences, and bingo at the Officers' Club
every Thursday night, and cinemas showing *Kind Hearts and
Coronets*, and book-binding or flower-arranging or Japanese
grammar classes, and church on Sunday, and jeep-trip weekends, and a monthly magazine called *Gen* to which I contribute
—under compulsion from Army Education—polysyllabic and
esoteric articles on Japanese theatre. I can, however, feel the ship
slowly sinking, weighted with the regret of those whose jobs
have folded up, and who have left, and the increasing unhappi-
ness of those whose time is running out in a fascinating country
and a fantastic organization. Houses become empty. Grandiose
projects at Nijimura remain unfinished, the curving concrete
avenues sweep up to huge prefabricated buildings with locked
and dusty windows, to parks of tree-guards filled with weeds. In
Kure, The White Rose Curio Shop has its shutters up; other
curio kiosks have always the same execrable trinkets on display
for there are no new mug buyers arriving; more and more
Japanese are dismissed from jobs, and return to the day before
yesterday, to the destructive nobility of poverty, to the acceptance that although the tree may have many branches the bird
requires only one twig. Directly downhill from B Mess the
Officers' Club which was once, so old-timers tell me, bursting
at the seams every night is still, every night, lit up like a casino,
and the faint dance-band smoke of "Some Enchanted Evening"
drifts from it, and yet, night after night, no jeep or staff Hum-
ber stands in the car-park, no colonel and his lady walk the
terrace, no gaggle of army nurses and canteen girls on the tiles
can be heard tipsily singing to the "Glow-worm" tune "I
Wish I Were a Fascinating Bitch".

One night, I am bored with the Mess Bar, which is noisy

286

with some officers I don't much care for, and empty of those who have become friends; walkabout seems the thing. The night is icy. The moon is full, a plaque of frozen tin. What to do? Shall I visit Baby, the youngest and chubbiest prostitute in one of the brothel beer-houses off the Hondori, Kure's main street? She is in the middle of teaching me to sing the words of a Japanese jazz-tune called "One, two, three, four!"

I start off, maybe Baby-wards, maybe anywhere and anything, through a little shoulder-high gate, unguarded, in the wire fence. From here an almost vertically breakneck path leads to the Officers' Club level down a precipice of bomb debris—shards of rice-bowls, roof-tiles, saké-bottles, and teapots, and rusting spirit stoves, and shattered shutter-frames. It is from this slope, the guards and bar-boys tell me, the ghosts of children can be heard weeping and deploring, ghosts of those killed in the bombing of a children's hospital. Ground-level reached, I decide to visit the Club for I can hear the band playing with nice aptness "Baby, It's Cold Outside", and the Club is ablaze with lights.

The doors are swung open for me on the warmth and the carpets and the bowls of fresh flowers on lacquer tables and the armchairs and the glittering standard ashtrays of the foyer. I am helped off with my overcoat and gloves. The cloak-room attendant gives me the little disc. In the drink-lounge I choose to sit near the row of french windows which look on to a Japanese garden with its rocks and azaleas and girlish pines and twisting brook. While one of the stewards is getting a whisky I send another to ask the dance-band, which can be heard playing in the dining-room, to play some of the maudlin "Night and Day" kinds of tune I am given to. After three slow drinks I go into the dining-room, merely to eat a supper snack for it is now half-past ten and, whatever charms and comforts the Club has, the food is—like all Occupation food—revolting: frozen meat and fish, tinned or dehydrated vegetables, menus based on the dishes served in Australian cabarets of the sort patronized by bookmakers and advertising men. I have some sandwiches, and several more whiskies, and watch the dance-floor, and try out the orchestra on such dating tunes as "Begin the Beguine" and "The Lullaby of Broadway". I stand up when, at eleven o'clock, "God Save the King" is played. All the others I can see also stand stiffly to attention—the waitresses in uniforms of mauve starched cotton, the drink stewards in their monkey-jackets, the orchestra in its black trousers, all a bit baggy as though everyone has on the wrong pair. I, and all the Japanese staff, stand. There is no one else to stand just as there was no one to dance on the shining floor, or eat the abominable food, or sully the ashtrays in the drink-lounge, or hang a coat near mine, the only one on the rows of empty hooks. I learn from a drink steward that there has been no Occupationnaire in the Club since five, and that the chefs and pantry-maids and kitchen-boys are in the kitchen, and that the orchestra goes on playing to the empty floor just as he goes on waiting to wait on empty tables.

One of my harmless vanities is to enjoy plugging myself into the current of infinity, into time's and space's continua, in rather twee circumstances such as being the only human being for a quarter of an hour at three in the morning in the Piazza San Marco, or the only one outside Gogol's house in the Via Sistina, Rome, or the only one sailing like a bird in the Luft-sellbahn Zürichsee high above little masted boats with names like *Lucky*.

The enjoyment of being the sole drinker at the enormous Officers' Club, that bureaucratic facsimile of luxury, is, how-ever, a forlorn enjoyment from which the writer gets an unholy *frisson* I do not. The warmth and flowers and lights and music and iced drinks, the Rose china-ware and mass-produced coffee-pots and production-belt food, the well-ordered trees, and rows of coat-hooks, and platoon of attendants with brilliant smiles, all brought into being to be seen and heard and used, have lived beyond their reason, have become the appurtenances of the hollow behind an impermanent institution that pretends per-manency.

I do not go downhill to Baby, and do not toil up the cliff of smashed china and child ghosts to B Mess which is suddenly seen to have as dreary an impermanence as the Club, but cut across to the cobbled road down which I tumbled excitedly into Kure once upon a time, and begin to climb it. As I pass the guard at the B Mess gate the officers are roaring out "She Was Poor But She Was Honest". I keep on uphill in the freezing moonlight, pass the unceasingly brilliant House that Jack Built, and see the road go narrower, feel the cobbles change to earth.

Beyond the crumbling Buddhist temple where the muscular guardian deities gesticulate with fiendish love behind their bars on each side of the gate, the road of earth begins to run deeper, trenched by generations of feet, runs narrower, no wider than a pair of pilgrim soles, between a bluish fur of grass, runs more raggedly and steeply among boulders and their blue shadows, and the anatomies of bushes and their blue meshes of shadow, into a short valley cracked crookedly down the centre by a sibilant and ageless stream.

I have climbed here often before in daylight, never by moonlight at midnight.

A dozen stone images, knee-high, waist-high, shoulder-high, have squatted among the spheres of rock for centuries, and their eyelids are blotched by lichen, their equivocal smiles half-erased by rain, their coiffures blanched by thousands of noonday suns, their long ears netted by spider-webs. They are of the family of down-to-earth images one sees up and down Japan, wayside deities who audit the prayers of pregnant women, and crippled fishermen, and children with whooping-cough, distraught peasant virgins, and mother-in-law-hating wives, and balance these prayers against inevitability.

I have not climbed up from the Club of servants without guests, from the vacancy of a shoddy dream that drags on although it is over, to visit this zoo of stone beings anchored in stone and time, these never-sleeping simplicities. Too easy an emotional and mental device of symbolic contrast, that. I have climbed in the ice-blue moonlight to visit what seems to me, then, that night, and still seems—though I cannot define why—the one piece of sculpture in the world that best expresses the earth itself while also expressing Man.

By the stream, among the rocks and weeds, a vast hand of stone, palm upwards, rises out of the ground.

Thrust calmly and inevitably as a growing thing through the very flesh of the earth, this human gesture in stone is at one and the same time a gesture of offering and acceptance open to

289

heaven and any mortal interpretation, and a gesture relaxed and earthbound.

I climb on to the moon-frosted palm, and lie there like a lizard, looking over the fingertips down on to the Inland Sea the colour of an eye suffused with silver, down on to the minute twinkling world below from which rises the scent of wood-smoke and sleep, and there, symbolically mesmerized by the far-off, perhaps I still remain.

The stone palm accepts because it cannot reject me.

The stone palm offers because it cannot hide me.

It could be a table for beer-bottles or the Last Supper, a bed for love or death, a platform for dictators, an altar for sacrifice, the perfect dais for never-ending contemplation. Leaving myself there for ever, I climb out of the hand, and go down down down into the world where there is too much to do.

I make no qualms about doing too much. The smallness of the country, the months of school holidays, the weekends free from half-past-three on Friday afternoons, the finely meshed network of trains and buses and ferries, allow me to become familiar with the main islands and to explore many of the smaller ones. All that I see haunts me yet—here, more than anywhere on earth, are people who know what the earth and the dead and time and humour and pain and beauty are. Philosophy and the relative do not distract them. Beauty is beauty, for example, and no words can undo it.

What I see is often, to me, absurd—Francis Xavier's relic of a Basque arm on tour like a bottled mermaid; Nagasaki's jealousy of Hiroshima for having so completely outshone as an atomic-bombed city that Nagasaki might just as well never have been bombed; Lafcadio Hearn's dumb-bells and old flannel singlets preserved in the samurai house he lived in at Matsue; strip-tease shows of almost wanton sexlessness; all-female musical comedies like Ziegfeld productions of *Oedipus Rex*; and the hundreds of fluorescent-lit cocktail bars with names like Ronsard, Soirée, Prunier or Bel-Ami jammed side by side like chocolate boxes under the shadow of bombed department-store skyscrapers in Tokyo. If these things seem absurd, they also haunt, and most absurd and most haunting is the Kiss Dance.

In 1950 I am quite unable to foresee that adolescent school-girls in trousers, or that tinned vegetables and deep-freeze meat, will become acceptable in Australia. They seem no more than ugly fads brought about by something unusual in Occupation circumstances, something Yankee and perverse. I do, heaven knows why, have singular premonitions, particularly in family-dominated Japan, about the Kiss Dance, because the kiss, in pre-Occupation Japan, is a taboo indecency.

One night, in Tokyo, I get a pedi-cab driver with an Oxford accent to cycle me to what he considers the wickedest place he knows—even writers as pure as milk like to think they have a taste for mud—and finish up at a neon sign which, because the Japanese have some confusion about R and L, brazenly says in acid-green, *Florida Cabalet*. The cabaret is in a huge basement brimmed with a raddled-and-ruby sultriness, and solidly packed with dancers. At each end of the hall, sulphurously illuminated, is a dance-band. From the ceiling depend rotating spheres patchworked with pieces of looking-glass which throw flak-like dapples of light over the dancers. On the outskirts of the mass, taxi-girls perform tango-like steps with their partners, or sit drinking with them at tables.

It is the whirlpool of young dancers at the centre of the floor that makes my mental eyebrows lift. Schoolmasterishly I sense a form of defiance. There, mouth to mouth, soldered together, boy and girl, boy and boy, girl and girl, the adolescents in Western dress, scarcely progressing, are doing the Kiss Dance. This imperceptibly wheeling stew of minors is my first sight of mass juvenile delinquency, and I can understand why the middle-aged pedi-cab driver thinks it outrageous. It is not sex that would disturb him but the erotic defiance, the lawlessness and decadence of the public kiss. Having been an adolescent among adolescents, having lived day by day and cheek-by-jowl with adolescents for years, I am surprised, right there and then in the *Florida Cabalet*, to find myself faintly distressed *for* rather than merely bored by them and their mutiny. No adolescent male is worth listening to until he is at least thirty-five, no adolescent female ever, but the nature of this mutiny says something to listen to because nothing is said. Deeds committed in such suggestive silence cannot but bounce off older sounding-boards to make words: "Youth is nothing. Future is nothing. Life is nothing."

As children of a half-destroyed city and a defeated nation, as blackmarket's messengers, and eavesdroppers on the corrupt *Florida Cabalet* side of the Occupation, they are entitled to their gestures—youth is anyway always giving pimply ego names like idealism, radicalism, modernism, and so on. This fazes no adult who recalls that youth is flash-in-the-pan and useless to the young. What does disturb me, then, in 1950, is that the first juvenile delinquents I ever see are self-destructive, cannibalistic and, more horrifying, completely uncynical. The writer wants me to stay and see the Kiss Dance evening through to the end. I renegue. There are other things to do while the young city Japanese poison will with kisses.

I get the same pedi-cab cyclist who is still lurking outside the *Florida Cabalet*, he and his Michelangelo muscles, and return to the Marunouchi Hotel, and telephone Olivia's actress sister who is also in Tokyo. She and I spend the rest of the evening pretending that I am to marry Olivia again, that love has to live in one house and one bed. It seems believable even with Olivia not there. Lies about what one wants to do are, however, always outweighed by the truth of what one has to do.

The past is always criss-crossing the gadabout Japanese present. I leave flowers on John Ward's grave at Yokohama. Boys I caned keep on turning up as burly brutes in uniform who could crumple me like a newspaper. Weddings occur with the frequency of Occupation nervous breakdowns which are frequent enough. A former Williamstown drinking-mate, with less taste than he should have had, uses the Emperor Hirohito's white horses to draw his wedding coach; the Adelaide doctor who met me at Iwakuni has a glossy marriage to the Belgian consul's daughter; the fat "You Are My Sunshine" teacher marries a British Embassy employee; I am best man at the wedding of a former Williamstown pupil to a Japanese girl. More and more Australian men are marrying Japanese girls. Those who do not marry return to Australia leaving broken-hearted mistresses or, more heart-breakingly, their half-caste bastards. In a country where all hair is black and straight, all eyes the same brown, it jars some national fibre to see a blue-eyed or

curly-headed demi-Aussie child playing alone in the street of
some one-pig village, or paddling in the gutter-muck of a city
back-alley. I feel this jar because it is obvious that, however
earnestly the Japanese of the Occupation years appear to be
subscribing to General Macarthur's imperial notions of democracy, however civilized and modern they are as a nation, they
are also traditionalists, contemptuous of the rest of the Asiatic
world, and as disdainful of by-blow Occupation half-breeds as
they are of their own untouchable Etas. Most of the illegiti-
mates are the children of stupid women not only incapable of
protecting themselves but incapable of protecting the child
from the anguishes of ostracism, from becoming a child of the
streets, a garbage-eater, an outcast with blue eyes, a beggar
with a shoot-through barbarian father it will never know.

The steadily sinking ship of the Occupation becomes increasingly burdened with the agonizings of small-time Cho-
Cho-sans left high and dry by rough-as-guts-Aussie Pinkertons
as well as by the remorse of many of these returned-to-stock
Pinkertons. The luxury-cruise promiscuity, albeit accepted,
and provided for by the House that Jack Built, is nevertheless
subject to certain restrictions. For instance when one of the
most accomplished of the Nijimura teachers, an intelligent
woman skilled in most profitably playing the black market, and
forthright about sexual free-lancing, is given a donation of
gonorrhoea by her spivvy little Japanese blackmarket agent,
she is sent back to Australia. Her error gives her only a short
start for home. Within the next few months more of the teachers and most of the children are also sent back because war has
done its cut-and-come-again trick, and is making a noise just
next door.

Late in June 1950 I hold a small party in B Mess for a friend,
an enthusiastic gourmet who has spent a day haggling in the
Kure markets for cucumbers which he proposes to pickle on
board the frigate *Shoalhaven* of which he is a commodore. He is
giving details of his recipe when a jeep arrives to collect him
with dramatic immediacy because the Korean War has started.
He tosses down his drink, and goes. It is fifteen years before I
see him again, still a food-enthusiast, in Jimmy Watson's bistro
in Melbourne.

Four or five weeks later the Kure Occupationnaires gather in the rain to farewell the first shipload of Australian brigade volunteers, permanent army men and World War II veterans of the Occupation forces, on their way to Korea. As the ship at last slides away like a curtain, the damp Australian seers-off standing under the rusted derricks have revealed to them, as on a stage, what lies on the other side of the curtain, the other side of the ship. Dressed in their best kimono, each wearing two flowers, one red, one white, are the sweethearts of the soldiers. The formality of their obeisances, the control of distress, are moving but more moving is their gesture of farewell. Western hand-waving suggests a shooing-off, Japanese hand-waving is a painful and restricted gesture, a clutching back towards the warmth of the body and the emptiness of the vacated heart.

It is mid-autumn when the time arrives for me to leave Japan. Blindly passionate as I am about the place, I have no deep regrets. There are not many stones left unturned. By going flat-out, often in the company of pain, the most tiresome of travelling-companions, I have covered much of the country. It is now necessary to arrange the machinery of living so that I can see much more of the world, continue my paper-chase career. How else can I be certain that Japan is what it seems to be? Apart from a little time in Tasmania, and a few hours in Manila, Japan is the only place whose exotic enchantments I have been able to set up beside my own country's familiar but powerful ones. In fact, it is for the very reason that this foreign civilization so deeply affects me that I compel myself to turn down a job on a Tokyo newspaper. Anyway, whatever colour-print-and-*haiku* notion the writer has of being a latter-day Lafcadio Hearn watching the shadow of the pine-tree on the paper shutters while the blind masseur's flute cries like a bereaved bird in the moonlight outside is not for me. I cannot bear raw fish, blood-warm rice, aubergines, or the stench of pickled radish. Moreover, I have been an infatuated expatriate long enough and, were there room for the emotion, could even be getting homesick.

The one painful thing to be done is to part from Ikuko-san.

There is no way of assessing the degree of practicality or cynicism with which the army decides to give each officer a

house-girl. It is certainly not the cheapest or only way of dealing with the housework and laundry of a group of men. On each
side of the coir-matting-covered corridor of B Mess Officers'
Quarters are ten rooms, a total of twenty rooms, twenty officers, twenty house-girls. It is easy to spot which of the men
sleep with their house-girls, which do not. More do not than do.
There are faithful-unto-death married men, and bachelor virgins; there are discreet men who make love elsewhere than in
their own boarding-house nests; there are men with moral or
fastidious or officer-and-gentleman standards; there are men as
wary as I of allowing the body to commit them to the razza-
matazz and fatiguing by-play of a settled amour. No one comments on the sexual inclinations of anyone else; unwritten law
makes us in this matter behave like the Three Wise Monkeys.

The golliwog Mess-Sergeant gets round to me after a week,
and his is the only comment, "You don't have to keep Ikuko-
san. She was only a kitchen-maid we were turfing out. She's no
bloody oil-painting, but you caught us on the hop. If you find
anyone else you'd rather have..."

Only a kitchen-maid, no bloody oil-painting ... Ikuko-san.

Ikuko-san ... not much of a body, not much of a face, one
that is willing to go anywhere.

When, waking after the first night of the Kure festival, I
pull up the blind, there is immediately the lightest of taps on
the door.

"Come in!"

The door-handle turns slowly as though someone is opening
the gate to the infernal regions. The door opens slowly as
though reluctant to reveal what it must; closes behind what is
revealed.

"Well-come, Por-ter-san," says Ikuko-san, faint and high,
smiling brilliantly with nervousness, and bowing and bowing
and bowing.

Yes, not much of a body, not much of a face, to have been
waiting outside for three hours, ears strained for the awakening
of the unknown boss. Not much of a face; and it has looked at
itself in looking-glasses. Ikuko-san stops bowing, stops smiling,
puts her hands by her sides, licks her lips, and:

"Porter-san, I speak, please?"

"Of course."

"Me, Ikuko-san."

"Welcome, Ikuko-san!"

Somehow, I expect her to bow again, to give one of her nervous but heavenly smiles. Not so. She has something she must say. She says it.

"You see, no make-up?" She indicates her broad pentagonal face, bare and polished. "For Porter-san today no make-up. Porter-san see not pretty. Not young. Twenty-eight years."

I catch on. At least, I catch on to two possibilities. This homely creature making a deliberate début without make-up is either being a wily Oriental female angling for sympathy, or someone whose nature compels her to be direct. Simple enough to find out.

"But you're very pretty, Ikuko-san, very pretty."

She gives me a look I am often to be given during our year's relationship, a chastening one that says, "You don't have to lie to me."

"Excuse, please," says Ikuko-san. "Mirror says not pretty."

"Okay, Ikuko-san. You say not pretty. Mirror says not pretty. I say, 'Welcome, Ikuko-san!' "

She smiles. I am a gone coon.

She giggles, putting her hand over her mouth.

"Ikuko-san ancient spinster," she says. I fall for her there and then.

To write of a woman who is, objectively, very plain, and yet who has great beauty because an inner self of even greater beauty lights up the coarse shell, requires ability I haven't got. Moreover, I am uncertain of the ultimate source of the illumination.

It is not difficult to put her on the dissecting-slab—there are the stubby feet with stubby toes, the hairless bow legs mottled like bamboo, the wide hips, the narrow waist, the flat chest, the slender neck, the round head covered with a pelt of hair mutilated by a do-it-yourself *permanento*, the deft little paws capable of the most deliciously succinct gestures.

It is not difficult to list the virtues Western writers since the nineteenth century, virtues trained-in for centuries, have credited women of her race with, and which she possesses:

296

obedience, grace, sweetness, femininity, domestic wisdom.

Since, however, there are so many women in Japan who resemble her in appearance and accomplishment, these common-factor elements are no more than the soil in which grows the more dazzling Ikuko-san flower. Throughout our relationship I am selfish, experimental, always coming and going, as obsessed by time as Macbeth, and offhandedly accept her rare and out-of-the-ordinary qualities as though such qualities are always lumped-in with the usual house-girl ones, as though she is not a special individual making a special offering. What is at the white heart of the illumination, what is the flower of light? Intelligence and wit? Unusual delicacy of feeling? Honesty untinged by self-interest?

Why am I uncertain of the source of her beauty? Why can't I see her clearly?

My actual eyes, of course, see what is in front of me, but the eyes of consciousness, as I hurl myself about Japan, see only behind me, see the road through the back-seat window, see the essence of Ikuko-san only as a will-o'-the-wisp far back.

What my actual eyes see is not to be forgotten. Her clothes hang in the wardrobe with mine: a couple of exquisitely darned kimono, a couple of schoolgirlish pre-Occupation dresses in which the dye has run like tears, clothes I have bought for her or which she has made from cast-offs sent by Olivia and my sister. The two top drawers of the tall-boy are hers—one for cosmetics and sewing-basket, one for her hoardings: Bovril bottles, balls of wool, canteen goods she will sell on the black market, discarded shirts and socks and underpants of mine, fans I have collected as inn-*presentos*, postcards I have sent her from famous places in her own country which she'll never be able to visit.

I see her in all sorts of daily situations: rump in air, walking dog-like on hands and feet to polish the linoleum with dark-tan shoe polish; absorbed in a flower-arrangement; filling the ash-trays with water; scuttling across the snowy Mess compound from the bar with a bottle of whisky for me; hanging my laundry near the gingko-tree outside the window; teaching me to fold frogs and pagodas and cunning little boxes from paper, how to tell the time in Japanese, how to sing the Rain Song.

My feeling for her is deep enough for me to try to keep on emotional no-man's-land, to play happy-ever-after in what is only a here-today-and-gone-tomorrow dream, to be honest and laugh because there is no time to be dishonest and cruel, but there are times when pain or meanness or unprincipled wickedness takes charge of me. Control slips. The gears grate.

Any day, and in one moment, I toss away my hard-earned wisdom and splendid hopes and tainted love, become the sort of middle-aged man I despise, and lash out with cunning insensitivity and sensitive cunning at the angel in my room. For a man to take an interest in a woman is to make her suffer. Any pretext at all serves, because there is none ever, except that Ikuko-san is a woman. Any pretext serves to disguise fear, and the fact that my love for her is the thread the child ties to the beetle's leg. Any pretext—a song she sings at what I choose to decide is the wrong hour in all the years, tomato-juice in a chipped tumbler, a button missing, a towel not to hand.

"I've told you before not to wash the towels every day."

"*Hai.*"

"That's all very well. You're always saying '*Hai.*' *Hai, hai, hai*! Yes, yes, yes! But you still wash them. Now listen, Ikuko-san. No wash tower-u, no wash tower-u. Understand?"

"*Hai.*"

She is bewildered, quenched.

She bows.

"*Hai.* No wash Porter-san tower-u."

She does not flinch. She knows I have set the alarm at dishonesty. Her face sets at nothing o'clock. Her honesty stiffens. She goes about her tasks. From where I sit in the armchair I can see her dodge out between the showers of rain in her worn-down wooden clogs to pick cosmos from the Mess garden. She brings them in, and arranges them—Western style. She takes my shoes from the wardrobe, and leaves the room to polish them in the corridor. She does this job and that job, silently, a sham ghost called up by my own spleen. The door opens. The door closes.

Her silent exits and entrances become unbearable. Distress makes her colossal and portentous although she is attempting

298

invisibility. Guilt and weakness drive me to lash at her guilt-lessness and strength. Once again the door opens.

"Oh, for God's sake, Ikuko-san. . . ."

No need for these words, no need for such a tone in my voice, but there we are, the showers stopping and starting outside, the tree-frogs exulting as though they believe the world and the sweet rain and the sheltering leaf also belong to them, there we are, Australian and Japanese, thirty-nine and twenty-eight, boss and servant, unbombed and bombed, con-queror and conquered, Church of England and Shinto, dis-honest man and honest woman, half-civilized male and civilized female.

"Oh, for God's sake, Ikuko-san. . . ."

She is fearless and wise but she can bear no more.

With a primitive movement of flight she turns to the ward-robe, and stands behind its half-open door, her back to me.

She makes no outcry, but the outcry she is wrestling with agitates her body, making me aware of the strength of will which so often lends her slight frame the semblance of a physi-cal strength it has not got.

I see her legs quiver as her toes press into the linoleum; her body in its scanty rotten work-dress now and then violently shudders.

I will not will not will not be affected. I remain sitting in the armchair, glaring at what I think I am reading. I have gone too far. The air is volted with misery and guilt.

Presently, from the wardrobe comes the rustle of a paper handkerchief. She is crying. I say nothing, and do nothing.

Now that the initial wrestling with her pain is over she has, in a backwash of tears, begun to test the atmosphere, to gauge the depth of my pretence of not being affected by her. She rustles the handkerchief again, purposely loudly, and sniffs designedly. It is an offer for me to accept, a chance for me to stop being false and selfish, to make a warm move. I do nothing. I am somehow—why?—appeased. For me the thing is over.

For her?

She cannot stay in the wardrobe, yet to turn to me with un-veiled eyes requires a swagger and immodesty beyond her; she cannot punish me by the knowledge in those eyes that I have played vilely with her integrity.

As though she were pretty and arch and false she must be oblique, she who is weary of the world's obliquities, and history's leftovers: a bed-ridden air-raid-crippled father, a purgee brother Occupation-humiliated to the verge of a suicide he never commits, a mother vaporized at Hiroshima, dead without a grave to visit, lacking even a certified ghost.

Weary—and yet she coddles me:

"Porter-san."

"Yes."

"You *pisto*?"

"No. No, not angry any more."

"True?"

"True." At last, my throat oiled by a woman's tears, I can speak as though nothing has happened. "Ikuko-san."

"*Hai?*"

"You hubba-hubba off, and get me some soda-water from the bar-boy."

She whirls from the wardrobe, and falls on her knees by the armchair, noisily sobbing.

She grips my hand in her paws—how cold and work-cracked. She is not sobbing for herself, but this she cannot let me know, so:

"Me not happ-ee. Me bad girl."

"There, there, there—everything's okay."

"Me bad girl. Too much washing tower-u."

"Come on, now. Wipe your face."

"Oh, me die . . . me die. . . ."

"Ikuko-san, soda-water, please."

"Last night me pray for Porter-san . . . today bad girl. . . ."

"Soda-water, *please*. And you can ask the bar-boy for a bottle of lolly-water for yourself."

"*Hai?*"

"Get some lolly-water from the bar."

"*Hai.*"

She is at the tall-boy. She opens her cosmetic drawer, and powders her face. She rakes her frightful hair with the brush of rusted wire teeth, paints her lips. Then, for the first time since my persecution began, we look at each other. Her eyes glitter with the ebb of tears, and the dark sparkle of another anguish, and yet her eyes are still saying, "You don't have to lie to me."

To conceal the rebuke she cannot conceal she smiles—a smile that shocks me by its loveliness.

I cannot see what my face and eyes express, but shame should be there for that is what I feel, and wonder at forgiveness of such purity. With her intimate sense of presences she observes what is to be observed.

She must not leave me so.

To restore me fully she mocks herself.

"Ikuko-san ancient spinster," she says.

I do not speak because I cannot.

"Ikuko-san very ancient spinster," she says.

"Yes."

"Ikuko-san paint-ed hussy," she says. This is my teaching.

"Yes, indeed."

"Ikuko-san Jez . . . Jez . . ."

"Jezebel."

"*Hai*! Jez-eb-el. Ikuko-san ancient spinster, paint-ed hussy, Jez-eb-el!"

She has made me smile.

She is gone.

I hear her running on the coir-matting of the corridor, even though her bare feet make no sound.

She is gone.

I, too, am gone.

The clouds arrange and rearrange their untruths between me and Japan in which I have left a broken fountain-pen, empty Bovril bottles, tossed-out clothes, a trail of cigarette butts, the dust of filed fingernails, the ashes of burnt letters, little else one can prod with the ferrule of an umbrella, nothing that is not useless.

Anything else?

Only equally useless spectres of myself, poetic ones drifting down cryptomeria avenues or temple stairways or village streets or the neon-drunk Ginza, through pheasant woods or maple forests or back alleys, in and out of theatres and shrines and inns and dives, useless spectres for I alone still see them just as I alone see myself—a morsel of myself—left like an invisible signature on the stone palm of the great hand in the little valley above Kure.

Anything else left?

Little else. There is little else to leave—some thrown-away convictions and tired habits, some illusions and stupidities and weaknesses I shan't need any more.

There is, on the other hand, much to bear away and, like a thief who has lost his head, I bear much away, too much.

I sit in the aeroplane, gorged and drugged with experiences, every last and highest shelf of my mind overloaded with information it will take time to sort out, a long long time, for beneath the multicoloured junk, among the heaped-up gew-gaws, lie what seem to be hand-carved and time-burnished treasures, seeming truths I have found nowhere else, and have put aside to find again in my own country, dispassionately to examine in a sardonic and hypercritical light that will reveal any flaw.

Every filament of my being throbs and burns with sensations it is not yet the hour to evaluate: what appears noon's delight may well be midnight's revulsion, what is today opaque and dubious may tomorrow be crystal and luminous. Am I enriched or bombed-out? It is too early to know, or to know how much. Instinct for the moment is blindfolded with stars and rubbish. New beliefs jostle old ones. An innocence I do not yet trust gnaws at the foundations of the chromium-plated cage I have built about myself. The future is already littered with what I nearly know: glittering scraps which may be tinselled half-lies or gold-leaf verities blow ahead of my feet.

I bear away, too, as though bearing away a life or a heart, the small parcel Ikuko-san has given me.

She stands, in her best kimono and obi, formal Japan, bowing beneath the gingko-tree outside the window of the room I shall never enter again.

She must enter again, for the last time, must take off the kimono and obi and the white tabi and the sandals lacquered vermilion, and get into her work-dress. Her clothes, once jammed in the wardrobe as closely to mine as the leaves of

302

a bible, hang free, un-elbowed, surrounded by air. She must pack them, for she is no longer my house-girl, and is not to be anyone else's. She is out of work, back on the market.

The flute so full of sweetness is silent until blown, and she is once again the silent flute.

She must open the only two drawers not empty, and take out her bits and pieces, the brush with rusty wire teeth, the hair-distorting devices, the hoard of Bovril bottles I never remember to ask the reason for.

Before the sun sets she must scour a year of my life and her life from the room, and close the door.

She stands, in her best kimono and obi, formal Japan, bowing for the last time beneath the gingko-tree.

The jeep arrives.

From her sleeve she produces the little parcel, ritualistically tied, an object of beauty itself, even if it contain vipers and vitriol.

She makes her last request.

"Porter-san, please not open now. Please?"

I am in the jeep. Where am I going? What am I leaving? What can be said?

"Sayonara, Ikuko-san."

"Sayonara, Porter-san."

As the jeep moves away towards the wire gate in the wire fence, she raises her hand to wave, to wave with that gesture which fumbles imploringly on the air, beckoning back. I see no more. The paper chase goes on.

In the aeroplane which Japan can still hear, I open the parcel.

It contains a long fringed sash of silk so fine as to be weight-less. I recognize it as a little girl's first going-out sash, and with-out being told—who is now to tell me?—know that it is hers. Wrapped in the sash are two letters.

One is written in ink on the beige paper provided by the Australian Comforts Fund:

Dear Porter,
I wish you good luck and good health forever.
Sincerely yours,
Sakamoto.
I wish you many thanks for your great kindness on behalf of my daughter.

Startled at the smooth man-to-man tone of the letter, and its subtly correct-for-the-occasion style, my distress at leaving her abates for a second at a conception of the father as educated, intelligent, even distinguished. A second, no more. I recall that he is bed-ridden and all-demanding, and that Ikuko-san's forays into the blackmarket world with canteen goods are on his behalf.

The other letter is from the purgee brother. It is written in pencil, and I see Ikuko-san standing behind his shoulder, making him write what she cannot make her father write and what, despite her fearlessness, she traditionally cannot write herself:

> *My dear great teacher,*
> *I am very glory to be able to write to you.*
> *I am a elder brother of Ikuko Sakamoto.*
> *She has no money to buy things with, but she has had from you many present.*
> *If it had not been for your care, she never has happy.*
> *Thank you very much for your kindness.*
> *Thanks a lot for every thing.*
> *She said it is a pity she say goodby, but it's no use any more.*
> *Goodby great teacher.*
> *I hope your happyness and health.*
> *Oh, God save for my great teacher.*
> > *Sincerely yours,*
> > *Chihiro Sakamoto.*

Great teacher!

Teacher!

I have taught nothing except that I have to be taught.

In a year I have learned to read half-a-dozen Japanese words, placard-Japanese—Beer, Tobacco, Ice Water, Lavatory, Entrance, and Exit, and have learned to write none.

I have not learned to write, have not asked to see written, did not even know the surname of Ikuko Sakamoto.

Entrance! Exit!

There are other words to learn, even in my own language, even for one whose life is more doors than rooms.

Entrance, yes. Exit, of course. In between, the other one in the room. In between, Ikuko Sakamoto, the ancient spinster, the crippled father's daughter, the neurotic brother's sister, the flighty civilian-officer's house-girl, the earthy angel plain as bread and beautiful as flame.

As the aeroplane carries me towards Australia and forty it comes to be that what lies between unavoidable entrance and inevitable exit—life, Ikuko Sakamoto, anyone, anything—is equally unavoidable and inevitable. This has not come to me so clearly before. Life has seemed avoidable. The knowledge that a child's sash and a purgee brother's pencilled letter can scarify the conscience, that soft silk and cheap paper can plough deep and bloody, proves otherwise.

Nothing is avoidable, not even one's own ignorance.

The farther I cross the wilder and deeper and blacker the water, the higher I climb the more perilous and tempest-bitten, the steeper the mountain.

Here, having seen more than I have ever seen, I know that I know less than I have ever known.